Unrivaled

Unrivaled

UConn, Tennessee, and the
Twelve Years that Transcended
Women's Basketball

JEFF GOLDBERG

Foreword by REBECCA LOBO
Afterword by ALYSA AURIEMMA

University of Nebraska Press • Lincoln & London

Library of Congress Control Number: 2014957528

Set in Lyon Text by Lindsey Auten.

Dedicated to the memory of Ruby Dadarria, and to all those who fight daily for their dignity in the face of Alzheimer's disease, and for those who love and care for them.

CONTENTS

ILLUSTRATIONS

Even though the teams haven't played since 2007, UConn-Tennessee will always be the best rivalry in women's college basketball. I was there from the beginning, when the Lady Vols visited Storrs for the first time. We didn't know the game was going to turn into a rivalry. We didn't know the rivalry was going to come to define women's college basketball. We just knew that the number-one-ranked team and most storied program in college basketball history was coming to Gampel Pavilion to play our undefeated team. We saw it as a game, not as the beginning of something special.

Now, with the advantage of 20/20 hindsight, I see how special the rivalry became and how special it was to be there for the first contest. I played in the first two UConn-Tennessee games, called several more of them for CBS, and watched the rest as a fan. (I even watched a VHS copy of the second matchup in 2001 from my apartment in Spain a week after it was played. I knew the result—a Lady Vols win—but still had to watch.)

People who didn't care about women's basketball would watch UConn-Tennessee because the game always mattered. Both teams were always ranked and often both were undefeated. When they met in the regular season it was assumed to be a preview of a Final Four matchup down the road. The game was compelling. The coaches were compelling. And the respect-filled distaste the players had for one another was palpable.

I called the last regular-season meeting between the two teams for CBS, a January 6, 2007, game played at the Hartford Civic Center. Often, after I called games in this rivalry, Tennessee fans would tell me I sounded like I was rooting for the Huskies. And UConn fans would tell me I sounded like I was rooting for Tennessee. Unlike the players in the actual game, I couldn't win.

The day before the game I watched Tennessee practice at Trinity College in Hartford. While I watched I chatted with long-time Tennessee Sports Information Director Debby Jennings. She said to me, "What would you think if UConn and Tennessee didn't play anymore?" I said, "That's ridiculous. They'll always play each other." Debby said, "The contract is up after this year."

I didn't think much of her comment at the time. After all, it was absurd to think that after twelve years and twenty-two games the teams wouldn't play. Wasn't this rivalry meant to go on forever?

I write this in 2013, six years after UConn and Tennessee last played. Fortunately, we have Jeff Goldberg's book to remind us why this was the rivalry that came to define—and in many ways still does define—the best in women's college basketball.

Rebecca Lobo

ACKNOWLEDGMENTS

After the success of my first book, *Bird at the Buzzer: UConn, Notre Dame, and a Women's Basketball Classic*, I was thrilled in the summer of 2013 to have the opportunity to work once again with the great editorial and promotional team at the University of Nebraska Press. Led by Rob Taylor, the UNP staff has always made the writing process much easier to complete with confidence. Courtney Ochsner is always there for advice and counsel, which never goes unappreciated.

None of this happens without the hard work and guidance of Barbara Collins Rosenberg, who took a novice author under her wing in 2009 and has represented me since with professionalism, honesty, humor, and, at times, compassion. She has always supported and nurtured my ideas and helped guide me through the trials and tribulations of the proposal process.

So many former UConn and Tennessee players, coaches, and media members graciously gave up their time and memories to the cause of telling the story of the great UConn-Tennessee rivalry. Some, like Semeka Randall, Carol Stiff, Geno Auriemma, and Rebecca Lobo, were particularly generous and are featured throughout the narrative. But they were only a fraction of those who helped, and I offer my deepest gratitude to all.

Alysa Auriemma offered one of the most heartfelt tributes

to Pat Summitt when the news of the Tennessee coach's illness became public. She was kind enough to grant me permission to reprint her wonderful essay as the afterword of this book, and I am honored to do so.

Special thanks go out to Patrick McKenna and Luanne Dunstan at the University of Connecticut's media relations department for their assistance in gathering the vintage box scores and photographs reproduced in this book.

Thanks also go out to Ben Adamson, Assistant Director of Athletics Communications at Missouri State University; Bill Tavares, Media Relations Manager for the Connecticut Sun; Chuck Sullivan, Director of Communications for the American Athletic Conference; Rachel Margolis, Senior Publicist at ESPN; and M. Adam Waller, Director of Community Relations at the Pat Summitt Foundation.

A special thank-you goes to my parents, Bob and Carole, for their guidance—and occasional lodging in Connecticut—during the research process.

And then there is Susan, my wonderful wife, who has encouraged me through every phase of both literary ventures. She now knows more about women's basketball than she ever dreamed could be possible.

And last, but not least, Rocky.

INTRODUCTION

In March 2014, on the eve of the NCAA championship tournament, the University of Connecticut's women's basketball team
was precisely where it had been four times before over the previous nineteen seasons: undefeated and the odds-on favorite
to win the championship.

Technically there had been five previous UConn teams to
enter the tournament undefeated under Hall of Fame coach
Geno Auriemma, but the first, in 1995, was hardly considered
the favorite. That distinction belonged to Tennessee, and when
UConn completed the program's first perfect season by knocking
off fellow Hall of Famer Pat Summitt's Lady Vols in the title game
in Minneapolis, the greatest rivalry in women's basketball—and
arguably in all of women's team sports—was forever forged.

Over the course of thirteen seasons, from 1995 to 2007, the
UConn-Tennessee rivalry was, for all intents and purposes, the
only game that mattered in women's college basketball. Certainly it was the only game the media cared about, the only game
the networks cared about—even people who never watched or
even respected women's basketball cared about the UConn-
Tennessee game.

And, lest anyone try to convince you otherwise, it was the

only game that UConn and Tennessee fans, players, and iconic head coaches ever truly cared about.

Desire, passion, admiration, jealousy, and hatred were hot-wired into twenty-two matchups over those thirteen seasons, with UConn leading the series 13-9. Seven times they met in the NCAA tournament, six times in the Final Four, and four times for the national championship.

UConn would win all four of those title matchups, in 1995, 2000, 2003, and 2004. But Tennessee won two of the other three March Madness matchups, in 1996 and 1997, en route to becoming the first three-peat champions in women's basketball history. UConn would follow suit by winning three straight titles from 2002 to 2004, beating Tennessee in the national semifinals in 2002, then in the championship game for each of the final two titles.

How dominant was UConn and Tennessee's lordship over their sport? Over the first decade of the rivalry, from 1995 to 2004, they combined to win 8 of 10 national championships, posting a record of 86-5 in NCAA tournament games not played against each other.

They were, in a very real sense, the women's incarnation of the Celtics-Lakers rivalry of the 1980s that was credited with lifting the sagging popularity of the NBA to the stratospheric level it still maintains today.

The UConn-Tennessee rivalry performed the same life-giving function for women's basketball, bringing the sport unprecedented national attention and television ratings.

UConn was the Lakers of Magic Johnson and Pat Riley, running an offense like Showtime with silky-smooth guards and athletic forwards, running away from all comers to win five titles between 1995 and 2004. Tennessee was the Big Three Celtics of Larry Bird, Robert Parish, and Kevin McHale, punishing opponents in the paint with tremendous rebounding and inside play to win four championships over the rivalry's thirteen seasons.

As in any great sports rivalry, UConn-Tennessee had heroes and villains on both sides, classic games and cantankerous controversies. And when it abruptly ended in the summer of 2007, it left a void that the sport was still attempting to fill in the spring of 2014, with some even clinging to a hope that, with a new coach at the helm of the Lady Vols, the rivalry might resume as early as 2015—the twentieth anniversary of the first UConn-Tennessee game that changed everything.

This book is about those thirteen seasons, the story of how it all came about in the summer of 1994 and how it all ended in the summer of 2007, and what it means now, all these years later, with Auriemma having moved past Summitt for all-time national championships with nine, upon completing another undefeated season in 2014.

For those of us who had the opportunity to cover the rivalry, it was the single highlight of the season—the only regular-season game to garner the attention and coverage of a national championship.

As a sportswriter for the *Hartford Courant* during the rivalry's thirteen seasons and UConn women's beat writer from 2001 to 2006, I had the pleasure of attending thirteen of the twenty-two games, including national championship games in 2000, 2003, and 2004.

My first UConn-Tennessee game was the regular-season game in January 1999 at UConn's Gampel Pavilion, when Tennessee sophomore Semeka Randall tangled on the floor with UConn sophomore Svetlana Abrosimova, a Russian émigré and emerging darling of UConn's ferociously protective fan base. After Randall appeared to push Sveta's head to the floor like a dribbled basketball, the Gampel crowd serenaded her for the remainder of the game with boos, a blast of angry emotion almost never seen in the women's sport, so out of character—yet so indicative of the white-hot emotions attached to UConn-Tennessee—that Lady Vols players and fans would forever fondly refer to Randall by the nickname Boo.

Beyond the great games, All-American players, and Hall of Fame coaches that were part of the furniture of this great rivalry, there was one element, especially from the UConn perspective, that took hold forever in the psyche of the rivalry. Whenever UConn played at Tennessee, or if they met in the NCAA tournament, the Connecticut Yankees were subjected not only to a wide expanse of orange but to the nonstop playing of Tennessee's fight song, "Rocky Top."

The Tennessee band would play "Rocky Top" so many times by 2000 that Connecticut media members would conduct a pool, at five dollars per entry, to guess how many times the song would be played during the course of the game. (I recall winning the pool for the 2000 national championship game in Philadelphia; I believe I picked twenty-three playings.)

In the summer of 2011 my wife Susan and I adopted our first dog, a ten-week-old playful mix of Italian greyhound, chihuahua, and Jack Russell terrier. His foster mom had temporarily named him Theo, but since we lived in Boston we didn't feel right naming him for the outgoing general manager of the Red Sox, Theo Epstein. Too corny and clichéd for our little guy.

As I contemplated the name change one August afternoon, I took into consideration that the pup had been born and rescued in Morristown, Tennessee, just a bounce-pass away from Knoxville. Instantly I could hear the Tennessee band in my head like a siren song. Twenty-three times.

We named him Rocky.

Unrivaled

1

For the Good of the Game

The irony was that UConn and Tennessee weren't supposed to play each other in the first place.

Not far from the bucolic campus of the University of Connecticut, just forty-five miles west via Interstate 84 in the town of Bristol, lies the most powerful sports campus on the planet.

ESPN doesn't call itself the "Worldwide Leader" for nothing. In the first fifteen years of its existence, from its humble beginnings in 1979—the same year the Big East Conference began playing basketball—to the launch of ESPN2 in 1994, the Entertainment and Sports Programming Network had evolved from a small network showing Australian Rules Football and high-stakes billiards to a sports and television behemoth broadcasting the National Football League, Major League Baseball, the National Hockey League, and major college football and basketball twenty-four hours a day, with its highlight show, *SportsCenter*, turning athletes and anchors alike into household names.

ESPN had not just been a mirror for the sporting audience, but had proven itself an influential vehicle for taking heretofore niche sports and turning them into national phenomena. This was perhaps never more evident than with the America's Cup yachting races—by covering first the United States' shocking upset loss to Australia's "Winged Keel" in 1983, then the

Americans' triumphant reclaiming of the Cup in 1987—making Dennis Conner one of the most recognizable figures in sports.

By 1994 men's college basketball had become a staple of ESPN's daily winter lineup, with color commentator Dick Vitale bringing a manic announcing style oft-mimicked by a nation of hoop junkies. The sixty-four-team National Collegiate Athletic Association tournament, covered by CBS, had become a national obsession over the fifteen years of ESPN's existence, with office tournament pools only adding high-octane fuel to the madness of March.

However, reflecting the gender gap in American society at large, the women's game lagged woefully behind the men's product in popularity, financing, and media coverage.

Changing the landscape for women in sports was the last thing on Carol Stiff's mind in the summer of 1994. In charge of programming women's basketball coverage for the network, Stiff was just trying to change on the fly.

Stiff had always had a close connection to women's basketball, growing up playing the game in Bernardsville, New Jersey, and later for Southern Connecticut State University.

"I was the youngest of six, grew up being sort of the tomboy of the family," Stiff said. "There were no girls in the neighborhood, so the guys always let me on their teams, it was no big deal. I grew up in a really small town. All the dads commuted in and out of New York."

Stiff's uncle, Don Donoher, was an Ohio basketball coaching legend, leading the University of Dayton to the 1967 national championship game before losing to John Wooden's emerging dynasty at UCLA. Donoher, who was named an assistant coach on the 1984 U.S. Olympic men's basketball team by Bobby Knight, would later have a basketball facility named for him at Dayton Arena, where several NCAA women's tournament regional finals would be played, including one in 2003 that sent UConn to the Final Four.

Donoher also had an enormous influence on the future of ESPN. In the late 1970s he cut a broadcast journalism major named Dan Pugh, who had transferred from Eastern Kentucky University after playing for two seasons. Fans know him today as Dan Patrick.

Patrick and Keith Olbermann were a match made in heaven for *SportsCenter* in the summer of 1994, when Stiff set about to make a match of her own.

Stiff had joined ESPN in 1989, after a brief stint coaching the Southern Connecticut women's basketball team. "My first position [at ESPN] was to work on the [network's] tenth anniversary party through the Communications Department, under Rosa Gatti, who had been the sports information director at Brown, so there was a connection there," Stiff said. "And from there, I went over for a short stint in sales, adding in commercial time, so I was learning the business, and then went over to programming, where I resided for twenty-something years.

"In that area I learned about Nielsen Ratings and programming and what I learned from the coaching and playing—and why I think they hired me for this area—I worked really hard, I put my nose to the grindstone, just that energy to excel, I had in me."

Tommy Odjakjian, who would later leave ESPN to join the Big East Conference, was in charge of scheduling all college sports. In 1992 he handed off the duties of scheduling ESPN's women's basketball coverage to Stiff.

"He came over to me one day and said, 'Hey, I know you coached, I know you played college basketball, I know you have a great love for the game,' and he handed me all the files and said, 'Can you schedule all our women's basketball games?'" Stiff said.

There were two ways ESPN went about scheduling its regular-season lineup, which consisted entirely of weekend games, mainly on Sunday afternoons, up against the NFL, NBA, and NHL.

"One is where you have contractual obligations through a contract that had been written and executed with a conference," Stiff said. "That could be football and basketball, and under those contracts would fall women's basketball and Olympic sports. That's one way, by contract, schedule three SEC games, eight Big East games, etc., for all the conferences we own the rights to.

"The other mechanism was being afforded an opportunity or pitching a good idea or a good date for a game and pitching our programming department on, 'If I can get X team to play Y team on this date, I think it will be a really good game.' We started putting matchups together, noticing which teams rated well, which teams had good depth charts and recruiting classes. I had a big notebook on different conferences and different teams."

Both elements would come into play as the summer of 1994 got under way. While the nation was transfixed by the O. J. Simpson murder case—and highway chase—Stiff was making the case to her ESPN bosses about creating a marquee women's basketball game to be played during the winter doldrums of January. And, for a change, it would be a game that had a sports audience all to itself.

Since 1986 the third Monday in January had been designated as Martin Luther King Jr. Day, a federal holiday recognizing the life and achievements of the civil rights leader who had been assassinated in April 1968.

ESPN had in years past tied a national holiday to the scheduling of a college game. On Presidents' Day, for instance, it was always a good bet that an ESPN audience would tune in to find George Washington University taking the court.

For the 1994–95 season Stiff envisioned staging a women's game on January 16, one day after King's actual date of birth, and the observance date of his holiday in 1995. The game would feature two of the top teams in the nation that had just squared off in the 1994 NCAA East Regional final—UConn and North Carolina.

The Tar Heels, coached by the legendary Sylvia Hatchell and featuring a speedy guard named Marion Jones, had defeated UConn en route to capturing the national championship over Louisiana Tech on a dramatic three-pointer at the buzzer by

Charlotte Smith. North Carolina, trailing by two, inbounded from under Tech's basket with 0.7 seconds left, with Smith nailing the three-pointer that might or might not have truly beaten the clock, but was whistled good in the days before instant replay.

A holiday rematch fit all of Stiff's criteria. A contract ESPN already had in place stipulated a televised game between an Atlantic Coast Conference team and a Big East school. Now it was just a matter of arranging it with the two schools. Stiff made her first phone call to Chapel Hill, North Carolina.

"I knew North Carolina had just won the championship and I had my eye on UConn, with Jen Rizzotti and Rebecca Lobo, I knew they were bringing back quite a good class," Stiff said. "So I made the call to Sylvia, because it had to be an ACC–Big East matchup. I made the first call to her, because I didn't think UConn would turn it down. But she turned it down."

In fact, Hatchell had been in favor of playing the game, but only under the condition that North Carolina be the home team. But Stiff knew that would be a problem. ACC teams had hosted the previous two games against Big East opponents. This game, by contract, had to be played at the Big East site, which in this case would be Gampel Pavilion, the 8,200-seat arena on the UConn campus that had first opened its doors in 1990.

"She wanted the game on her home court," Stiff said. "I looked in my files and noticed the previous two years were on ACC soil, and I said, 'No, no, it needs to be on a Big East campus.' I was physically looking at the file. She said, 'No, I don't want the game.' I repeated myself. 'Are you sure you don't want this game?' I pitched her on it being Martin Luther King Day, on ESPN, Robin Roberts calling the game, and she declined the game.

"You have to remember, it was [scheduled for] mid-January, teams are into their conference play. We still have a little of that today. Teams would rather not meet a tough opponent while in conference play.

"I was surprised that she wouldn't take it, but I understood. So I said, 'Okay, now what do I do?'"

Stiff dug back into her contract files. She still intended to keep UConn as one-half of the matchup. Now she turned to another conference under ESPN's control, the Southeastern Conference. And in the SEC the biggest name was Tennessee.

But first Stiff reached out to the athletic department at UConn, which agreed to take part.

"At the time, it was more of Carol bringing it to us and wanting to have a Martin Luther King Day event and they approached us at first just about playing the game," said UConn coach Geno Auriemma. "There was no opponent at the time. And I said, 'Sure, we'd love to play in the game.' Getting the opponent was up to them.

"I guess the people they contacted, for whatever reason, didn't show any interest in playing the game, and when they came back to me and said, 'Do you think Tennessee will play you?' I said, 'I'm sure they will, you just have to ask [Pat Summitt].' They play a great nonconference schedule, there's no reason for them not to. That's kind how it evolved. I had no idea they would be the opponent."

Stiff placed the call to Knoxville. Summitt had already earned the reputation for playing a difficult nonconference schedule, and Stiff was confident this matchup with UConn would be no different.

"I moved on and made the call to Pat and I think I started, 'You might not know who I am, but do you want this game?'" Stiff said. "And I gave her the same pitch I gave to Sylvia, and then I laid low, didn't say a word. There was this awkward silence, and she goes, 'You know, I'm in the SEC schedule that time of year, that's going to be tough. It's a Monday night, we play on the weekend. . . .'

"I didn't say a word. And that's when she said, 'You know, for the good of the game, I'll take it.'"

Stiff breathed a sigh of relief. ESPN had its marquee matchup. Tennessee's Lady Vols, the most dominant women's program in the nation, winners of three national titles over the previous eight seasons and the favorites to win the 1995 national championship, would travel to Storrs, Connecticut, for a Monday afternoon game on January 16, 1995, against the upstart Eastern power, the UConn Huskies.

"Obviously her program was legendary and she was a legend," Stiff said. "I knew they were going to be good and I knew I wanted a marquee representation on that day. She would take games at any given day and time. She knew the importance of television. She was very savvy, from wearing microphones to letting us into her house for [NCAA tournament] selection shows. So she stated it, 'For the good of the game, I'll take the game.' I think I said, 'I really appreciate this, I think it's going to be a great game and a great showcase for women's basketball.'"

2

Birth of the Dynasties

The two greatest women's basketball coaches of all time, the two coaches who guided their teams to a combined seventeen national championships in the first three decades of the NCAA tournament, had humble beginnings. But both Pat Summitt and Geno Auriemma, although total strangers in the coaching world before 1995, were determined to lead their respective programs to the pinnacle of their sport.

Born in 1952, the only daughter among five children, Pat Head began her basketball career as a youngster shooting around with her three brothers in the loft of her family's barn in rural Henrietta, Tennessee, forty miles northwest of Nashville.

Her father, Richard, was known as a disciplinarian, the source of the fierce intensity that Pat would bring to the game as a player and coach.

Richard had moved his family from Clarksville to Henrietta so that Pat, a five-foot-nine-inch guard, could play at Cheatham County High School, since Clarksville did not have a girls' team in the late 1960s.

Her collegiate career lasted three seasons at the University of Tennessee at Martin, where there were still no scholarships for women in the pre–Title IX days of the early 1970s.

There was also no NCAA tournament for women in the 1970s,

and high school girls in Tennessee still played six-on-six, with three players on each team allowed to play on only one-half of the floor at any one time. By 1980 Summitt would help eliminate the archaic rules and bring the sport into the modern era.

In the fourth game of her senior year Summitt tore the anterior cruciate ligament (ACL) in a knee, but her team had gone 64-29 in her four seasons and she graduated in 1974 as the school's leading scorer with 1,405 points.

While rehabbing the knee and waiting for the U.S. Olympic women's basketball trials to begin, Summitt, age twenty-two, took a job teaching physical education and coaching basketball at the University of Tennessee in Knoxville, making $250 a month.

"I fell into it," Summitt said. "When I tore my ACL, I thought, 'What am I going to do? I don't have basketball. I'm not going to have it for the rest of my life. Coaching could be the avenue that I take.' I have great passion for the game. I love it."

Summitt was the do-it-all for the program, like an old-time barnstorming baseball team. She coached the games, washed the uniforms, and drove the team vans.

Her first season, in 1974-75, ended with a 16-8 record.

In 1976 the knee was fit and so was Summitt. She made the Olympic team and, as a cocaptain, helped lead the team to a silver medal in Montreal.

The next spring the Lady Vols went to their first Final Four as part of the Association of Intercollegiate Athletics for Women (AIAW), the forerunner of the NCAA. Two fellow Olympians, Trish Roberts and Cindy Brogdon, as well as a walk-on guard named Holly Warlick, became the nucleus of Head's first great team, one that was ranked first in the nation in 1978.

Tennessee made the semifinals of the AIAW tournament in 1978 and 1979, losing both years, then began its domination of the SEC in 1980, the year she married to become Pat Summitt and finally reached the AIAW final, losing to Old Dominion. Tennessee would lose again in the AIAW final in 1981, but Summitt's reputation for building a collegiate powerhouse was cemented, and in 1984 she coached the U.S. national team to the gold medal at the Los Angeles Summer Olympic Games.

Soon Tennessee began to collect national championships, winning their first in 1987 over Louisiana Tech, then again in 1989 against SEC rival Auburn, led by Sheila Frost and Bridgette Gordon.

Summitt would become the first coach to win a third NCAA title in 1991, defeating Virginia in overtime in New Orleans.

That year a little-known program out of New England had reached the Final Four for the first time. But it would not be the last time the women's basketball world would hear from Geno Auriemma and the University of Connecticut.

UConn had always been a hotbed for basketball, and the men's program enjoyed tremendous popularity in the mid-1980s, when Auriemma was hired as a thirty-one-year-old from Philadelphia who had spent the previous four seasons as an assistant to Debby Ryan at Virginia.

Auriemma was born in Montella, Italy, in 1954 and did not come to the United States until the age of seven. Growing up in Norristown, Pennsylvania, just outside Philadelphia, Auriemma, who spoke no English, learned to assimilate quickly and found his place in his new country through sports. He played basketball at Bishop Kenrick High School and, though he did not have the talent of Summitt as a player, quickly took to coaching both boys' and girls' teams.

Soon he was hired by Jim Foster, the women's coach at St. Joseph's, who also mentored Muffet McGraw, who would go on to win the 2001 national championship for Notre Dame. From there Auriemma headed to Virginia. In 1985 he interviewed for his first head coaching job, at the University of Connecticut.

The school didn't even show him the dilapidated field house that the basketball programs called home. The women's program, as well as its building, needed a total makeover.

Auriemma assured the search committee that he could be the man for that job. He was hired to begin the 1985–86 season.

"Those early years, every year his program got better," said future University of Hartford athletic director Pat Meiser-McKnett, who was on the UConn search committee. "He was maximizing potential with the students he had when he arrived and he laid the groundwork by recruiting a kind of student-athlete that could be molded and could grasp the vision of being a winner."

After Auriemma hired former Rutgers standout Chris Dailey as his associate head coach and top recruiter, the program began to make strides.

Among the first major recruits was swingman Kris Lamb, soon to be followed by forward Kerry Bascom, who would score 2,177 points in her career. In Auriemma's second season UConn finished over .500 for just the second time in program history. By 1988 his team was competing for the Big East title.

The 1988–89 season was a breakthrough. The Huskies went 24-6 and won the Big East regular season and tournament titles. With the latter came the first NCAA tournament appearance in program history.

In 1991 UConn reached the Final Four, losing in the semifinals as Tennessee won its third straight title. But now both programs were on the map. Soon, together, they would redraw all the lines.

3

Dog Day Afternoon

When Rebecca Lobo woke up on the Monday morning of January 16, 1995, in her dorm room on the campus of the University of Connecticut, she had no grasp of the magnitude of the event in which she would take part in a mere matter of hours.

In fact UConn's senior All-American center was concerned whether she'd be able to grasp anything that day.

The previous Friday night UConn had beaten Seton Hall on its home court in Gampel Pavilion, raising its record to 12-0.

But the victory came with a price, as Lobo had jammed her right pinkie finger so badly during the course of the 44-point victory that it was bent at a forty-five-degree angle.

It was certainly not a tune-up for number-one-ranked Tennessee, coming to Storrs for the hotly anticipated Martin Luther King Day game on ESPN. But worries about the Lady Vols took a backseat to the crisis of the moment.

"At the time, it was more like, 'Holy cow, my pinkie finger is shaped like an L,'" Lobo said. "It was pointing to the side. I remember going to see the doctor while the game was going on and he was using every bit of force that he had, with his foot up against the table, trying to pull this thing back into place. So at the time, it was more like, 'Get this digit pointing in the direction it's supposed to be pointing.' And then after that, what does this mean? When am I going to be able to play again, how is this going to affect how I play? But the initial thought was, 'This thing looks crazy.'"

But Lobo would not be missing the game against Tennessee. It seemed as if no one in Connecticut was going to be missing this game. Since Geno Auriemma had taken over the UConn women's program a decade earlier, his team had been incrementally building itself toward this moment.

The Huskies began winning Big East tournaments in the late 1980s. They made their first NCAA tournament appearance in 1989 and surprised the basketball world by reaching the Final Four in New Orleans in 1991, losing 61–55 to Virginia and a guard named Tonya Cardoza, who would later become a longtime assistant coach at Connecticut.

Had UConn won that national semifinal they would have faced Tennessee in the championship game. Instead Cardoza's Cavaliers fell to Pat Summitt's Lady Vols in overtime, 70-67.

It was Summitt's third national championship at Tennessee in a five-year span, giving her program the most titles since the women's NCAA tournament had begun in 1982.

And though Tennessee would not return to the Final Four over the next three seasons, their run of titles between 1987 and 1991 established the Lady Vols as the premier women's program in the country. The Huskies, who had fallen one game short of reaching their second Final Four in 1994, enthusiastically welcomed the opportunity to test their mettle against the leading power in the sport.

UConn would enter the game ranked second in the country, just behind the top-ranked Lady Vols. It would be just the third time in program history that UConn would be facing the number-one team in the nation, the first two against Virginia— the 1991 Final Four semifinals and a loss in Lobo's freshman season of 1992. But Virginia was a recent power, with no real history beyond the fact that Auriemma had been an assistant coach there in the early 1980s. Facing Tennessee was a much different prospect. "This was the first time that we were playing one of the traditional powers that I had grown up watching," Lobo said. "As a kid I watched Louisiana Tech or Tennessee whenever they were on. Those were the big teams that left an impression when you were a kid. So it was the first time playing a program that I had a tremendous amount of respect for. So we were all just kind of eager to do it.

"We were excited, but I remember being really nervous and anxious as well. It was still Tennessee, and even though we'd been to the Elite Eight the year before, we still weren't a 'program' really. We were a team that was starting to get attention and starting to come together, but we sure weren't Tennessee, with the number of Final Fours and championships they had. So I think there was a combination of excitement, let's test ourselves against the team considered to be the best.

"But there were also some nerves. This isn't Providence or Seton Hall. This is Tennessee and this is a big deal. This was Pat Summitt and she was a legend even then. She had this aura around her and there was some of that."

More importantly, perhaps, it was the first time UConn would enter a matchup with the top-ranked team while ranked second. And it was the first time UConn would play a top-ranked opponent at home.

"You know, Auburn had been to three straight Final Fours and we had them in our building [in 1990] and beaten them and gone on to the Final Four in 1991," Auriemma said. "We had Stanford in Gampel [in 1993] coming off a couple national championships, so we had played really good teams at Gampel before that. But [Tennessee] was really the first game that was nationally televised and really hyped up and the game lived up to the billing.

"I think all the talk and all the hoopla about the game coming up made it an even bigger game than it would have been—the fact that number one and number two were playing, national television, it was still kind of relatively new. TV hadn't really done a whole lot with women's basketball up to that point. So everything was kind of in place and then the game lived up to the hype."

Perhaps not surprisingly, the attitude of the Lady Vols was of a more curious nature. Tennessee had just played SEC rival Auburn two days earlier, before flying to Connecticut on Sunday to play this rare nonconference game against a program with little recognition outside the Northeast.

"The game didn't jump off the schedule when they scheduled it," said Dan Fleser, who for two decades has covered the Lady Vols for the *Knoxville News-Sentinel*. "I'm looking at this game knowing Connecticut had a little more history, they'd been to the Final Four before. But that was like 1991 and I knew they were okay, but I didn't know what it was going to be like. [Tennessee] would go places to play people. I think Summitt liked [it]. They once played in a Thanksgiving tournament in Vermont, because they'd never been to Vermont. They would go places and play people, because they knew it would help that program.

"To me, it was like the circus coming to town. They would go to these places and invariably, the setting would work against the home team. They would be so nervous, they wouldn't play well. But they would have a big crowd, and there would be a lot of energy. I think the year before they played at Arizona and won a close game, and the Arizona kids came into the post-game like they had won the game. I remember looking around, going, they lost. But they were so excited."

Tennessee entered the UConn game the top-ranked team, but the early portion of their season had been tumultuous.

Injuries and suspensions—both team and NCAA variety—forced Summitt to use ten different starting lineups over the Lady Vols' first sixteen games, all victories, including nine against teams ranked thirteenth or higher, six of these on the road.

"We like playing in hostile environments because the fans are there to see good basketball," junior guard Michelle Marciniak said at the time. "I think we've handled it well because we practice so hard—Pat challenges us every day—and that's motivated us. The team is very mature, so nothing really bothers us. We've turned negatives into positives."

Despite All-American Nikki McCray missing time and Dana

Johnson playing with a slightly dislocated left shoulder, the Vols were off to the best start in Summitt's twenty-one years.

"We've had a set of unusual circumstances, and I've been very pleased with how we've handled everything," Summitt said before the game. "I think that's a real credit to this team and their ability to handle adversity. But when you think about it, this is a veteran team and should be able to handle it."

But for all their experience in road venues, nothing could have quite prepared Tennessee—or even the home team Huskies, for that matter—for what was taking place this holiday afternoon.

"We used to just walk from our dorms over to Gampel and I do remember for the really big games, when we got there two and a half hours before the game, there were already people lining up outside," Lobo said. "I remember Robin Roberts and the announcers watching practice, which didn't happen very often. We weren't on TV all that often, so there was a big feel to what was going to happen that day.

"I remember my sophomore year we played Stanford at home on CBS and even though it was billed as a sold-out game, there were still a lot of empty seats. For this one, there was not an empty seat in the place. The fans being there a couple hours before the game, there was this real energy about the building that I hadn't even felt there watching our men's team play. It was really electric."

Not only was the game a sellout, filling the 8,241 seats to capacity, it was essentially a media sellout as well, with an unprecedented 123 credentials issued for this one game, including those for the ESPN crew that would broadcast the game live to the nation beginning at 1:00 p.m.

Adding to the drama of the day was the fact that the Associated Press, which normally released its Top 25 women's poll early on Monday morning, was holding off on its voting until the completion of this matchup of the two top-ranked teams, giving the game as close to a championship-level feel as a regular-season game could get.

"I remember coming to the arena that day, and immediately

the atmosphere was more juiced than any of the other ones," Fleser said. "The governor was there, there were politicians there. There were people of note there. But I knew what Connecticut was. I knew about the Horde [the large UConn media contingent] and that the men's team was really popular and had a lot of coverage and it was a novelty in that area, and this was an extension of what's happened with the men."

But true to his coaching philosophy, Auriemma refused to make the game bigger than it really was—a regular-season game in January against a quality opponent. There were no film studies, no special preparations.

"At the time, we weren't looking at it as a defining moment for us," Auriemma said. "That was never the case. We knew we had a good team, that we had a chance to be a Final Four team, we had everybody back, pretty much, from the year before.

"So I remember that when we played that game, that was the first time that those players had actually seen Tennessee play, when the game first started. My guys had never seen them play. We just felt like, what's the point? It's not about them, and we're still that way today."

What Auriemma did stress was to keep the relentless Vols frontcourt off the boards, a job for the six-foot-five Lobo, six-foot-seven center Kara Wolters, and six-foot forward Jamelle Elliott.

"Whenever we played Tennessee, the focus was on rebounding, because that was their bread and butter, especially at that time," Lobo said. "You had to keep them off the glass. But in the regular season, Coach Auriemma's philosophy was, let's focus on us. If we do what we do well, we'll win the game."

But in the early moments the focus was on guard play. The raucous crowd, many wearing "Battle of the Best" T-shirts, were momentarily silenced as Tennessee seized the early initiative, taking a 6–5 lead.

"The game started, and it had to be the first minute of the game and [UConn's] Pam Webber is bringing the ball up against Latina Davis, and she just takes it away from her like stealing lunch money, just a clean steal, you could hear the slap of the ball it was so clean," Fleser said. "And she goes in for a lay-up, and I remember going, 'Okay, it's one of these deals again.' But that was my first impression, and within five minutes, I realized that was the wrong impression."

Lobo started the Huskies on a 10–0 run with a three-pointer, and Jen Rizzotti's three-point play completed it for a 15–6 lead. UConn would not trail again.

In Fleser's words: "[Auriemma] made an immediate adjustment, I think [freshman Nykesha] Sales started bringing it up, and they started attacking, and you could see they were well-coached and they were hungry. And it was like, 'Whoa, this is totally different'. So by the end of the game, I can't remember what I thought of Connecticut, but I knew that could happen again. That was a pretty good performance. And the rest was history."

Tennessee's Abby Conklin and Michelle Johnson each hit three-pointers to cut UConn's lead to 41–33 at halftime, but the Huskies maintained control through the midway point of the second half, when Lobo picked up her fourth foul and Johnson scored twice to cut UConn's lead to 58–53 with 9:19 left, prompting Auriemma to call time-out.

"When Tennessee was making a run and some of the calls were going the other way, I could see in their eyes and their body language that there started to be a little doubt," Auriemma said after the game. "There was a little apprehension like, 'Uh-oh, here they come. Now they're playing their A game.'"

Auriemma brought the foul-saddled Lobo back and she found Wolters for a hook shot. Wolters then hit two free throws before Lobo made a steal off a rebound and hit a lay-up, giving UConn a 64–53 lead with 7:43 left.

UConn led by 12 points with just under five minutes to go when Lobo fouled out. She gathered the Huskies together before exiting to the bench.

"I told Kara to post up hard, I told Jamelle to get every

rebound," Lobo said. "I'm sure they didn't hear a single word I said and I really don't care because they just played unbelievable."

Even with Lobo out, Tennessee could not cut into the lead. Final score: UConn 77, Tennessee 66.

"The game played out like two really, really good teams," Auriemma said. "I know that when the game ended there was an incredible atmosphere in the building. The players knew we had done something that was pretty significant. We had beaten a great team, a great program with a great coach. The kids knew that and the fans made them feel that way as well. The fans knew that something special had happened. And I think the people on T V knew something special had happened, too."

With one minute left and UConn leading by 11 the fans began to chant, "We're Number One! We're Number One!" After Elliott made two free throws Lobo hugged reserve guard Missy Rose and both tripped over Kim Better, who was on the court.

When the buzzer sounded Lobo led the bench onto the court. Her arms were raised, her index fingers pointed skyward. She and her teammates collapsed in a screaming heap on the polished wood floor to be swallowed up by television cameras and photographers.

The fans stayed, dancing, screaming, and waving homemade signs and banners. One read, "2 vs. 1 = UConn."

"Today was a perfect example of what 'team' means and what women's basketball can be," said Lobo, who had 13 points, 8 rebounds, and 5 blocks. "And I can't say enough about our fans, the greatest in the country."

The Lady Vols committed 25 turnovers, one off its season high. Its key perimeter players, All-American McCray (2 for 10) and Marciniak (5 for 14), shot a combined 29 percent.

"We had more Connecticut than we could handle," Summitt said after the game. "Rebecca Lobo is the most versatile post player we've faced and brings a lot of confidence to their team, but they're just not Rebecca Lobo and I think they understand that. It's probably good for them to play and win without her down the stretch and at critical times."

Indeed, as ESPN's Carol Stiff made her way off press row and into the postgame press conference room in the bowels of Gampel, she could hardly contain her excitement. This game had been her brainchild the summer before, and it had played out beyond even her highest expectations. The game would bring a 0.8 Nielsen rating, almost unheard of for a women's basketball game, with an estimated 965,000 viewers tuned in.

"The story itself of the game on Martin Luther King Day in 1995 was the electricity in that building," Stiff said. "That's when I knew this was something special. I remember sitting there, looking around, capacity crowd, the *New York Times* was there. They held the AP poll, because they were one and two. I remember hearing Robin's [Roberts] voice at the end, 'Ladies and gentleman, we have new number one team in the nation,' as they piled on at half court. I could just feel it, this is something.

"Then going in the back and watching Geno's press conference. He had this huge smile. And then I went down the hall and saw Pat and she was looking at the stats and said, 'For the good of the game.'"

Meanwhile the celebration continued out in the stands, where the fans refused to leave, as if a mythical national championship had been captured.

"More than anything, what I remember is that after the game, nobody left," Lobo said. "We won and people stayed around forever, just celebrating the moment and there was a feeling of, 'I don't want this to end,' like being at a great rock concert or something. There was just this real energy and it was real amazing."

The emotions would not ebb, even into the evening hours. The UConn men's team had a game scheduled for that same evening at the sixteen-thousand-seat Civic Center in Hartford, about twenty miles west of the campus, a game also televised on ESPN.

The crowds for the two teams differed greatly, with more

senior citizens and children likely to attend the women's games, but few students, who saved their rooting allegiance for the men's program. It was into this different atmosphere that the women's team entered en masse early in the men's game. But when they were shown on the Jumbotron above center court, the reception was very familiar.

"After we beat Tennessee and things had finally cleared out, Jen Rizzotti had a car, so we would ride with her to go to the men's games," Lobo said. "I remember her saying when we were still at Gampel, 'Do you think if we get pulled over on the way to the men's game tonight, there's any chance we get a ticket?'

"And when we were at the men's game our seats were behind the basket and I don't remember if they announced it, but there was this big roar in the crowd and someone saying they mentioned that we were there and congratulations on beating Tennessee. That was pretty cool for us."

"That's still the high-water mark of those early years of Connecticut basketball and people want to look at where's the launching pad for everything that came after that, that was it," Auriemma said. "That afternoon, that's when it all happened. It was just the perfect circumstances, the two right teams and the game was played perfectly and then it took off from there."

It was immediately clear within the world of women's college basketball that something more than special, perhaps seismic, had just occurred, its epicenter the tiny campus in Storrs.

Women's basketball had certainly had more than its share of great players (Nancy Lieberman, Ann Meyers, Anne Donovan, and Cheryl Miller) and great teams (USC, Texas, Stanford, and Louisiana Tech). Only ten months before North Carolina had won one of sports' most dramatic games, as Charlotte Smith buried a three-pointer at the buzzer to give the Tar Heels the national championship.

But there had been nothing quite like this UConn-Tennessee game.

All one had to do was pick up the Tuesday *New York Times* to know the sport had passed through the looking glass. Right there on the cover—not the sports cover, but the lower corner of page A1—was a story about the undefeated Connecticut women's team and its stirring 11-point victory over powerhouse Tennessee to claim the number one spot in the AP Top 25 poll.

Overnight this became a story about women's basketball and how one exquisitely-played game between two top teams in a frenzied atmosphere could appeal to far more than just the sport's purists.

"I just thought it was absolutely great," said Louisiana Tech coach Leon Barmore. "I watched Rebecca Lobo run out on the floor after the game. She and UConn showed real personality on TV. This game had charisma and fun. It was good entertainment. It's obvious you've got a good thing there. It was good for women's basketball."

"I like it any time our game is treated as it should be," said Jim Foster, Auriemma's best friend from their days in Philadelphia and head coach at Tennessee's SEC rival Vanderbilt. "We've been there. Our game with Tennessee was on CBS. It's good, because the games don't disappoint. Women's basketball has reached that point."

Stanford coach Tara VanDerveer, who would be coaching the U.S. Olympic team in 1996 in Atlanta, had a delayed reaction, with her team practicing while the game back east played out live.

"I saw the tape," said VanDerveer, a two-time national champion. "It was very good. Anyone who watched saw more than a lot of women running up and down the court. There was so much enthusiasm and interest. That's what people like about sports.

"Those women showed a lot of heart, and a lot of important things came out of it. It showed that it is not just one place that this is happening. Not just Texas Tech or Stanford. No, this is not the standard just yet, but we're making progress.

"UConn is a spectacular team, and I hope their fans continue that wonderful support when there is no Rebecca Lobo or no Nykesha Sales. Also, it is important that the men's team is so strong. This shows fans can be enthusiastic about team success regardless of gender.

"Women's basketball still has trouble [getting attention]. We have been in [number one vs. number two] games that were not even broadcast live. It's tough to get our scores on TV. We're still fighting those battles. But we're making progress. I hope the sponsors took notice of just how good this was."

The impact was perhaps felt most keenly at UConn. Tennessee had won three national championships and were the established national power. But this was all new for UConn. Even the men's program, which had exploded onto the national scene under Jim Calhoun just five years earlier with its "Dream Season" and Final Eight appearance after Tate George's miracle buzzer-beater in the Sweet Sixteen, had never encountered the intense emotional outpouring the women's team had so suddenly unleashed.

"They just felt good about themselves, about our team," Lobo said. "Here came big bad Tennessee and this little school up in Storrs, Connecticut, still came out triumphant. It's easy to embrace a team that never lets you down, and we didn't because we went undefeated, which was the first time it happened in so long.

"We validated people cheering for us. They felt pride, like if you have a kid who does well in sports or has a good report card. You feel full of pride and for some reason those fans felt like that, probably because of the different ages of the people in the stands, they had this maternal feeling about us. It's weird, you don't often feel pride in a team you root for, but I feel like that's what they had for us."

The bond only grew stronger as UConn continued to win, ending the regular season 26-0 and then ripping through the Big East tournament, every single one of their twenty-nine victories coming by double digits. The media demands on Lobo, UConn's charismatic All-American, increased to the point that the coaching staff and media relations department agreed to limit Lobo's access to two days a week.

Interestingly, Lobo and her teammates found their greatest sanctuary from public attention in the shadow of the arena where they played their games.

"On campus, it didn't exist," Lobo said. "We were still just the girls' basketball team. Because even at the time, at that Tennessee game there were at the most—at the most—100 students there. It still wasn't something that students were coming to watch, it was the community. So when we are on campus, nothing changed. No one asked for my autograph or a picture. Maybe after the season, a couple people asked us to sign the copy of the *Sports Illustrated*. But on campus, we were still treated exactly the same.

"It was only if we went to the local mall where there were nonstudents there that we got treated differently. And we hardly ever did those things, because only a couple people had a car and we mostly stayed on campus. We really didn't get a sense of that until after the national championship."

But the cozy confines of Gampel Pavilion almost became a house of horrors in the NCAA East Regional finals.

Because the NCAA scheduled their tournament regional sites years in advance, it was a happy coincidence for the Huskies that the 1995 East Regional would be played at Gampel Pavilion, where the NCAA knew, even before the UConn-Tennessee game, that fans were likely to sell out the 8,200-seat arena, even for games not featuring UConn.

And with the top-seeded Huskies given home games in the first two rounds of the tournament, UConn would get to play four straight games for the right to reach the Final Four in a place where UConn had won thirty-three games in a row over the past two seasons.

But when the Huskies played Virginia in the regional final, it almost all came undone.

Over the first ten minutes UConn raced to a 29–10 lead, and a ticket to Minneapolis appeared all but punched. Then Virginia punched back, outscoring the Huskies 34–8 in the remainder of the half to take a 44–37 lead. It was the first time in forty-eight games that UConn trailed at the half.

"I remember coming into the locker room at halftime and we're down and it's like, 'Oh crap,'" Lobo said. "And I remember Jen having this rah-rah attitude, 'We're not going to lose this f—ing game!' And I remember in my brain and my body, 'Oh, we've got this. I've got Jen on one side and Jamelle on this side and they're not going to let us lose this game.'

"And the vibe in the locker room, as soon as Jen spoke, we just got this renewed belief that no one was going to stand in our way. That's my most vivid memory of that game."

Lobo may have been UConn's biggest and brightest star, but Rizzotti and Elliott were the team's heart and soul. The two fierce competitors would often fight one another in preseason games, but that was better than the alternative. When they played together their combined talent and drive to succeed made every pickup game unwinnable for the opposition.

In 1995 the same could be said of the real games. Rizzotti, the junior guard from New Fairfield, Connecticut, was UConn's fiery leader. Elliott, the forward from Washington DC, was the most underrated player on the team, often doing the dirty work in the paint while frontcourt mates Lobo and Wolters got the most media attention.

"[Rizzotti] would refuse to let her team lose or admit she could miss a shot or commit a foul [in preseason]," Lobo said. "But once the season started you were on her team all the time and it was phenomenal. She was the one talking in the huddles. Jamelle too, but mostly Jen. Coach would be all over us and she would be the one to bring us all together and say, 'F— him, he doesn't think we can do it, and we're going to do it.' She was, without question, the fiery leader.

"[Elliott] was not underappreciated at all by us. We understood her value. She's undersized, but she always got it done."

It was Elliott who got the Huskies going to start the second half, scoring twice early in a 14–5 run that re-established the lead.

Elliott then capped the scoring with a late free throw, while Lobo and Wolters combined for three blocked shots in the final two minutes to preserve a 67–63 victory and a trip to the Final Four.

Tennessee also ripped through the rest of its season unscathed except for one other loss in the SEC tournament final against Foster's Vanderbilt squad, when their reliance on their rebounding and inside game left the Lady Vols one-dimensional and unable to adjust when Vandy stifled them inside.

"We learned a valuable lesson in the SEC tournament about our perimeter game," Summitt said. "That really helped us and made me a better coach. If we don't give the perimeter players the green light to shoot fifteen-footers, we wouldn't have had a chance to get to Minneapolis and the Final Four."

The Lady Vols then enjoyed the same four-game run at Thompson-Boling Arena to reach the Final Four, but without the drama UConn endured against Virginia. In the Mideast Regional Tennessee dispatched Western Kentucky by 22 points and Texas Tech by 21.

Tennessee and UConn were now forty minutes apiece from a dream rematch in the finals.

"We would [like to play UConn again]," said Tennessee's Dana Johnson. "I've been thinking about it since January 16. I don't think about it all the time. But once a week it will pop into my head, that Connecticut game."

There would be no stopping it. In the national semifinals Tennessee again dominated the glass against Georgia, outrebounding the Lady Bulldogs by 18 and winning the game 73–51.

"One of our things this year is, 'No rebounds, no rings,'" Summitt said. "Early in the game, we set the tone on the boards and maintained our aggressiveness offensively."

Two-time All-American Nikki McCray had 22 points and 8 rebounds to lead the way on offense.

"We had to keep our focus to be in the position that we wanted to be in, which is playing [in the finals]," McCray said. "We just have to concentrate and stay focused and not relax."

UConn had an even easier time against Stanford in the other

semifinal, destroying the Cardinal inside in an 87–60 victory. Wolters had 31 points, the third-highest total in a national semifinal game, as the frontcourt combined for 69 points and 24 rebounds.

"But even then, they asked Tara [VanDerveer] the next day to predict the winner and she said Tennessee was going to win it," Auriemma said. "And I'm like, 'Damn, we just beat you by 30 and you still don't think we're capable of beating them?' I don't know if that was a slight against us or if that was more the respect that everyone had for Tennessee back then."

Now the fateful matchup was set. For the final time in women's Final Four history, the teams would only have to wait one day to play the final, as CBS broadcast the semifinals on Saturday afternoon and the final on Sunday so as to not interfere with the men's Final Four schedule.

"It's all so much of a blur, because the games were back-to-back and there was very little downtime for me and Jen," Lobo said. "We were both named All-Americans, so we were going from this awards ceremony to that thing. I don't remember which awards thing we were at, but we were both there and we hadn't even showered. It was this constant going from here to there.

"I remember the night before, I couldn't sleep. Jen was my roommate and I've never been a person who has difficulty sleeping and I could not sleep. I don't think it was nerves. Maybe it was eagerness, but I did not get good sleep, and maybe that's why I played well because I was just running on fumes and I wasn't thinking because my brain stopped working."

Lobo would have plenty of opportunity to rest in the first half of the championship game. She was called for three personal fouls in a span of ninety-four seconds and did not play the final 11:58 of the first half.

"I don't remember how I got my first two, but I clearly remember my third," Lobo said. "It was on a pick-and-roll and [referee] Dee Kantner called it on the roll. I have a great relationship with Dee now and I give her a hard time about it with her to this day, how she almost cost us a national championship by calling a bogus third foul on me."

Soon Rizzotti would join Lobo on the bench with three fouls of her own. Wolters had two. For the second time in three games UConn trailed at the half, this time by 38–32.

"Believe it or not, it wasn't that big of a shock to me," Auriemma said. "People can say what they want to say about officials being impartial, that's a bunch of bull when you really think about a team in its first big-time championship game playing against a storied program. Everyone is affected by it. There were some calls made in that first half that were just unexplainable. If you went back and watched that game, you would be hard-pressed to explain some of that stuff.

"When was the last time you saw a national championship game, men's or women's, where three All-Americans are on the bench with fouls? That just doesn't happen under any circumstances ever, or anywhere, before or after. So the way the game was being played, it almost didn't surprise me. I'm like, 'Okay, if you guys thought this was going to be easy, you've got another thing coming, because they're not going to just let you walk in here and win this thing.'

"So, to be honest with you, for us to go into halftime down by just 6, under those circumstances, I told those kids at halftime, 'They've got no chance to beat us.' If they can't be up 15 on us after what just happened to us, they have no chance to beat us in the second half. It's going to even out. The calls are not going to stay the way they are, and they didn't stay that way. The game was decided on the court and we were better than them that day and we deserved to win a national championship."

In the second half, in the final twenty minutes of her collegiate career, Lobo did not let UConn lose.

Tennessee led 52–46 with 11:32 left when Lobo made a post move for an easy lay-up. After a steal Lobo scored again on a driving lay-up. With 9:03 left Lobo hit an eighteen-foot jumper from the baseline. With 7:40 left, she scored again on a sixteen-footer from the left wing.

Instead of allowing Tennessee to run away with the game, the Huskies stayed within 3 points thanks to those 8 from Lobo.

"It was one of the few, rare times that I just didn't think," Lobo said. "I don't know if it was because of my lack of sleep from the night before, but my brain shut off and I ran around, caught the ball and shot it. I don't even know if it was in the framework of the offense. That spot over there is open, I went over there and got it. There was no hesitation at all. Coach Auriemma would always say to me, especially my first three years, you've just got to play. I think that was the moment where it finally made sense. I just stopped thinking and played basketball."

But it would be Rizzotti who made the play of the game, the signature move of her career. With 1:51 left and the score tied at 61–61, Rizzotti tracked down a long Tennessee rebound, blew past Marciniak with a crossover dribble, and scored the lay-up that put UConn ahead for good.

And because the officiating swung hard the other way in the second half, putting UConn in the bonus early and often, the Huskies' free-throw shooting in the final ninety seconds secured a 70–64 victory, a perfect 35-0 season, and the first national championship in UConn history.

As the clock ticked down to zero Lobo raised her fists to the sky and ran around the court in celebration.

"I remember looking up at the clock and it was ticking down 4 . . . 3 . . . 2 and quickly doing the math in my head and realizing there was no way now we can lose this game, and that's when I just started running," Lobo said. "It was just pure joy and time to celebrate. It was a phenomenal feeling. Just jubilation when you realize you've reached a goal that you've been striving for, for a long time."

For Tennessee the defeat was particularly bitter. Losing to UConn once, on the road in mid-January, was tolerable. Losing a second time, with the national championship at stake, was unacceptable.

"I don't know if they were necessarily surprised [in January]," Fleser said. "They probably thought in the back of their minds, 'We'll get these guys in Minneapolis.' I don't think the players took what happened in that first game seriously. I think they thought it was, if not a fluke, a product of the environment, them shoe-horning this game [into the schedule], having to travel. That was to their detriment, because they got every break in the book in Minneapolis—foul trouble in the first half, they should have been ahead by 15 points at halftime. And then they got it handed to them in the second half. After Minneapolis, they realized, these guys are different."

So, apparently, did the rest of the nation. UConn's perfect season was not the first in women's history. It was fewer than ten years since Texas had accomplished the feat in 1986. But this title season captured the imagination of the sports world as no women's team had done before.

Within days Rizzotti would appear on the cover of *Sports Illustrated* and Lobo would appear on *Late Night with David Letterman.*

And already people's attention turned to the next time UConn and Tennessee would play, in Knoxville in 1996.

"I think pre-UConn-Tennessee there wasn't a women's game that non-women's fans cared about on a yearly basis," Lobo said. "There wasn't a game that people pointed to as must-see. There wasn't a game that players, coaches, and fans said, 'This is what I look forward to. This is going to be a great showcase.'

"If there hadn't been so much at stake, it wouldn't have become a rivalry. It would have just been another game. It was one vs. two, made for TV the first time we played. Then it was the rematch everyone wanted to see when it came time for the national championship. At the time, we had no idea it would turn into what it became. We just knew it was special to us, beating this team twice when the stakes were really high was special to us."

4

1996

Semi-Tough

When ESPN created the UConn-Tennessee series back in the summer of 1994, it was not intended to be a one-hit wonder. The game at Gampel Pavilion on Martin Luther King Day in January 1995 was merely the first half of a home-and-home series, with the second game scheduled for cavernous Thompson-Boling Arena in Knoxville on January 6, 1996.

At the time, Thompson-Boling Arena was unquestionably the toughest venue in the nation for an opposing women's team, as Tennessee entered their game against UConn with a record sixty-nine-game home winning streak. Certainly the championship-level play of the Lady Vols had a lot to do with that, but it didn't hurt to be playing in an arena that held twenty-four thousand of the most rabid women's basketball fans in the nation.

Of course, much had happened between January 16, 1995, and early January 1996. In a game that no one had planned, but everyone anticipated, UConn completed its undefeated season by defeating Tennessee in the national championship game. While the state of Connecticut basked in the glow of a fairy-tale championship season, Tennessee and its star guard Michelle Marciniak were left to pick up the pieces of a stunning defeat.

The relationship between Summitt and Marciniak was probably always destined to be a bit chaotic after the way it started. When Marciniak was in high school in Allentown, Pennsylvania, in September 1990, Summitt and Tennessee assistant coach Mickie DeMoss came to Marciniak's home for a recruiting visit.

Also making the trip was Tyler Summitt, although he had not been officially named yet. He hadn't even been born yet, and wasn't expected to be for another two weeks.

But while Summitt could control almost everything within her basketball program, some things were beyond anyone's best plans. Summitt's plans were to have her baby in the state of Tennessee, where she could share the moment of birth with her husband.

But shortly after the home visit began, Tyler had a different plan.

"I had tried not to think that it could remotely happen," DeMoss told the *Knoxville News-Sentinel*. "Then Pat started to have some contractions."

And they weren't letting up. Soon it became clear that this home visit was over, and the race against the clock was just beginning.

"My heart started beating faster," DeMoss said. "I felt like we were in the last two minutes of a game."

They managed to get Summitt back on the plane headed for Knoxville. But with the aircraft over Virginia, Tyler's full-court press was continuing. The pilot suggested making an emergency landing in Roanoke.

Summitt grimaced, but not because of the contractions. There was no way, no how, that Summitt was going to have this baby anywhere other than Tennessee, and it certainly wasn't going to be born in Virginia, where, six months earlier, the state university had knocked Tennessee out of the NCAA tournament with the Final Four scheduled to be held at Thompson-Boling Arena.

"I know it sounds crazy," Summitt later said. "But there was no way. No, ma'am. Don't land anywhere but Knoxville. Put your pedal to the metal."

They made it to Knoxville with moments to spare. She was almost fully dilated when she arrived at the hospital.

"If you know Pat, you know that once she makes up her mind, it's hard to change her," DeMoss said.

The same could probably have been said of Marciniak, who wound up not going to Tennessee after high school, but instead chose Notre Dame.

Her time in South Bend lasted just one season, however, and, after reaching out to Summitt in the summer of 1992, Marciniak transferred to Tennessee, one of the rare times that Summitt accepted a transfer into her program.

Because of the transfer rules Marciniak could not play for Tennessee until the 1993–94 season, but in her three years with the Lady Vols she would become one of the greatest guards in program history, scoring over a thousand points and earning the nickname "Spinderella" for her patented spin moves to the hoop and her flowing blond hair.

But Marciniak would be best remembered for the constant clashes with Summitt, as the headstrong coach and stubborn star guard.

"Pat and I had a love-hate relationship when I played for her at Tennessee," Marciniak told cnn.com in 2011. "I had a tremendous work ethic and a passion to play the game like no other, but I was young and tried to do things 'my way,' while Pat was coaching me 'her way.'"

Their disputes would become legendary, as Summitt struggled to mold Marciniak into the player she needed to lead the Lady Vols to their first national championship since 1991.

"Marciniak was very high maintenance, and Summitt is not a high-maintenance coach," said Dan Fleser, who covered Marciniak's career for the *Knoxville News-Sentinel*. "By that fact alone, it was certainly one of the more dramatic player-coach relationships, because you have to take into consideration all that stuff, the recruiting trip and her going into labor, then Marciniak coming here to begin with. They don't take many transfers.

"There was the drama, her and [Tiffany] Woosley competing for the same position. I remember it seemed those two would even compete for my attention sometimes. It was always something going on with Marciniak. She was a little a bit of a diva."

The divide between player and coach was never greater than after UConn's 70–64 victory over Tennessee in the 1995 national championship game. The iconic play from that game came with just under two minutes to go, when UConn's Jennifer Rizzotti went coast-to-coast and blew past Marciniak with a crossover dribble to score the basket that snapped the game's final tie.

The battles with Summitt would continue through the summer and into Marciniak's senior season.

"I think a lot of people had put a lot of pressure on her to be this amazing player that she was supposed to be," said Kellie Jolly (now Harper), who was a freshman guard on the 1995–96 Lady Vols. "I think it was hard for her. She had to work hard to be a good basketball player and be the kind of player Pat wanted her to be. There were stretches where there were struggles there. Pat and Michelle butted heads at times. But at some point they were able to get on the same page."

UConn would face Tennessee on the Lady Vols' home court in January, but they had an unusual opportunity to take Thompson-Boling Arena for a test drive the preceding November.

The 1995–96 edition of the Hall of Fame Tip-Off Classic was awarded to Knoxville, with Tennessee hosting Virginia—"Do not land this plane!"—and UConn taking on Louisiana Tech.

It was in the leadup to the Tip-Off Classic that a different side of Marciniak's personality was revealed. After the national championship game in Minneapolis, Marciniak scribbled out a note and gave it to Rizzotti as the Huskies prepared to leave the Target Center.

"I just said 'Congratulations on your championship. You deserve it,'" Marciniak said. "I guess it was just a part of my personality. I felt the other team was better that day, and I wanted to compliment her on a good game."

Rizzotti said she won't forget Marciniak's gesture.

"I can't say enough about a player who does something like that, especially at a moment like that," Rizzotti said. "We'd never met, and here she was, after a really tough loss, making the best day I've ever had even better."

But that story would be the extent of the warm and fuzzies on this trip to Knoxville. In an outcome that would prove eerily prophetic for the top-ranked Huskies, the Lady Techsters wasted no time ending any hopes of a repeat undefeated season, with Debra Williams's coast-to-coast drive and lay-up with five seconds left in overtime propelling Louisiana Tech to an 83–81 victory.

After UConn's Kara Wolters (29 points, career-high 20 rebounds, 7 blocks) put in a rebound to tie it with twenty-six seconds left, Tech's Kendra Neal threw the ball inbounds to Williams, who dribbled the length of the court, eluded a steal attempt by Rizzotti, and put in the lay-up.

"I guess I shouldn't have gone for the steal, but she hit a tough shot," Rizzotti said. "You have to give her credit."

Rizzotti took the ensuing inbounds pass and tried to duplicate Williams's feat. But Williams knocked the ball loose as Rizzotti drove the lane, and it bounced out of bounds as the buzzer sounded.

"I was looking to go to the basket because I knew they wouldn't want to foul," Rizzotti said. "I tried to just create a lane to the basket, but someone knocked it out of bounds and the buzzer went off."

UConn sophomore Nykesha Sales (20 points) sent the game to overtime by making two free throws for a 73–73 tie with 4.9 seconds left. It would not be the last time that season that Sales would tie a game with seconds remaining and Tennessee in the building.

The loss snapped UConn's thirty-five-game winning streak. And UConn would lose again in shocking fashion at Syracuse in early January—only the Huskies' second conference loss over the past three seasons—in the week leading up to their rematch with Tennessee in Knoxville.

"Everybody was a little bit surprised," Marciniak said the day after UConn's loss. "I think it gave us a boost of energy, to know they are beatable."

Said freshman forward Chamique Holdsclaw: "I was kind of excited. I thought maybe they were thinking about us too early. But everybody loses a game here and there."

Summitt was not as gleeful. The coach knew drawing UConn off a loss was not the mindset she wanted to face.

"Certainly I was surprised," Summitt said. "Then my second thought was, 'That's going to make it even tougher for us Saturday.' When you lose, you look at what you did wrong and correct it. Your players just listen better after a loss."

Tennessee, which had been picked sixth in the AP preseason poll, its lowest ranking since number seven on December 24, 1990, and the first time it had been out of the top five in eighty weeks, entered their home showdown with UConn ranked fourth, with a record of 11-1.

The lowered expectations were in part because Tennessee graduated two of its key players from the 1995 season, All-Americans Nikki McCray and Dana Johnson.

"We're in a different position, but I'm enjoying it," Summitt said. "But we do have high expectations and know we have to be overachievers."

To offset the losses in personnel, Summitt had one very important new arrival. In freshman Chamique Holdsclaw Tennessee had a potential player for the ages. The six-foot-two-inch forward, who had been a star at New York's Christ the King High School and won state titles in all four of her seasons, chose Tennessee after canceling a visit to UConn, having expressed a desire to leave the East Coast.

"I didn't want to stay around New York and felt Coach Summitt would be the best person to develop my game. . . . It's not that I didn't like UConn after being there for the Big

East tournament my junior year. I just felt I needed some space to grow."

It was the South's gain. Holdsclaw would score in double figures in her first twelve games as a freshman, leading the Lady Vols in scoring (15.2) and rebounding (9.3) entering the UConn game.

After Holdsclaw dominated the Kona Classic in Hawaii, Summitt said that the freshman "was like a woman among girls."

"You could tell from the start how talented she was," said UConn freshman Amy Duran, who played against Holdsclaw in high school. "She's so athletic, can dunk, and is such a team player. She's really hard to guard because she has so many weapons, which is why I'm sure she's doing so well."

Holdsclaw was just the fourth freshman in Summitt's twenty-two seasons to start her first game for Tennessee.

"I've not had a freshman come in and have the numbers across the board that Chamique has had," Summitt said, "which indicates she can play both ends of the floor and make a difference for us this year. She accepted a lot of responsibility right on, which took up the slack on the offensive end with the loss of [All-Americans] Dana Johnson and Nikki McCray."

In the days leading up to the UConn game, Holdsclaw could not contain her desire to avenge the two losses from the season before.

"College basketball is about rivalries, and we've been thinking about this game for a while," Holdsclaw said. "I wasn't on the team last year, but I was kind of crushed when they lost to UConn in the final and Michelle helped relay how much the loss hurt."

But Duran had a ready response for her friend.

"Last year, she kept saying, 'UT is number one,' even after UConn beat them the first time," Duran said. "We're going to end their record home win streak and her own win streak."

In what would become a trend with UConn-Tennessee games, the weather would play a role in the outcome. Thompson-Boling

Arena can hold as many as 24,600 fans at capacity, but only when they can actually get there.

A major storm arrived in Knoxville about the time the Huskies did, wrecking Tennessee's plans to use its vaunted home court as a sixth man. As it happened, only 10,184 were able to make it for the Saturday afternoon game, and the small size of the crowd took the edge off the proceedings.

At the outset it looked as though Holdsclaw would get the last laugh against her friend Duran. Tennessee's man defense forced UConn into 16 first-half turnovers and Holdsclaw had 10 of her team-high 15 points to lift the Vols to a 31–27 halftime lead.

But Duran and senior cocaptain Jamelle Elliott each scored 6 points in a 12–2 run that enabled the second-ranked Huskies (12-2) to win their third consecutive game against the three-time national champions, snapping Tennessee's sixty-nine-game home winning streak with a 59–53 victory.

"I'm trying to figure out how we won when we had more turnovers [26] than baskets [22]," UConn coach Geno Auriemma said. "But today was a win, not because it looked pretty. Not because it was executed beautifully. Today was a win because of character and tremendous willpower.

"Other than the national championship win last year, this is probably the most satisfying victory our program has ever been associated with."

After UConn opened the second half with a 7–0 run, the Lady Vols responded with an 8–1 run capped by a Marciniak jumper that gave Tennessee its biggest lead, 39–34, with 13:53 left.

"In the middle of the second half, things were not going well," said Mike DiMauro, the UConn women's beat writer—and later columnist—for the *New London (CT) Day*. "Tennessee got into the bonus pretty fast and we're directly across from the UConn bench and Geno yells over, 'Hey, now do you see why they've won sixty-nine in a row here?'"

After sitting out three minutes with four fouls, Rizzotti returned with 8:27 left and hit a jumper and a lay-up to get UConn to within 47–45. After Latina Davis made a jumper with 6:41

left to give Tennessee a 51–47 lead, the Lady Vols missed nine consecutive shots and were 1 for 12 the rest of the way.

"We didn't come out ready to play in the second half, and they obviously did," Summitt said. "You can't shoot 28 percent and then go to the other end and let Rizzotti penetrate without giving any help."

Said Marciniak: "We tried to stay within the frame of our offense, but no one could hit. We just didn't have that fire we needed at the end, and they did."

It was the freshman Amy Duran who would ultimately play the hero for the Huskies. After Davis's jumper, Auriemma called time-out with 3:24 left and inserted Duran for Nykesha Sales, who was bothered by a cold. Auriemma said he put in Duran because of her passing ability, but she was also UConn's best three-point shooter.

"We set up a three-point shot, but the wrong guy took it," Auriemma joked. "As I was drawing it up during the time-out, I said to myself, 'We're going to get a three-pointer from the corner, and that's Amy Duran's favorite shot.'

"When Amy caught the ball in the corner, everyone knew it was in because that's her shot. But I wasn't comfortable setting up something for a freshman on the road in this environment, so I set it up for Jennifer. It just didn't work out that way."

Though she had missed her only two shots in the game so far, Duran didn't hesitate.

"I knew I had to take that shot because we were behind and weren't going to get a better one," Duran said. "I was hoping I could make it because I needed something. I had been getting support from the coaches. They weren't telling me, 'Hey, pass it up if you're open.' [Associate head coach] Chris Dailey had told me, 'I think you're going to make one.' I felt confident."

"I think the one thing that sort of broke our backs was the three-pointer from the corner," Marciniak said. "We were in our zone defense, and when she made that they got kind of fired up. Then we didn't come back and capitalize, and they made the three-point play [by Elliott].

"They made the shots they had to, and we didn't have anyone step up and make a shot, especially in their final run."

The snowstorm stranded the Huskies in Knoxville for an extra day. They spent their Sunday watching the NFL playoffs in their hotel bar, shooting pool and playing cards with the UConn media, and basking in the glow of yet another victory over their new rivals.

"That game, to me, above all, showed Connecticut's stature," Fleser said. "This is the real deal. Because they had lost Lobo, they weren't the same team. And yet, they come in here and Tennessee had Holdsclaw. I thought Tennessee had improved, adding a great clutch player, and Connecticut had lost its All-American. And they still come in here [and win]. That game, as much as the 1995 games, cemented that, 'Okay, here's the rival.'

"I think them winning those first three meetings was pretty important. I wonder where that series would have gone if that hadn't happened, if Tennessee had come back and beats them in Minnesota, or whatever. But the fact Connecticut won those first three games was big, because it got Tennessee's undivided attention. I think it also immediately cemented Connecticut. They got a real boost from that. Not that they wouldn't have been good anyway, but it was like a greenhouse and they just took off from there."

For Tennessee the loss was an enormous step back, with the sparring between Marciniak and Summitt resuming anew. But now the coach and the star guard reached an understanding. And Tennessee began to click as it anticipated another shot at the Huskies at the Final Four in Charlotte.

"Her and Summitt were still brawling through the 1995–96 season," Fleser said. "There was still enough drama that year, with Summitt still on Marciniak and [Marciniak] finally saying, 'You have to lighten up on me.' That was part of it."

For the second year in a row UConn and Tennessee breezed through the first four games of the NCAA tournament to reach the Final Four. But this time they would not meet in the championship game. The layout of the bracket demanded that the Huskies and Lady Vols play each other in the semifinals.

On the Friday morning of the semifinal game, a headline blared in the *Hartford Courant*: "Is She Tough Enough? UConn Needs Sales to Step Up." The story examined the reputation that the sophomore guard had been saddled with toward the end of her second season: that she tended to coast, could be lazy, and shrank from the big moments when her team needed her most.

But the true moral of the story was that as the season, and ultimately the NCAA tournament, had worn on, Sales had increasingly picked up the pace of her game, scoring a combined 37 points in the regional semifinals and final to help punch UConn's ticket to Charlotte.

Now, in her fourth career game against Tennessee in a span of fourteen months, the pride of Bloomfield, Connecticut, would flower as a star.

On the other side, Michelle Marciniak was gearing up for what could be the final game of her college career.

In what would have been the irony of all ironies, her final game was almost played in the regional finals against Virginia—in Virginia. The Lady Vols had trailed by as many as 17 points. But Marciniak scored 10 points in the second half, including six enormous free throws in the final forty seconds, to secure a 6-point victory.

"That's where people have to make big plays," Marciniak said. "Not to put any pressure on myself . . . to make big plays, but somebody has to step up. I look at my job this year as making sure somebody does. If it's me, that's fine."

Big plays? There would be plenty when UConn and Tennessee took the floor in Charlotte. Whoever made the last one would almost certainly go on to play for a national championship.

And for most of the night it appeared that Tennessee would be that team. In a game defined by alternating runs, it was the Lady Vols who drew first blood, ripping off 11 straight points to take a 22–13 lead. It was 28–17 when UConn scored 7 straight, but Tiffani Johnson hit a pair of shots late in the half to give Tennessee a 34–30 lead.

Rizzotti's three-pointer with one second left on the shot clock got UConn to within 53–52 with 11:45 left before Pashen Thompson, Brynae Laxton, and Jolly sparked a 9–0 run that gave Tennessee a 62–52 lead with 9:27 left.

Then UConn made a final frantic push, playing the final 6:19 of regulation time without Kara Wolters, who fouled out, forcing UConn to play with no players taller than six feet. But Rizzotti capped a 13–0 run with a lay-up with 5:42 left that put UConn ahead, 65–62.

Tennessee would fight back once again to take the lead, then Marciniak hit a pair of free throws with twelve seconds left to put the Lady Vols up 75–72.

On UConn's ensuing possession, with the clock running out on her career, Rizzotti made a dangerous pass to the top of the key for Sales. Marciniak, always the aggressor, lunged for the ball, looking to make a game-clinching steal. But Marciniak missed and Sales had an open look at a game-tying three-pointer. And the sophomore stepped up, burying the shot with 4.2 seconds left to tie the score at 75–75, sending the game to overtime.

"You don't make that three-pointer unless you've got the, ah, special qualities," Auriemma said. "When Kesha nailed that three, put yourself in Summitt's, Marciniak's, Latina Davis's head. They're probably saying, 'What the heck to we have to do to beat these guys?'"

Indeed, when her team came back to the bench before the overtime, Summitt knew she had a problem.

"The mentally tough ones will win," Summitt told her team. "And I don't like the looks on your faces."

For the final time, and at the perfect time, Marciniak got the message. A year earlier Marciniak had folded after Rizzotti blew past her for the crucial basket late in the championship game. This time Spinderella did not turn into a pumpkin. In the overtime she scored 5 of Tennessee's 11 points.

This time Rizzotti did not make the big play to steal a win. With UConn trailing 86-83, Rizzotti's three-point attempt was blocked and Tennessee added two clinching free throws with three seconds left for an 88-83 victory.

"[Marciniak] did not let her mistakes affect her," Summitt said. "She overruns the basketball in regulation, they get a three. She comes to the bench and a year ago, she might have been out of it. Tonight, she was able to put that behind her and say, 'We're not going to lose this game.'"

Both teams were drained at the end. In a series that had already seen three games worthy of classic status, Tennessee's first win over UConn stood as the best of the bunch. Even in defeat Auriemma had no regrets. His team had not lost. It had just been beaten.

"When I shook hands with Pat Summitt at half court after the game, she said, 'It was everything I thought it would be,'" Auriemma said after the game. "And I said 'Damn right.'

"It's like how many times can you run across the street and not get hit? One of those days they were going to win because they hit the shots and free throws and get the rebounds. We made some huge plays and they made some huge plays, but unfortunately they just made a few more. The team that played the better game won."

Two nights later Tennessee reclaimed their throne. Facing SEC rival Georgia, Marciniak and the Lady Vols could not be denied the program's fourth national championship and first since 1991 with a convincing 83-65 victory.

With forty-eight seconds left Marciniak pounded the Charlotte Coliseum floor three times and leaped into the arms of coach Summitt. Named the Final Four MVP after adding 10 points in the final, after scoring 21 against UConn, Marciniak could finally lay her burden down.

"Probably not until today can I forget the loss to Connecticut," Marciniak said. "This definitely will erase it from my memory. Last year hurt so bad, and I just wanted to get back here so bad. Our team has been through a lot of ups and downs and so many people doubted us. But we just kept going and going. I'm just so proud of the whole team and the entire staff.

"Ever since I was a little girl, I had that dream of cutting down the nets and being out on the floor with a national championship team," Marciniak said. "When I decided to transfer, it was because I wanted to play for one of the best coaches in the country. I'd like to thank Pat for sticking with me."

Said Jolly: "For Michelle, she needed that national championship. We don't win that national championship without Michelle Marciniak playing good basketball. It just doesn't happen. But she doesn't play good basketball if she doesn't get on the same page as Pat Summitt. So at some point I think she figured things out. The thing for me, I was blessed that I didn't have many teammates that fought Pat. We just did what she asked. And I think that's something that Michelle learned and we were all benefactors of Michelle learning that. I love her to death. I was so excited she got that championship."

Tennessee's victory was not just redemption for a great player. It was another critical building block for what was becoming the marquee women's sporting event. In a matter of months the U.S. national team would capture the gold medal at the Atlanta Olympics, sparking the formation of the WNBA and the ABL as professional leagues in the United States.

But it was the UConn-Tennessee rivalry that was driving the popularity train.

"I don't think it became all that special until we had played each other a couple of times," Auriemma said. "Them being the undisputed heavyweight champions of women's basketball at that time, and then we beat them three times in a row. I don't know if anyone had ever done that to them. Here the first three times we played them, and next thing you know, it became, hey, wow, this is a real rivalry. This isn't going to be one of those fly-by-night things.

"And then we played them again in the Final Four in '96, so in a span of one year, we played them four times. And all four of those games were on national television and all four were great games and now all of a sudden that became the game to watch in women's basketball."

"Everybody talks now about the 'perfect storm.' They didn't talk about it back then, because they hadn't written the book about it. There wasn't a movie about it. But looking back on it now, it was perfect. The perfect people, the perfect scenario, the perfect outcomes. That wasn't the plan going in. That wasn't the plan by ESPN, by me, by anybody else. It was just something that took on a life of its own and it evolved into what it became."

5

1997

An Imperfect Tenn

It had been five long years since Tennessee had reached the summit. Five years of close calls, disappointments and, most recently in 1995, the denial of a championship from an East Coast upstart who had suddenly come to be a thorn in its side.

But that all was forgotten in Charlotte after the Lady Vols dispatched UConn in an overtime thriller, then spanked conference rival Georgia to once again cut down the nets, the fourth national championship in Pat Summitt's twenty-one-year career.

Now there was a new challenge in Knoxville. Could they do it again?

Ultimately, led by super sophomore Chamique Holdsclaw, the answer would be yes. But for a program that had done it all over the previous decade, this championship run would be unlike anything done before or since, and, for coach Pat Summitt, one season like this would be more than enough.

After two years and four electrifying meetings between UConn and Tennessee, the rivalry had taken root as a sports phenomenon, and women's basketball in general was entering into a golden age.

"I thought at first that this rivalry had a lot of potential," Summitt said in 1997. "I knew UConn had the atmosphere and would become nationally competitive, like other rivalries we've enjoyed in the past with Texas, Louisiana Tech, and Old Dominion. But in terms of the national perspective, there probably isn't any more interest in a matchup right now in the country than there is in this one."

The UConn-Tennessee overtime thriller in the national semifinals produced a 2.5 Nielsen rating, and Tennessee's title victory over Georgia rated a 3.7, the highest ever for a women's basketball game. More than 2.5 million sets around the country were tuned to ESPN.

"I noticed that more men were talking about it, outside of our basketball family," said Carol Stiff. "For people in *SportsCenter*, at the assignment desk, it seemed like more people knew when it was coming and looked forward to it. That part of the legacy solidified for women's basketball. It was The Game. If you were a sports fan, and even outside people, you were watching that game."

So popular had the rivalry become in such a short period of time that the sport became the subject of an early foray into reality TV. Over the course of the 1996–97 season the Lady Vols were followed by camera crews from HBO, which was making a behind-the-scenes documentary about a year with the top women's collegiate basketball team in the country, titled *A Cinderella Season: The Lady Vols Fight Back*.

HBO had originally approached UConn about being the subject of this new brand of visual storytelling, but the program declined. Summitt, always game for a way to showcase the sport—she was already known for letting network crews film her pregame and halftime talks—happily accepted.

And just months after Tennessee's victory at the 1996 Final Four, the U.S. women's national team, led by Stanford coach Tara VanDerveer and with Rebecca Lobo on the roster, captured the gold medal at the Summer Olympics in Atlanta.

It had been a stirring Olympic Games, with the heroics of track star Michael Johnson and a repeat championship for the U.S. men's basketball team, known as Dream Team II, after the first wave of NBA talent had taken Barcelona by storm in 1992.

But for all that, it was the U.S. women's team that stole the show.

"In the course of history, there's the first UConn-Tennessee game, then the Olympics," Stiff said. "We knew, if they didn't win the gold, we might not have a WNBA. But to see at the 1996 Olympics—they were primetime, the last event, the women's team. I think that's my most memorable moment in basketball. The level of that game never dipped."

The early UConn-Tennessee games had struck such a chord with the sports culture of the mid-1990s, it is not unfair to say it played a direct role in the formation of the WNBA, which debuted in 1997.

"[Lobo] was our Mia [Hamm] when we started the league and she handled it beautifully," former WNBA commissioner Val Ackerman said in 2006. "When I look back, there were two primary developments in the 1990s that helped make the WNBA possible: the explosion of women's college basketball and the 1996 Olympics in Atlanta. With those two, the WNBA was teed up, and what happened at UConn in winning the [1995] championship was a seminal event.

"There's no question that the early victories and championship by UConn helped put women's basketball on the map. They caught people's attention and energized the Northeast media. And they captured a dormant public on the subject of women's basketball. Rebecca was an icon and still is. Once a household name, always a household name."

What Lobo started, Holdsclaw now carried on. The sophomore from New York was rapidly emerging as the premier player in women's college basketball entering the 1996-97 season.

As a freshman in 1995-96, Holdsclaw became the first Tennessee freshman to start and play in every game and lead the team in both points and rebounds.

In her sophomore season, her exploits were already becoming the stuff of legend. In an early-season 94-93 loss to Georgia

Holdsclaw scored 15 of her 34 points in the final two and a half minutes of regulation time and another 8 in overtime.

When Tennessee came to Hartford to play the Huskies in early January, Holdsclaw was leading the team in scoring (20.4 per game), rebounding (10.8 per game), steals (32), blocks (19), and minutes (470).

"I want to be able to make a contribution in every way possible," Holdsclaw said. "I want to be able to say I helped women's basketball become more competitive and exciting. I want to bring flair to the game. I want people to say, 'That Holdsclaw kid, she could really play.'"

In 1997, Holdsclaw was getting no argument.

"Tennessee had always been a balanced-offense team," said Georgia coach Andy Landers. "But with Chamique, they haven't tried to disguise her importance. They rely on her. They really try to take [the offense] to her. And when the offense doesn't generate things for her, they let her be the offense. For the first time, there is a star system in place there."

"In terms of talent, athleticism and skill, she's one of the best I've ever coached," Summitt said. "She has the potential to be the best player we've ever had in the program or maybe ever in the game. But for her to do that, she needs to become more of a student of the game; make reads, be smarter on the floor. She's already improved, though. She's better with the basketball than she was just two weeks ago."

This season Summitt and the Lady Vols would need every ounce of Holdsclaw's energy and every point she could put on the board. Even before the season started it was clear that this year was going to be an enormous struggle.

Kellie Jolly was no stranger to overcoming long odds. Just before her senior season in high school the future Tennessee point guard tore the ACL in her left knee. Having suffered an injury that normally took up to nine months for full recovery, Jolly returned to playing in eleven weeks.

Then in October 1996, as she began to prepare for Tennessee's title defense, Jolly woke up the morning after a pickup game with a throbbing pain in the same left knee. Upon examination it was determined that Jolly had torn the ACL graft from her previous surgery.

For a second time Jolly had the knee repaired, with the patellar tendon of a cadaver inserted into her leg. Now Jolly would again aim for a quick recovery.

"For me, it was just really focusing on what I needed to do for my team," Jolly said. "And I think having the confidence that I had done it before, I'd recovered before and come back 100 percent, and then having confidence in my athletic trainer, who was fabulous, was a huge plus for me.

"It was hard. Sometimes when you sit out with an injury that long, when you're missing games, it's really hard, because you don't feel as much a part of the team. So I tried to do as much as I could to be around the team as often as I could. I lot of my rehab was done during practice time, so I was thrilled when I was able to get back onto the court to practice."

But with Jolly missing from the lineup, the HBO cameras captured a team in turmoil.

Just four games into the season, the Lady Vols suffered their first loss, 66–64, at Louisiana Tech. Then came a shocker: A week after dropping the overtime thriller to Georgia at Thompson-Boling Arena, Tennessee lost consecutive games at home for the first time in Summitt's career. It was VanDerveer's top-ranked Stanford Cardinal that performed the deed, making 11 of their first 13 shots and cruising to a 17-point victory. Holdsclaw scored 24 points but shot 1 for 12 in the second half. It was Tennessee's worst home loss in a decade.

By the time the Lady Vols arrived in Hartford for their January 7 matchup with the undefeated Huskies, their record stood at 10-4.

"I don't think we were as tough as we needed to be and people were taking advantage of that," Jolly said. "I'm sure Connecticut went through this as well. When we played teams, they were either going to play their best game against us because they were so fired up to play Tennessee or we were going to intimidate them before we got started, because we were Tennessee, and we'd win easily.

"And I think because we lost some games early, we lost some of that aura and we were a little timid, a little too nice. We had some young, inexperienced people playing. The personality of the team was passive. We didn't have an edge about us that every other year, we had that. We walked into the gym and we knew we were Tennessee. We knew that meant something to everyone looking at us. And that team lacked that early on."

And it would get worse before it got better.

As time has moved on, more than fifteen years since the 1997 UConn-Tennessee regular-season meeting, there is tendency to talk about the early games of the rivalry in terms of Huskies milestones. The first game in 1995 resulted in UConn's first number-one ranking in the AP poll. The second meeting led to UConn's first national championship. In the third game UConn ended Tennessee's sixty-nine-game home winning streak.

And the fifth game would bring another famous first, another giant leap for women's basketball. This game would be played not at Gampel Pavilion, which had just expanded its seating from 8,241 to 10,027 for the 1996–97 season.

Instead it would be played at the 16,294-seat Hartford Civic Center, heretofore the domain of the UConn men's basketball team and—for a few more months in 1997, anyway—the NHL Hartford Whalers.

Indeed, it was a seminal moment for UConn's program and for the sport. Only three other times in UConn history had they played before larger crowds, and only their game at Kansas in January 1995 had drawn a bigger attendance figure for a regular-season game.

And even that one needed an asterisk, as the women's game was actually part of a doubleheader featuring the top-ranked UConn men's team, led by Ray Allen, against the Kansas men, featuring a future NBA championship teammate of Allen's named Paul Pierce.

So this January 1997 event would be the highest-attended UConn women's regular-season game. But it was actually not their first at the Civic Center, even if UConn's 62–46 win over Boston College on January 4, 1989, was entirely forgettable.

Game attendance: 287.

"If you count my wife and kids, we had a couple hundred people," Auriemma said. "It was awful. You feel like one of those traveling sideshows. You show up and go, 'Where is everybody?' That ball. Boomp. Boomp. Boomp. So loud. And the one lone guy in the back. Clap. Clap. Clap. God, it was terrible."

UConn's return engagement in Hartford was decidedly different.

"Like a Civil War game between interstate [sic] rivals," said Tennessee point guard Laurie Milligan.

"It's still a rivalry with us, regardless of whether or not it's for the number-one ranking or for the national championship," UConn point guard Rita Williams said. "It's probably always going to be the biggest game."

"Usually, a [big] game never lives up to the hype," Auriemma said. "In this case, it always has. It's unusual. But at some point, you say, 'There's going to be a clunker in there.' One of these times there's going to be a blowout and everybody's going to go home disappointed. I hope it's not [today]."

This time, Auriemma proved prophetic. The game would be remembered for those who watched it, both in the arena and on television. But what they watched was a UConn rout.

Led by their defense and a successful suppression of big-stage jitters, the top-ranked Huskies shut down all Lady Vols not named Holdsclaw and cruised to a 72–57 victory.

"This was kind of like the day we went to Washington to meet the president [after the national championship in 1995]," Auriemma said after the game. "People kept telling me how exciting it would be. And honestly, I couldn't understand what the big deal was all about. That is, until the president came over to shake our hands. Then I got really nervous."

Auriemma's team reflected the coach's mood early, as

Tennessee took a 10-7 lead. At one point Auriemma asked his freshman guard, Shea Ralph, if she was scared.

Then the Huskies went on the first of two runs, 12–0 over 7:47—featuring 7 Tennessee turnovers and 8 points from Ralph—to leave the Volunteers in a 19-10 hole.

"We knew how to break a press," Holdsclaw said. "We were just playing a little scattered."

In the second half, a 9–0 run made it 39-18. With ten minutes to play, UConn led by 23.

Holdsclaw had 23 points on 9-for-23 shooting. UConn junior Nykesha Sales finished with 22 points, 16 in the second half.

As usual Tennessee outrebounded the Huskies, 51-37, but they shot horribly, finishing with a season low percentage of 30.7.

"I told Chamique after the game that we have to handle these times," Summitt said. "We've handled success. I hope we can handle this. We lost to a better team. It's just how we lost that disappointed us as a team and as a staff."

The loss to UConn was just another setback for the defending champions, who were still without Jolly and seemingly unable to respond to a challenge. Their 57 points was a season low, their 24 turnovers a season high.

"I'm not going to put down my teammates," Holdsclaw said, "but we need some people to step up their games at the offensive end. Last year, [opponents] just let me float around. This year, they're getting between me and the basket and making me work a lot harder. That should create some openings around me."

The Lady Vols were also paying the price for one of the most of ambitious schedules Summitt had ever put together. Never afraid to play a tough opponent, Tennessee had over-extended itself for a squad that had just lost Michelle Marciniak and Latina Davis to graduation.

Tennessee's five losses through January 5 now included number-one UConn, then-number-one Stanford, then-number-five Georgia, then-number-eleven Louisiana Tech, and then-number-twenty-two Arkansas. And the team was still in the midst of a six-game road stretch that would end two nights later with their sixth loss, at number-two Old Dominion.

It all amounted to Tennessee dropping out of the AP Top 10 for the first time since 1986.

"Last year we were the national champs—we knew how to handle success," Holdsclaw said. "Now we have to learn how to handle adversity. It's not easy, you know. I mean, the University of Tennessee has a lot of history. You don't want to be the team that sets all those bad records."

While Tennessee suffered, the sport as a whole continued to thrive. Despite the rout, and despite going head-to-head against the New England Patriots' first postseason victory in a decade, the women's game owned a significant share of the Connecticut sports television audience.

UConn-Tennessee received a 12.9 rating and a 22 share in overnight figures. The Patriots-Steelers game got a 25.7/49. Nationally, the football game won the time slot easily, as expected, but the basketball game still achieved a solid 1.0 rating.

"For me, I don't remember when that moment was, but there were people talking about the UConn-Tennessee rivalry on ESPN and *SportsCenter*, and somebody said something about it in the paper," Jolly said. "People were excited about women's basketball. That was huge for our sport. At the end of the day we want people talking about women's basketball games and no game was talked about like Tennessee-Connecticut."

Soon people would be talking about Jolly. After just three and a half months the sophomore guard returned to the Tennessee lineup on January 12 against Kentucky. After losing six of its first sixteen games, Tennessee would rip off ten wins over its next eleven.

"For me, my motivation for getting back was, 'How can I help this team?'" Jolly said. "Obviously, I felt like we were struggling and I could help them if I could get back on the court. By no means was I an All-American, but I felt like I could be a part of a spark, halfway through the season, if I could get back."

But the struggles were not over. The one defeat in their 10-1 stretch came against Florida, the first loss to the hated Gators in program history. At the end of the regular season Tennessee for a second time lost back-to-back games, denying it a first-round bye in the SEC tournament for the first time. In the semifinals Auburn scored with two seconds left for a 61–59 win, saddling Tennessee with its tenth loss of the season—the most for the program in eleven years.

And now the Lady Vols were faced with a formidable challenge. No team with double-digit losses had ever won a national championship.

"I distinctly remember about that season, we lost in the SEC tournament and we had about two weeks until we played in the NCAA Tournament," Jolly said. "I remember Pat coming in to us saying, 'We have to get better in two weeks. We have two weeks.' And I remember thinking okay, we'll just get better in two weeks. We'll just make up for all this lost time in two weeks.

"She was just so confident that that's all we had to do. The way it was presented to us, we were very motivated in that time. That's a tough time for college players to be motivated. You're not playing games, it's just practice. It seems like forever before you're going to play a game. But she had us very motivated and we did get better. There's no way we would have won if we didn't get better."

Up in Storrs the Huskies would be hard-pressed to get much better after capturing their fourth-consecutive Big East tournament to raise their record to 30-0.

UConn played the Big East tournament without Auriemma, who had returned to his hometown of Philadelphia after the death of his father. When he returned his sentiment was much different from the urgent tone he had taken in Knoxville. Such is the way things are for a team with no losses, as opposed to ten.

"Frankly, I think the layoff we're having is a little too long this year," Auriemma said. "In many ways, it's a little unnatural. Sometimes it's hard to keep everyone's attention."

Senior Kara Wolters and junior Nykesha Sales were the leaders of this UConn group, gunning for their third Final Four together. But the player who had made the biggest impact on the undefeated Huskies was a freshman, a player Tennessee had tried valiantly to land, Shea Ralph.

A guard from Fayetteville, North Carolina, the daughter of a former player named Marsha Lake, Ralph brought to the Huskies an intensity and drive that had just left with the graduation of Jennifer Rizzotti and Jamelle Elliott.

It was early in the January Tennessee game that Auriemma challenged Ralph, asking the freshman point-blank on the sidelines if she was scared. Thirty seconds later she drove the lane and scored. Then again. Then another. Ralph's 8-point run erased Tennessee's early lead and the Huskies rolled from there.

"She saved our life," Auriemma said. "The scouting report on Shea is that she's going to go to the basket. Well, that's like saying [Bob] Cousy was going to go right. She's going to go to the basket all right, and I don't think there's too many people that are going to stop her from going to the basket."

Ralph's determined play was no surprise to Summitt.

"I've watched Shea Ralph play a lot of basketball in summer camp," she said. "She's a very confident offensive player. It's unusual to find a player that can come into a big game like this and put up the points and demonstrate with her offensive skills the type of aggressiveness and finish—I mean, she finishes plays."

And it was in the first round NCAA tournament game at Gampel that the hard-charging freshman looked to finish a play. But as Ralph drove to the basket on a fast break in the first half her right knee suddenly buckled, and she crumpled to the court with a frightening scream of pain.

UConn would go on to an easy victory, but it proved extremely costly. For the first of three times in her UConn career, Ralph had torn an ACL and was lost for the season.

"In my mind, I've always had the fear of injuring my ACL," Ralph said the next day, after the diagnosis was confirmed.

"Unfortunately, it did happen to me. It happened on a fast break. I stopped. The top of my leg went one way, the bottom went the other. But I'm a freshman, I have three more years. What I'm going to do is concentrate this summer on getting better and I'm going to come back even stronger."

But in the here and now Ralph, who averaged 11.4 points, 4.5 rebounds, and 1.8 assists and provided the Huskies a solid emotional lift, was ripped from the lineup with no time to adjust.

"Shea's injury will have a huge impact on us in purely basketball terms," Auriemma said. "What you lose is versatility. Losing Shea is not like losing just one player. You lose a point guard, a scorer, a rebounder, an excellent passer. You're losing someone who can easily score 20 if you need it.

"Losing Shea means we'll have to change much about what we do. I don't really know the eventual effect this will all have on our kids. But hopefully we'll find a way to band together, find a way to compete. I'm sure we'll be able to do that."

Meanwhile, Summitt's two-week crash course in Basketball 101 was netting the desired results. Tennessee won its first-round game with ease as well. But as at UConn there was an injury scare. It was Jolly, but fortunately for Tennessee it was not the knee. However, her sprained ankle was serious enough to limit her to fifteen minutes in a second-round victory.

After two years of arranging the bracket to allow UConn and Tennessee to meet in the Final Four, the 1997 pairings called for an earlier encounter. Both teams, placed in the Mideast Regional in Iowa City, were put on a collision course for the regional final.

And both teams fulfilled their destiny. With senior Carla Berube helping to pick up the slack for the injured Ralph with 17 points, UConn held off Illinois, 78–73. In the other regional semifinal, Holdsclaw's 20 points helped Tennessee draw away from Colorado for a 75–67 win.

UConn was 33-0, but the Lady Vols had renewed momentum and confidence from their four straight wins.

"There was a 100 percent chance, going into that game, every fiber of my being knew we were going to win that game," Jolly said. "Everybody on our team knew we were going to win that game. Now, looking back, I have no idea how that happened. I guess our coaches brainwashed us, because given what we'd gone through and how that Connecticut team was playing, we shouldn't have won that game. But we were convinced that we were just as good, or better.

"I will never forget running down the tunnel in Iowa, and I was so anxious to get out there and play them, I almost forgot my team. I was running out there and had to turn around and tell them, 'C'mon, c'mon!' because we were about to win. We had nothing to lose and we went out there and played with a lot of confidence. [Assistant coach] Al Brown has talked about how ready we were for that game. I do remember in warm-ups thinking we were going to win."

Tennessee then went out and proved Jolly's intuition correct, taking the ball inside against Wolters and hitting the offensive glass, sprinting to a 21–11 lead. UConn cut the deficit to 26–19, but another Tennessee run pushed the lead to 15 before the Lady Vols settled for a 45–33 halftime lead.

After Jolly opened the second half with a basket, UConn outscored the Vols 13–5 to close to 50–48. A few minutes later UConn had a chance to tie when Holdsclaw committed her third foul as Rita Williams (14 points) scored. But when Williams missed her free throw, the Huskies still trailed 53–52.

And then the game, and the season, turned.

"I remember one play," said Mike DiMauro of the *New London Day*. "UConn was down quite a bit and they made their run in the second half and they're coming. Tennessee had gotten the lead because of a couple of their lesser players made a couple of big shots. And now they're not making them anymore and here comes UConn.

"They had the ball down one and Kara Wolters pins her man in the post, wide open, and Carla [Berube] sort of lobbed a pass in there, instead of giving her a nice, hard entry pass, and it got tipped away. And I remember Geno in front of the bench, jumping up and down, going '[crap, crap, crap, crap, crap],' five times, jumping up and down."

Off the turnover, Tennessee scored 9 straight points to re-establish a 10-point lead.

"They were never heard from again after that," DiMauro said. "In a ten-second span you could go from, 'Here they come, they're not going to lose,' to 'There they go, they're not going to win.'"

Appropriately for the ten-loss Lady Vols, 10 would the final margin this night, 91–81. A year earlier UConn had felt it had done all it could but had still lost in overtime to the Lady Vols in the Final Four; however, this loss was different. The injury to Ralph had left UConn shorthanded at the worst possible time, and the team did not respond as they had hoped.

"I remember standing in the hallway [after the game], and whenever Geno is in distress, he runs his hands through his hair," DiMauro said. "He was doing that. He was blaming himself for a strategic thing in that game. But mostly, it was because they didn't have Shea."

"It's just so hard," Auriemma told reporters. "When you're a freshman or sophomore, you think it's going to last forever. Then it dawns on you your senior year that time is precious. I just so feel bad for Kara and Carla. They've meant so much to our program. I don't want them to leave thinking this night symbolizes UConn basketball. It's only one small part of a big picture."

For Holdsclaw, who led Tennessee with 21 points, and Jolly, who chipped in 19, the victory was a stunning validation of a season teetering on disaster as well as payback for their defeat in Hartford in January, when the losses were piling up.

"I remember when everything was going wrong for us in January," Summitt said. "Abby Conklin said, 'If there's a championship in us, that woman's going to drag it out of us.'"

"We just played with intensity," Holdsclaw said. "But I think Connecticut was scared. That's the first time I've ever played them when they looked scared."

Tennessee moved on to play Notre Dame in the national

semifinals. How concerned was Summitt about her team's chances of reaching Cincinnati? Summitt didn't purchase a Final Four outfit—a task she usually performs in January—until the day after beating UConn in the regional final.

"When Kellie Jolly went down with an injury, I was concerned more so than ever about our chances to be a contender in March," Summitt said at the Final Four. "I think when she returned to the floor we felt she and Laurie Milligan, we were obviously in that group of people that could make a run. Then Laurie goes down five games later. I never felt totally out of it. My concern in January is, we have to win enough games to get into the tournament. Once you get into the tournament, anything can happen.

"We played some of our best basketball in February. Once I saw we were in a position to make the pool, then I felt much better about our chances. Once I saw the bracket, I liked the bracket we were in because we were not playing against any SEC teams, and that's one situation that I really favored. Then obviously we knew we had a huge challenge ahead of us. I thought the possibility still existed that we could be in this position."

Tennessee then went out and handled the Fighting Irish in the semifinals, 80–66, before facing another traditional power, Old Dominion, in the championship.

The Lady Monarchs had handed Tennessee one of its ten losses earlier in the year, but now, with the team rolling as at no other time that season, the Lady Vols would again make history.

After seeing ODU turn a 15-point deficit into a 49–47 lead, Holdsclaw slammed the door, starting a 12–2 run that sealed the title with a 68–59 victory. It was Tennessee's fifth national championship and its first time winning back-to-back titles. Holdsclaw finished with 24 points and was named Final Four MVP.

"Of all our runs to a championship, this one is really the most unexpected," Summitt said. "It came from a team with tremendous heart and desire. This is a group that will always be very special to me personally as well as professionally. And to our staff and our team, I just applaud their willingness to work together to do something that was never done to the University of Tennessee, and that's win back-to-back championships. I just feel very, very fortunate to have had the opportunity to learn and to grow and to be challenged, and to come through in a championship way with this team."

6

....

1998–99

....

Boo Yeah

In the end it was really all Peyton Manning's fault.

Through the first three years of the rivalry, the relationship between the two programs had been hypercompetitive but cordial. Entering the 1997–98 season UConn led the overall series 4–2, but Tennessee led where it counted, rebounding from their three straight losses to UConn to open the series—including the 1995 national championship game—by beating UConn in the Final Four semifinals in 1996 and the regional finals in 1997 en route to the first two of an unprecedented three straight national championships.

At this stage, whatever back-and-forth banter that existed between the two programs was still rooted in mutual respect.

"The irony of it is, the way that series started, Connecticut beating Tennessee [the first three games], things were still good between those two coaches," Dan Fleser said. "You'd think it could have gotten off the tracks right then and there, but it didn't. There was a lot of mutual respect, not that it ever went away, but it carried the day. It was more in the forefront than it was later on."

The Huskies and Lady Vols were now considered the two leading lights on the national landscape, their annual game having become the marquee event of the women's basketball regular season. More eyes were on this rivalry than any other women's contest, and those eyes increasingly belonged to impressionable, talented teenage girls, dreaming of taking their abundant basketball talents to one to the two biggest stages.

As it had on the court in calendar year 1995, UConn also won the first two head-to-head battles off the court, convincing two top recruits, center Paige Sauer and guard Shea Ralph, to bypass Tennessee and sign national letters of intent that November to play at Connecticut.

The following year, in the fall of 1996, it was Semeka Randall's turn to decide.

Randall developed her toughness and swagger on the basketball court at a very early age. Growing up in Cleveland, Ohio, Randall, one of the few girls in her neighborhood to take an interest in the game, started playing basketball at the age of six.

"Growing up, playing against guys, every day you have to prove yourself to them," Randall said. "They weren't just going to let you play because you were a girl. You had to show something out there on the floor, and that's the mentality I took with me, and it's what made me successful."

Another great motivator was fear. One of the most popular variations of the game in her neighborhood was called "Booty"—the title referring to the part of one's anatomy that was constantly in peril for the defeated.

"It was 'Around the World'—make a shot, go to the next spot, etc.," Randall said. "But if you didn't win, there would be a ton of guys in the backyard, and you had to stand and put your hands on the pole and stick your butt out, and each person got an opportunity to hit you with the basketball five times.

"So if there's twenty guys in the yard, I'm getting a hundred hits. It got to the point where I went home crying to my mom about it. She's like, 'I told you not to be out there playing with those boys. You're crazy.' So I had to learn how to stay in there and take it, at the age of ten, like a woman. It got to the point where they felt sorry for me, and were like, 'We'll time you and make you run around the block,' because I would lose all the time. Over time, I got so focused and driven, I would make it all the way around."

Soon Randall, a five-foot-ten-inch guard, had made it to an elite level, becoming one of the top high school players in Ohio, starring for Trinity High School in Garfield Heights under the tutelage of legendary coach Pat Diulus, who won nine state championships—three with Trinity—over a twenty-five-year career before his death at sixty-seven in 2012.

Randall would be named Ms. Ohio Basketball as the top player in the state in her junior and senior seasons in 1996 and 1997, the latter also resulting in Kodak national player of the year honors. But even before suiting up for Trinity, Randall had caught the eye of Summitt and Tennessee.

"She started recruiting me in the eighth grade, and the reason why is because she was recruiting my teammate, [Na'Sheema] Hillmon, who went to Vanderbilt [from 1995 to 1998]," Randall said. "That's how she found out about me early. I didn't have a lot of exposure, like kids do today. I played in local stuff, but [Diulus] didn't let me do major things. I only did one AAU event and went to one camp in Rochester, New York, where I first met Chamique [Holdsclaw]. I didn't get that exposure like most people did.

"I was in awe of her. Even though she wasn't recruiting me, I'm like, 'That's Pat Summitt.' From there, she would show up and sit right in the front [at Randall's games]. And I'm animated, so I would let her know that I saw her sitting there. It really started with [Tennessee assistant] Mickie DeMoss just recruiting the heck out of me, to the point where I called Coach collect every day and we'd talk basketball, and I'd say, 'Coach, [the Lady Vols] need to be a little more aggressive.' I was very opinionated."

And Randall was not afraid to make her strong opinions very public, as Connecticut players, coaches, and fans would later discover. The first hints of Randall's uncommon candor came during her recruiting process, as the high school junior kept a running diary about her recruitment that ran in the pages of her hometown newspaper, the *Cleveland Plain Dealer.*

On September 12, two months before national signing day, Randall met Auriemma and UConn associate head coach Chris Dailey at coach Diulus's home. Summitt had made her official home visit the day before.

Randall wrote in the diary: "Geno seemed pretty easygoing, but yet a demanding coach. I know that's what I need. Our meeting lasted three hours. I don't think he caught my eyes like Pat did, but I told myself to give them a chance."

"Geno started showing interest in me, and my high school coach told me, I need to weigh my options," Randall said in 2013. "Even though I was excited about Tennessee, Connecticut is here. I know Geno always thought privately that my high school coach was pushing me toward Tennessee, but he actually wanted me to make a good decision. I had five schools when I started out, and it came down to the two schools where I thought I could win a championship. That was my goal. No disrespect to the other schools, but at that time, those two were playing at the highest level you could be at.

"I watched [UConn's] games, with Rebecca Lobo and Jennifer Rizzotti. I'm a basketball junkie, so I knew exactly what he did and who he was. I just didn't have that relationship. And Chris Dailey was awesome in the process. We would go up there to visit them and it was cool to have Nykesha Sales as my host [in Storrs] and getting to meet Rip Hamilton, and Ricky Moore was one of my favorite players, because I loved the way he played defense. I always thought me and him were the same."

But, in the end, Randall went with the program that had sought her from the start. On October 29, through her diary in the *Plain Dealer*, Randall announced her intention to sign with the Lady Vols. Just as had been the case months earlier in Iowa City, UConn was begrudgingly the runner-up.

"The recruiting process was kind of the way you expected it to be when recruiting a great player," Auriemma said. "For us, it was something we enjoyed doing—to a point. I got to know

Semeka and really liked her as a person and obviously as a player. I thought she had the ability to become a great, great player. That was evident right from the beginning.

"I think the guy handling her recruiting out in Cleveland [Diulus] was full of [it] and wasn't honest with us from Day One. So we were always battling uphill. The end result was she went to Tennessee. I didn't have a problem with that."

Randall would remember Auriemma's reaction to her decision to attend Tennessee a bit differently. Knowing how upset the Connecticut coach would be with her selection, Randall tried persuading coach Diulus to make the difficult phone call for her. No dice. For a player who would later be remembered for backing up her words with actions, it was time to back her actions with words.

"It was tough," Randall said. "My high school coach always made me pick up the phone and make that call to say I wasn't coming. He's like, 'No, you talked to these people all this time, you're going to learn how to tell people that you're not coming.'

"And I knew that was going to be one of the hardest things, for me at that age, to make that phone call, and it didn't go over so great. But I knew I had to do it. And that call was not fun."

According to Randall's diary, Auriemma's ire was not entirely focused on Randall and her high school coach. Buried deep within her prose lay one of the first shots fired in the war between the two coaches:

"Geno emphasized that I would get more national exposure [at UConn]. He said that when you hear about Connecticut, you hear about the players. And when you hear about Tennessee, it's Pat Summitt."

The entirety of Auriemma's rant left a lasting impression on Randall. Although she would have to wait almost fifteen months for her chance, she was already primed to exact revenge on the Connecticut program.

"Geno is Geno," Randall said. "He's going to always tell you how he feels. And he's going to give you the business. 'That's fine, you go there. We're going to kick your tail.' And when you're seventeen, eighteen years old, and you hear that, it hurts. For me, it hurt. But I was like, 'I'm going to show him something.'"

Tennessee had slogged its way through its ten-loss season in 1997 before cutting down the nets in Cincinnati, becoming the first women's team to capture a national title with double-digit losses.

But with Randall and fellow freshman Tamika Catchings, the daughter of former NBA player Harvey Catchings, joining forces with junior sensation Chamique Holdsclaw to become "The Three Meeks" in 1997–98, Tennessee embarked on an unprecedented season of a vastly different variety.

"The returning players had a lot of confidence, Chamique, myself, Kyra Elzy," said Kellie Jolly Harper, the Lady Vols' junior point guard in 1997–98. "And then the mix of the new players that were so super-talented. But that doesn't work if there's not good chemistry there, and the upperclassmen were so good at embracing the freshmen and the freshmen brought so much energy every day that the chemistry stayed great."

UConn had been the most recent team to go undefeated, in 1995, taking down the Lady Vols twice—including the epic championship game at the Target Center in Minneapolis—to finish 35-0. UConn nearly repeated the feat in 1997, winning their first thirty-three games before losing the thirty-fourth at the hands of Tennessee in the regional final in Iowa City.

UConn's stunning denial of a 36-0 season came in no small measure because of the injury to freshman Shea Ralph, who blew out her right knee in the first round of the NCAA tournament at Gampel Pavilion against Lehigh. And Ralph would be lost for the 1997–98 season before it started, re-tearing the ACL in her right knee during the preseason.

The Huskies still had senior All-American Nykesha Sales, who was closing in on UConn's all-time scoring record, and a newcomer and superstar in the making from St. Petersburg, Russia, named Svetlana Abrosimova. But when the third-ranked and 12-0 Huskies traveled to Knoxville in early January for the sixth edition of the rivalry, for the first time it was clear, despite their matching undefeated records, that one team had a decided advantage over the other.

Entering the second UConn-Tennessee game to be played at Thompson-Boling Arena, after UConn had ended the Lady Vols' sixty-nine-game home winning streak in its debut there in 1996, Tennessee was an emphatic 14-0 and ranked number one, led by Holdsclaw, the junior who entered the UConn game leading her team in scoring (20.6 per game), rebounding (8.2), and steals (3.3), but also by the talented freshman class of Catchings, Randall, Kristen "Ace" Clement, and Teresa Geter.

Catchings and Randall pumped in 28 points in Tennessee's early season victory over then number-two Louisiana Tech. They combined for 37 points during a late-November blowout of Stanford. They had 47 against Illinois in the championship game of the Northern Lights Invitational in Anchorage, Alaska.

"This is a unique situation," Summitt said before the UConn game. "There's no better way to put it. It's such a special class. I've never had [a freshman class] make such an immediate impact as this one, on offense, on defense, with rebounding. These kids are competitive along with being very gifted. It doesn't matter at all that they are freshmen. They don't back down."

In the final tune-up before UConn, the Vols had crushed twenty-fifth-ranked Arkansas by 30 points.

"There's no doubt we were very talented," Jolly said. "We had a lot of players who could do special things and we were all in it for the right reason, we all pulled for each other. And everything came together and went right. We didn't have major injuries. And once we started rolling, it was out of control in a positive way for us.

"We had some highly competitive people who thought we were going to win a lot of basketball games. And when we got into that season and we started winning, there was no doubt.

Pretty early on, we felt like we were going to win every game. It was either our competitive nature or we just didn't know any better, but that's where we were."

But for one of the only times in the history of the rivalry, the game on January 3, 1998, took a backseat in the minds of sports fans in Tennessee. On the evening before third-ranked UConn and the top-ranked Lady Vols renewed their pleasantries in Knoxville, the third-ranked Tennessee football team took on top-ranked Nebraska in the Orange Bowl in Miami.

For the Cornhuskers a shot at a share of the national championship with Michigan was at stake. Though Tennessee would fall short of the title, it had its own significant storyline: win or lose, this would be the final game in the illustrious career of star quarterback Peyton Manning.

So momentous was the occasion that the region's leading newspaper, the *Knoxville News-Sentinel*, chose to send Fleser, its women's basketball beat writer, down to Miami to supplement the coverage of Manning's farewell.

"That 1997–98 game, I didn't cover it, because I was at the Orange Bowl and I couldn't get back in time," Fleser said. "I was covering Nebraska down there. And that's the game where all the [expletive] started."

For the freshman Randall, this was the game she had circled on her calendar since the tumultuous phone call with Auriemma back in November 1996.

"I am so hyped, because I know this game is so bigger than the series," Randall said. "This game is about how he told me [Auriemma] was going to kick my ass. I'm ready. I can't remember if she started me or brought off the bench, but I didn't care what happened in that game, I was getting this."

Because of an experimental rule put in place by the NCAA, the game was played with four 10-minute quarters instead of two 20-minute halves. UConn entered the contest with a fifty-two-game regular-season winning streak, its last such loss coming against Georgia at Gampel in the 1996 Martin Luther King Day matchup, a major letdown for ESPN after the magical 1995 game.

For this UConn-Tennessee matchup, CBS once again held the television rights and would broadcast a blowout loss for the Huskies.

Playing in front of the largest crowd in the history of women's college basketball (24,597), the Huskies fell behind 10–0 and trailed by as many as 17 in the second quarter before ultimately succumbing to the Lady Vols, 84–69.

Randall did not start the game, her first since having a finger accidentally bitten in her previous game against Arkansas, but she finished off the Huskies as promised. The freshman scored 16 of her 25 points in the fourth quarter, after UConn had pulled within a point late in the third.

Randall hit 8 of 14 shots from the field, grabbed 10 rebounds, and was a key factor in Tennessee's full-court pressure defense that disrupted the Huskies.

"That was right up her alley," Jolly said. "I think the freshman class of Randall, Catchings, Geter, and Clement helped bring in a little bit of swagger. They had some edge about them. I think our team took a lot from them. That's what took us from the passive team that barely won a championship to going 39–0. Semeka had such a big personality on the court. Fiery, explosive, high energy, she was the player you loved to play with and hated to play against. She was an easy target for our opponents, but she was also very well loved if you were wearing orange."

And when it was over, the flamboyant freshman headed back to the floor, acknowledged the record crowd that stayed behind to celebrate the victory, and played to them in a radio interview from press row that was pumped over the public address system.

"When I made my final decision to go to Tennessee, Geno said, 'I am going to have to put the whammy on you when we play,'" Randall crowed. "I think Connecticut about ran off the floor, they were so scared."

By chance, *News-Sentinel* reporter Chuck Cavalaris, filling in for Fleser for one of the few times in his career with the Knoxville paper, made an unconventional but quite fortuitous decision to walk back out onto the court in search of Randall for postgame comments. Hearing her radio appearance, Cavalaris jotted down Randall's comments about UConn's composure and used them in his game story, which ran in the next day's paper.

But had Fleser, who never before or since missed a UConn-Tennessee matchup, not been on Manning duty in Miami, he would have written the game story that Cavalaris ultimately filed. And it would not have included Randall's inflammatory remark. Instead, splattered all over Knoxville, was the first shot heard round the women's basketball world.

"I think a lot of people forget that's really where it started," Fleser said. "The guy who covered the game for us went out onto the court and listened to her talk on radio and she threw out a bunch of Semeka stuff to play to the crowd. I'm guessing if I had been covering the game, I'd never gone out to listen to [Randall], to what someone was saying on the radio. I never would have written about that."

But Cavalaris did, and word of Semeka's smackdown, even in the early years of the Internet, quickly made its way to the basketball offices in Storrs. When they next held an open practice for the media just days after the loss, the Huskies did not hide their displeasure.

"Any real player would take that to heart," said Sales, who had hosted Randall during her official visit to UConn's campus during the recruiting process. "I don't know. She might have really meant it. But I think we'll remember it for the next time we play."

Added guard Rita Williams: "I don't know what she was thinking, but if that's what she took away from the entire game, that's up to her, I guess. If we had come back to win, would we still have been scared? Are those the words she would have used?"

But the biggest blowback came from Auriemma, who fired back at Randall and the Tennessee coaching staff with both barrels.

"I'm not sure what to think of what Randall said," Auriemma said. "How do you interpret something like that? I'd like to believe that kids aren't stupid, that they understand what's going on. Is it just a case of kids talking? Or do they sense a lack of aggression on our part?

"If she played for me, I'd make sure to talk to her about it. You shouldn't be making judgments about other teams. She's a little cocky, I'll admit. That's one of the reasons I recruited her. But if she had any guts, she would have said the things she did to [the Connecticut media].

"I think it's about personalities. What Semeka might have been alluding to is Tennessee's feeling we don't have kids tough enough to beat them. But I don't want to say our guys were scared. If they were, they would have fallen apart for the entire game.

"Hey, the year we beat Tennessee for the national championship, Michelle Marciniak looked like a wreck. But we never accused anyone of being scared. They can say what they want, I guess. Bottom line, they had the greatest team ever to play the sport at that time and we beat their butts.

"But we never said they looked scared. If that stuff is coming from their coaching staff, then to hell with them, too."

Just as quickly as Randall's "scared" comment had reached Storrs, now Auriemma's retort boomeranged back to Knoxville. For the first time—but certainly not the last—Summitt greeted Auriemma's bellicose blast with incredulity.

"I think [Randall] was trying to compliment our fans, not criticize an opponent," Summitt told the *News-Sentinel* days later. "These players are not trash-talkers."

Summitt took particular exception to Auriemma's comment about Marciniak in the 1995 title game.

"I find it hard to believe that he'd refer to Michelle from three years ago," Summitt said. "And the language [Auriemma used]. It's just hard to believe."

"That was the beginning of [the rift between the coaches]," Fleser said. "He responded and Summitt was totally blown away by his response. She goes, 'The language!' And I think that really took her by surprise."

Fifteen years later Randall claims her comments about UConn

being scared were taken wildly out of context—if she said them at all. It has been suggested that Randall was lauding the intimidation factor supplied by the record crowd at Thompson-Boling Arena as the source of her comment, although Randall herself offered no explicit explanation.

"I said, we scared them off the floor. I will say this: It was totally taken out of context, but I'll take it," Randall said. "We played hard. We just went at them. We were ready to go? Did they have something to come back at us? Obviously, you look at the scoreboard, they didn't. We were ready.

"Pat came after me and said, 'You got me in trouble. You got me in the doghouse.' Because that's not the way Coach Summitt is, about saying stuff. She was like a parent, like when you go in to meet with the principal, then the parents go in, and they only listen to the principal's side. I was sitting there like, 'But I didn't do that.' She was like, 'Randall, I can't believe you said that.' And I said, 'But Coach, I didn't do it!' I'm trying to defend myself, but it got to a point where, if I said it, I have to own up to it.

"I think, to this day, Geno knows that [I didn't mean it], because he's good at being the mastermind of stuff and it was good to get his team [fired up]."

Regardless of the content or tenor of Randall's remarks, for the first time in the rivalry's short history the basketball battle between North and South had turned into an uncivil war.

"That did add fuel to the fire," Auriemma said in 2013. "Kids being kids and players being players, you ask them a question and they tell you what's on their mind. Semeka thought that and said it. And during those years, they had the right to say whatever they wanted to say, because they were winning the championships."

"Something else probably would have touched it off eventually," Fleser said. "But the way it happened was really unusual and unlikely. This was the Lexington and Concord moment and it was purely unintentional and might not even have happened under normal circumstances."

But as quickly as tempers flared between the programs, they subsided. Semeka Randall and the Lady Vols were far from the minds of the Huskies and their fans in late February, when Sales was lost for the postseason with a career-ending Achilles injury. The controversy that surrounded the subsequent "gift" basket against Villanova that earned her UConn's all-time scoring record dominated the airwaves, but obscured the fact that UConn was left vulnerable entering the NCAA tournament. And when Abrosimova was injured during a regional final matchup against North Carolina State, the season was lost.

Meanwhile, the Lady Vols put UConn far behind them as they continued their inexorable march into history, steamrolling through the early rounds of the NCAA tournament, then beating Louisiana Tech by 18 points in the championship game in Kansas City to capture their unprecedented third straight national title and sixth in program history.

In the process Tennessee became the first program in women's history to go undefeated by winning thirty-nine games.

"The best team doesn't always win, but tonight I thought the best team won the championship that they deserve," Summitt said after the game. "And they've been the best team all year long. But I kept saying, 'Let's see what happens when we get into postseason and March Madness.' I am so happy for this team because of their love for the game, their competitiveness and their chemistry and love for each other. And it has just been an incredible year. I cannot imagine this team not getting what they deserve. They deserve a national championship. They came out in the opening minutes clearly ready to play. I felt good about it. I told them I've been to fifteen of these, I said I've never felt better going into a championship game than I feel tonight.

"I can tell you it's the quickest, the best defensive team I've coached and the best transition team overall that I've coached. I also can tell you it's a team unlike any that I've coached in terms of their competitiveness and their will to win. Also, they're willing to prepare to win. A lot of players say they want to win. But this team, their preparation was tremendous. As far as all those coaches out there that coach a lot of great teams, this one is a different style. But I like this style probably best of any I've seen."

Jolly and Holdsclaw were now three-for-three in national titles, fulfilling 75 percent of a goal they set out to attain upon arrival in Knoxville in 1995.

"We felt like from Day One, we were going to win a national championship," Jolly said. "Chamique and I, when we were in high school, she and I were talking and we said we were going to Tennessee and we were going to win four national championships. We actually stated that to each other. I don't know what fairyland we thought we were living in, but for us, we believed it."

Her sixth championship trophy added to the collection at Thompson-Boling Arena, Summitt went on something of a victory tour in the weeks after Tennessee's triumph. Her first book, *Reach for the Summitt*, had just hit bookshelves across the nation—and that included Borders Books in Farmington, Connecticut, just a bounce-pass away from Hartford.

On April 17, just three weeks after cutting down the nets in Kansas City, Summitt prepared for a dragnet of UConn fans deep in the heart of enemy territory.

"I teased [the book promoters] about it," Summitt said before making a three-hour appearance at the store. "I said, 'Yeah, so are you going to give me a police escort?'"

But any animosity that might have built up after Randall's 'scared' comment in January was nowhere to be seen in April. Nearly seven hundred people waited in line to meet and greet the legendary Tennessee coach. Many had copies of the book or *Sports Illustrated* covers that featured Summitt. It was the largest crowd for a book signing in the four-year history of the store, far surpassing appearances by radio icon Dr. Laura Schlessinger, 1994 Olympic figure skating champion Oksana Baiul, and even Rebecca Lobo, who only drew one-fourth of the crowd that came to see Summitt.

Even Auriemma extended an olive branch, in the form of flowers and a note.

"Congratulations on your great season," Auriemma wrote.

"We hope your next visit to Connecticut is not as pleasant as this one."

Tennessee's next visit would be in January at Gampel Pavilion, the Lady Vols' first return to the UConn campus since the historic first-ever meeting between the two teams in 1995.

UConn held a 4–3 lead in the series, but the Lady Vols had won three of the past four meetings, including the previous two in a row. But Tennessee had never won on Connecticut soil.

Presumably, if ever a Tennessee team was going to win such a game on the road, it would be the 1998–99 team. After all, they were the three-time defending champions, returning the core of the roster that went 39-0 the previous season.

But the Lady Vols found the road to a fourth-straight title a bit choppy as the calendar turned to January. They were ranked number two with a 12-1 record behind top-ranked UConn, which entered the Tennessee game at 13-0.

But though Tennessee had just one loss, the chemistry and intensity that had been the hallmark of the 39-0 team was not quite the same this time around. Randall and Catchings were now sophomores, and the growing pains were proving acute.

"Last year, we played with so much emotion because it was our first time out here playing. We were in college," Randall said the week before the UConn game. "Sometimes, now, being older, we might get complacent. I think sometimes it's a wakeup call, and it's good for us.

"I know sometimes I need to be the emotional leader instead of sitting back and waiting. That's what I've learned as I've gotten older. I've matured. I know when to do things, when not to."

UConn had its own blockbuster freshman class on display in 1999—at least the ones that could actually play.

UConn had recruited the top class in 1998, bringing in blue-chip forwards Tamika Williams, Asjha Jones, and Swin Cash, and guards Sue Bird and Keirsten Walters. The media had tried to label them the "Fab Five," like the Michigan men's class in 1991 that featured Chris Webber, Juwan Howard, and Jalen Rose. But the UConn freshman sought their own identity, taking the first initial from each of their names to become the TASSK Force.

However, injuries would force some of them to the bench as freshmen. Bird, the point guard, was lost for the season in December with a torn ACL in her left knee, forcing Walters to man the unfamiliar position. The Tennessee game would be just Walters's second start at the point. Cash would play against the Lady Vols, but with a stress fracture in her leg.

But Shea Ralph, after missing the 1998 season with her second ACL tear, was back, and sophomore Svetlana Abrosimova was developing into one of the smoothest scorers in UConn history.

Once again the game was scheduled for a national television audience on CBS. And already, plans were under way to take the rivalry to another level in 2000, with two regular-season games between the titans in each of the next two seasons—one for CBS, the other in prime time on ESPN.

But by now, with all the hype and hoopla placed on a nonconference game in January, the two coaches began publicly showing signs of rivalry fatigue.

"There's too much attention paid to this game," Auriemma said on the eve of UConn-Tennessee VIII. "And it happens every year. I guess, it's good. But it's also January 10. Then again, this is Connecticut. If we win, we're a lock to win the NCAAs. And if we lose, I realize we're not going to make it to the tournament. It makes a lot of people jump up and down and go, 'Aren't we great?' And another group of people go, 'Oh man, what a bummer.'"

But for the players the game was still vital. The Huskies were still smarting over Randall's comments from the year before. Some of the veteran players appreciated the rivalry as keenly as ever. "I do think toward the end of my career, the Connecticut rivalry was more important," Jolly said. "I don't know if it was just me maturing in the women's basketball game and understanding it, or if more people were getting on board of UConn vs. Tennessee. It became more of a national thing later on in my career. I felt like the intensity of that rivalry was increased as each went along."

If there was any doubt about where on the scale the intensity level for this game would reside, it ended before the opening tip. Looking to add a little more big-fight feel to yet another heavyweight bout, UConn paid $5,000 for legendary boxing-ring announcer Michael Buffer to introduce the starting lineups before offering his signature, "Let's get ready to rummmmmmble!!!"

UConn and Tennessee were ready. And then they did.

As always when they faced Tennessee, the Huskies' toughest task was to keep the Lady Vols off the boards. And so it was that Abrosimova, not known for mixing it up in the paint, battled early in the game for a rebound against Randall. As the two sophomores grappled for control, they fell to the floor in a heap yet continued to scrap for possession. As they struggled Randall rolled on top of the Russian, banging Abrosimova's head against the floor. Whistles blew, as did tempers in the partisan UConn crowd.

"Street basketball," Randall said after the game. "I didn't want to let it go. She didn't want to let it go. We rode around for a few and, I guess, it was a WWF match, huh?"

Years later, as coach at Alabama A&M, Randall recounted her encounter with Abrosimova.

"Let me say this: She had the ball. I had the ball. I'm not going to let go. She's not going to let go," Randall said. "But it appeared to look like I body-slammed her. I just didn't want to let go of the ball, and I'll get in trouble for saying this, but international players do that. I played international ball, and there's no knocking into international players. I mean, I did bump her, but I think she made it look a little worse than it was."

Intentional or not, hard foul or not, there was no turning back. Randall had already gotten under UConn's skin with her "scared" comments the year before. Now Randall's inciting words had become inflammatory actions. And after Randall knocked Abrosimova down a second time later in the game, the response of the Gampel crowd every time Randall touched the ball was undeniable—and for the women's game, shockingly unprecedented.

"Boooooooo!"

"I thought it was funny," Randall said. "At first, I couldn't figure out what they were saying. Then one time I had the ball, just for a second, and there was a "Boo!" And the next time I had it for about ten seconds, and it was 'Boooooooo!' And I was like, 'These people are really booing me. Are you kidding me? Okay, boo me then. That's fine. I'll take that.'

"And from that point on, it was history. I get back to Knoxville, our next home game, and we run out of the tunnel with the smoke and fireworks and all that. 'Semeka Boooooooo Randall!' And I'm standing out there like, 'I've got a new name!' And from there, it's history. To this day every fan in Knoxville calls me Boo. 'Hey, Boo.'"

The crowd's attempt to heckle Randall had the opposite effect. Randall would go on to tie her career high in points with 25. Abrosimova would make just 3 of 12 shots.

"That's Mike Tyson, baby," Randall crowed after the game. "Total knockout right there."

The real knockout wouldn't come until the final four minutes. UConn had managed to hang with Tennessee, the score tied at 76–76 with 3:53 left. But by then Walters, pressed into point-guard duties after Bird's injury two weeks before, had run out of gas. Tennessee dared Walters to shoot and she did, missing 11 of 14 attempts in the game. On cue, Tennessee rebounded the misses and launched on a 12–0 run that put the game away, ultimately settling for a 92–81 victory.

"For thirty-seven minutes we didn't blink," Auriemma said. "Over the last three minutes, a couple of their guys made big plays, which I expected. And some of ours made the type of plays I was afraid they might. And there went the ballgame."

Just as UConn had done to Tennessee at Thompson-Boling Area in 1996, the Lady Vols' victory snapped UConn's home winning streak at fifty-four games. It was also Tennessee's third straight win over UConn, knotting the rivalry at 4–4.

"Before I came to Tennessee, UConn kind of owned us," said Holdsclaw, who also scored 25 points. "We were kind of intimidated by them."

Said Summitt: "Glad you came, then."

Tennessee held UConn, who came into the game shooting over 50 percent from the field, to 41.1 percent (30 for 73). With forty-six seconds left Randall scored to ice the game, then dropped to her knees and put out her arms in celebration as the boos continued to rain down.

"It was a very physical game," Randall said. "It reminded me of street-side basketball. Somebody has to be the mentally tough one.

"I live for this. I'll do anything for Tennessee. And if I had gone to UConn, I would have done the same thing. I'll never change. Being built like I am, I'm not afraid to bump. If I get knocked around, I get knocked around. But I'm coming back at you."

"Semeka has grown so much in the last few weeks," Summitt said. "I know she's reading the papers. She's such a great competitor. It's like throwing gasoline on the fire. I'm very proud of her for being able to come here today and have the poise while playing an emotional game. She's emotional when she gets on the bus."

In retrospect, the UConn-Tennessee game was the last highlight of the season for both. Beset by their injuries and an uncommon lack of cohesion between the heralded freshman class and a senior class that had not been to the Final Four since their own freshman season in 1996, UConn was nearly knocked out in the second round of the NCAA tournament—at Gampel, no less—by Xavier, then was officially sent home by Iowa State in the Sweet Sixteen—UConn's earliest tournament exit since 1993.

But the biggest shocker awaited Tennessee, denied not only a fourth national championship for seniors Holdsclaw and Jolly but a return to the Final Four altogether, losing in a stunning upset to Duke in the regional final.

Nevertheless, as the twentieth century came to an end a new era for women's basketball was awakening. And leading the way were UConn and Tennessee, for better or for worse, in sickness and in health, till death would they part.

"I think you realize it now, when you're looking back, not to take anything away from the rivalries they have now—or even the rivalries Tennessee had against Louisiana Tech or Georgia—it was just at another level," Randall said. "It was bigger than us. We understood what wearing that uniform meant. Bridgette Gordon might have been at our game, or Michelle Marciniak, and you watched them growing up and appreciated what they did.

"I think I can speak for all Tennessee players that we respected that series. We knew that it was our duty to get up for every game and win or lose, give it everything we've got."

7

2000

Ready for Prime Time Players

For ESPN's Carol Stiff, the euphoria over the success of the first-ever UConn-Tennessee game on Martin Luther King Day in 1995 has proven bittersweet. Yes, the January 1995 game that she had created was a huge ratings hit for the network. And when the Huskies and Lady Vols staged their rematch in the 1995 national championship game at Minneapolis's Target Center less than three months later, it was clear that a potential yearly ratings bonanza had come to life right before Stiff's eyes.

"You couldn't walk away from the fact that [the Martin Luther King Day] game rated a 1.0, at one in the afternoon," Stiff said. "I was pretty thrilled with that number. I would love to get that nowadays. I'd be lying if I said I knew it then. I was just happy it rated well. Never knew that they would be in the Final Four that year and win the championship and go undefeated. We just hit it, I guess. It was just luck."

But ESPN's luck was about to run out. As it happened the NCAA and the major networks had signed a new contract in the spring of 1995, giving ESPN exclusive broadcasting rights to the women's regional finals and Final Four beginning in 1996. But the regular-season rights proved to be another matter.

"Obviously, history is made, they win in Minneapolis," Stiff said. "I'm watching this, knowing we have the contract for next year with a big smile. And we get into the springtime where we have to schedule again, and the contract stated that the [UConn-Tennessee] game was under the SEC contract and CBS gets first choice of women's basketball games.

CBS was obligated to broadcast three women's regular-season games a year, and the network chose to do so in one fell swoop, broadcasting a triple-header on either the first Saturday or Sunday of NFL wild card playoff weekend. On the day CBS didn't have its two NFL games it would show the three women's basketball games. But that guaranteed that even a hot matchup like UConn-Tennessee would battle head-to-head against an NFL playoff doubleheader on ABC and later on NBC.

And that got Stiff thinking of a new way to get UConn-Tennessee back into a place she felt it had always belonged. But that would call for an unprecedented scheduling maneuver, with two nonconference teams playing a home-and-home series within a single season.

"CBS would always schedule it up against the NFL playoffs, so no one really had an opportunity to see it," Stiff said. "It was sad to see that it could be a big marquee game in prime time. It just dawned on me to ask each program, 'Would you consider playing twice, a two-year deal, and both of you would get a home game? Go ahead and play on CBS in January and we'll put it on in Rivalry Week in prime time in February,' and that's how that happened.

"I was discouraged by the fact that the sports fan of basketball, not even just women's basketball, didn't have the opportunity to see this game and I didn't have a chance to grab it and it was put up against the NFL playoffs. So I don't think it took too long to come up with it. I don't think it was a big sell to the schools at all. I think they wanted the exposure on television, it helps them in recruiting, so why not? So, they did it."

The deal was finalized just after the Final Four in 1999. For the 2000 and 2001 seasons, UConn and Tennessee would play twice in the regular season with the hope—at least in Bristol—that there would be a third meeting each year in March or April to decide the national championship on ESPN.

"The only reason we did it was for television, and women's basketball needed it," Auriemma said. "ESPN got one and CBS got one, and everyone was going to be happy. The only downside to it was that you want both teams to always go 1-1. We did it because it was good for publicity, and it's great for the players. But it's not always great for the coaches."

For the first time since the first year of the rivalry, neither team would enter the 1999–2000 season as the defending national champion. UConn had limped to a Sweet Sixteen defeat against Iowa State, while Tennessee had ended the Holdsclaw Era with a stunning loss to Duke in the regional finals.

But both programs appeared poised to return to the Final Four in 2000, in no small measure because of the insertion of two of the top point guards in the nation.

Sue Bird had started the first eight games for UConn in 1998-99, but was lost for the season to a torn ACL in January. Now, after a lengthy rehab, Bird was poised to reclaim her role as the starting point guard.

Kara Lawson, who had been a friend of Bird's during their AAU days before college, was the heir apparent to Kellie Jolly in Knoxville. And Lawson came to learn quickly what it meant to be playing on one of the two premier women's teams in the nation.

"I can remember my freshman year going to a football game and there were all these people lining the sidewalks and I hadn't even played a game yet, and these fans were yelling my name, wanting me to sign stuff," Lawson said. "I'm just going to get the tickets for the upper-classmen. I remember Tennessee fans would come to watch me play in high school. It was definitely different."

So, too, did Lawson realize that playing against Connecticut was unlike any other game of her career, college or professional.

"You couldn't hear in those games," Lawson said. "I didn't realize that until when I first got out there, my freshman year.

Most games, you get out there and you can hear. But we had such big crowds at Tennessee, and we scored off the jump ball, I couldn't hear anything. I was yelling at the top of my lungs. I'm the point guard, trying to communicate something, and at that point I realized, no one can hear me, and no one is going to be able to hear me for the rest of the game. That was a challenge, just to communicate.

"I remember my rookie year in the WNBA [in 2003], we sold out the first game of the season at ARCO Arena in Sacramento. It was sixteen thousand. It was loud. And after the game, some reporter asked me what it was like to play in front of a crowd like that. I tried not to be disrespectful, but that wasn't even two-thirds the size of where I played in college."

Following the graduation of Jolly and Holdsclaw, the mantle of leadership fell to Lawson and the two remaining "Meeks," Semeka Randall and Tamika Catchings. While Randall garnered most of the attention with her on-court swagger and off-the-court comments, Catchings, the daughter of former NBA player Harvey Catchings who had overcome being born with a hearing impediment, was developing into one of the top players in the country.

"If there was one kid who played at Tennessee who I always admired and had great respect for, loved the way she competed and played, it was Tamika Catchings," said Auriemma, who would later coach Catchings on the 2012 U.S. national team that won the gold medal at the London Olympic Games. "Of all the players who ever played there, she was the kind of kid I respected and admired and really enjoyed watching her play. I was a big of fan of hers, and still am.

"She did everything everyone else did. She just kept her mouth shut and played. She just played hard. She didn't have to say anything. In fact, she said little. She just played, both ends of the floor. She played with a lot of heart and emotion. That's something that describes a lot of players that we had, and that's why the rivalry was what it was, because you had a lot of players like that on both sides of the fence."

The same could be said for Bird, but not exactly in the way Auriemma would prefer. The UConn coach had given his guard a nickname, "Susie the Cruiser," because of what he perceived as too laid-back an approach to the game.

"I think it was part my personality," Bird said in 2009. "When I would enter a situation, I would like to stand back a little bit and assess the situation. And with college basketball, with my position and the expectations, there was no time for that. I wasn't really living up to my potential. Cruiser is the right word, because I was just there. I wasn't the worst player in the world, but I wasn't doing anything, either.

"I think that injury [as a freshman] was a wake-up call and brought a lot of things to the forefront. I didn't have basketball in my life for the first time since I was six. It was a wake-up call in that regard, and I also got to watch and learn by seeing and realizing what it took. And the minute I was able to play again, I vowed never to be in a situation where I regretted it. I look back on the games that I did play [before the injury], and in a way I regret the way I did play, because I know I could have done a lot more. I mean, it's hard when you're a freshman. You don't know any better. But I vowed that I would never want to play that way again."

As had been the case for Jolly under Pat Summitt the previous four years, Bird was expected to be Auriemma's coach on the floor, in good times and bad, despite her lack of game experience. Even on a team with All-American juniors Shea Ralph and Svetlana Abrosimova, as well as fellow sophomores Swin Cash, Tamika Williams, and Asjha Jones, the success of the season would largely fall on Bird's shoulders.

"That became my role," Bird said. "Coach Auriemma, obviously he's one of a kind and has a unique ability to manipulate. It sounds harsh, but he knows what buttons to push and he pushes them in the best ways possible."

On January 8, 2000, in Knoxville, Sue Bird answered all the questions. She thrived under the pressure Tennessee placed upon her, mental and physical. In a bruising first act of the new home-and-home series, Bird poured in a career-high 25 points as the top-ranked Huskies prevailed 74–67 over second-ranked Tennessee before a crowd of 23,385 at Thompson-Boling Arena.

"There was never any doubt, when Sue was coming out of high school, about her ability," Auriemma said. "But when she got hurt, I think everybody forgot about her. And we've already gone through October, November, and December and people aren't talking about Sue Bird and then all of a sudden, in that game, she reminded everybody—players, coaches, media, fans—what an incredible athlete she was and how tough mentally she was, and that was just the beginning of many, many more moments of that.

"For her to have that kind of a game in that setting, that was the foreshadowing of the rest of her career. I think it was that she was a big-game player and that was her first big game. That was the first time she was ever in that situation, on the road in Tennessee, and that was one of the best performances I'd ever seen. I know Diana [Taurasi] had one similar to that [in 2002], where she had 32. Those kind of moments, in that particular game, anybody who had forgotten about Sue Bird, they got reminded."

UConn had led by as many as 12 points in the second half, only to see the Lady Vols, led once again by a flurry of points from Randall, make a late charge, cutting the deficit to 55–50.

Then Bird took flight. She hit a deep three-pointer, then another. She made clutch free throws. She helped keep Tennessee guard Ace Clement scoreless throughout and forced the junior into seven turnovers.

"She was the difference maker," Summitt said. "She hit the big shots. She controlled the tempo of the game. She stepped up and made the difference when she needed to. It was apparent from the beginning today that Connecticut was very confident and very aggressive both offensively and defensively. They caught us back on our heels. They were more confident and aggressive and mentally tougher. The list goes on and on."

Bird finished 8 of 10 from the floor, including 2 of 3 three-pointers, and 7 of 8 from the line, all this despite being tossed around the court like a ragdoll in the final minutes of a brutally physical game.

"It was a lot of fun," Bird said. "I tripped, went into somebody's leg. I got hit in the jaw. I fell on my butt, too. I'm going, 'Oh God, it's a dead leg.' I couldn't feel anything. [Associate head coach] Chris Dailey is going, 'Don't be a whiner.'

"Most players thrive on pressure. Today we all showed a lot of heart. We all know that famous [Randall] quote, 'They were scared. We could see it in their eyes.' Even though my class and [freshman guard] Kennitra Johnson didn't experience it firsthand, we've heard the stories. Today, I think we wanted to come out and prove to everybody watching what we're all about."

After the game Auriemma was asked about the toughness of his "New York" point guard. Indeed, Bird hailed from the Empire State, and played her high school ball at Holdsclaw's alma mater, Christ the King in Queens. But she had been raised primarily in the cozy confines of Long Island.

"Yeah, she grew up on the mean streets of Syosset," Auriemma said. "I think the last thing somebody stole was a newspaper off someone's porch. I tell her the toughest thing she ever had to do was decide what sale to go to at the mall—Neiman-Marcus or no Neiman-Marcus?

"But when it gets very, very physical, she has the same thing Shea Ralph and Svet Abrosimova have. Only she doesn't let everybody see it until it's time to see it. I think it shocks people when it happens. But it's there."

Randall, who would one day be a teammate of Bird's in the WNBA, was not as impressed with UConn's victory, its second in three appearances against Tennessee in Knoxville, which gave the Huskies an overall series lead of 5-4.

"This is not March," Randall said.

It was not February, either. But Randall would have her day against UConn soon enough. That it would be Groundhog Day in Storrs when the two teams would meet again in the back end of the home-and-home series may not have been coincidence.

That the game would be played in prime time was not by chance either. Stiff had not just wanted two games a season so ESPN could get its share of the UConn-Tennessee ratings pie. If they were going to play this unprecedented second regular-season game, it was going to be a big deal. Indeed, when the teams took the Gampel Pavilion floor on February 2, they once again made women's basketball history, playing the first women's regular-season game ever broadcast nationally in prime time as part of ESPN's Rivalry Week.

It was a testament to how far the rivalry had come in five short seasons. No women's basketball matchup—college, professional, or Olympic level—had become as intense and universal as UConn-Tennessee. Even non-basketball fans knew who Pat Summitt and Geno Auriemma were. They knew when this game was on the schedule, be it once, twice, or three times a season.

"It's no question that it was the premier rivalry in the history of the sport," Lawson said. "You look back now, it might not be as long-running as some of the other rivalries, but when you talk about high stakes, quality of play, level of intensity, star players, it was must-see TV. Everybody looked forward to watching those games.

"And as players, we looked forward to playing in them. What is college basketball? It's a lot of lopsided scores, a lot of games where you could come and not play your best game and still win. By a lot. That game, both teams knew: If you didn't play well, no shot to win the game. As a competitor, you want to be tested in that way, to see where you are, as an individual and as a team."

Tennessee had taken a shot from UConn on their home floor in January and come out on the losing end. Now, in Randall's return to Gampel Pavilion after earning her nickname, 'Boo,' from UConn fans, it was the fourth-ranked Lady Vols' turn to knock off the number one team on its own floor and end another Huskies bid for an undefeated season.

"More than anything, they had beaten us earlier that year at our place," Lawson said. "So the focus going in, anytime you're playing a team that has beaten you previously that season . . .

payback and revenge is too strong of a word, but just have a better performance. So we knew going on the road was going to be difficult for us."

The early going proved especially difficult, as UConn built a 14-point lead in the early minutes. Tennessee still trailed by 9 in the closing seconds of the half before Catchings hit a three-pointer that made it 34–26 and started the Lady Vols on the comeback trail.

"I think UConn led in the first half and they kind of let up," said Dan Fleser, who covered the game for the *Knoxville News-Sentinel*. "That was the thing about that series, if one team let up on the other one, the other one was right back on you. That didn't happen. Imagine if one of those teams got up by 14 against another team. They were cooked. But that was the one game where you can be up 14 and if you let up, you could be in trouble."

Tennessee would ultimately score 14 consecutive points around halftime and led 63–56 with under seven minutes to play. Shea Ralph and Tamika Williams then led a UConn comeback, capped by a three-pointer by Bird with 2:48 left that gave UConn a 69–67 lead. Over the next two minutes Tennessee would score the only point.

Then, with the game clock under a minute and UConn still leading 69–68, Randall and Bird would exchange big baskets as if they were Magic and Bird in game four of the 1987 NBA finals.

Randall struck first, hitting a bank shot in the lane with twenty-eight seconds left to put Tennessee up 70–69.

"She kept us from having an undefeated season," Auriemma said. "I don't know that there was a time during the rivalry where Semeka had a bigger impact on a game. That was an incredible performance, on the road, at the end of a game, that was as good as anyone has ever played against us. And I'm not surprised. Semeka had that kind of talent and she was that tough."

But Bird, who had established her toughness in Knoxville, would respond to Randall's big bucket in Storrs, driving the baseline and pulling up for an eight-footer that put UConn back ahead by 1 with 17 seconds remaining.

"Sue was just steely," Shea Ralph said. "She had ice running through her veins. You could not shake her. And there were times where she would get really excited and pumped, but it wasn't all the time. She would always make that big play and that was her way of showing you, and I would be all over the place and crazy and emotional and that was the role that I played and it fit both of us well."

But Bird did not get the last word. Naturally, that would belong to Randall. On what proved to be a busted play, Randall drove into the lane and, despite having Bird draped all over the ball, hit a double-clutch jumper with 4.4 seconds left to put the Lady Vols back on top, 72–71.

"The play was designed where I come off a ball-screen and look for Catchings," Randall said. "But when it started, I rejected the ball-screen and went back and the funny thing is, it was probably the worst crossover ever. I crossed over with the same hand. I come off the screen on the left side, crossed over and shot it with the same hand.

"Sue Bird fouls me as I'm going up, and so I made the shot and I'm at the free-throw line and I stand and turn back to Geno and [salute]. That's what the series made you do. I think he had said something to me on the sidelines. He did say something to me, and it pissed me off. He was always saying something to me, but I knew I would get him."

Randall had actually not been fouled, but there was a whistle. With 4.4 seconds remaining, Bird had called time-out. An ill-advised time-out, as fate would have it.

"I remember that I shouldn't have called time-out," Bird said. "I should have just taken it and gone, because they scored and we could have inbounded it. The things I remember, I remember a press conference later and [Auriemma] and/or Svet had said something along the lines of, 'Maybe we should have given the ball to Sue.'"

On this night—and for the last time in such situations with Bird in a UConn uniform—the ball went elsewhere. Auriemma called for Abrosimova, his fastest player off the dribble, to rush upcourt, get to the foul line, and shoot.

Abrosimova complied with the first part, gliding up the floor and pulling up at the Tennessee foul line with the clock ticking under two seconds. But as she stopped and gathered, Abrosimova suddenly noticed the defense rushing to her, leaving forward Tamika Williams—a 70 percent shooter in her career—alone under the basket.

Instead of shooting as instructed, Abrosimova passed to the open—but completely unprepared—Williams, who fumbled the pass, allowing the bigger Michelle Snow to react and swallow her up. Williams could only manage to hit the bottom of the backboard as the buzzer sounded.

In seeming disbelief at the unfolding of the final play, Lawson's eyes went wild, her hands coming up to her face. As she skipped toward the ESPN cameras at half court, she suddenly realized the gravity of the moment and informed the world that Tennessee was once again number one.

"It was a big win for us, playing on the road," Lawson said. "It was right in the middle of our conference season, so it was a little out of the ordinary for both teams, but it was a great environment and we felt pretty good about where we were leaving that night. There's not too many teams that can go in there and get wins."

While Tennessee celebrated at its end of court, Auriemma fixed an icy glare at Abrosimova at the other end.

"From a coaching standpoint, I don't like giving the defense a chance to gather themselves," Auriemma said. "I'd rather attack when they're running back. I should have made sure that Sue understood that we didn't want a time-out in that situation. But, her calling the time-out, there's nothing wrong with that. We're down 1. And we got the ball to the foul line in two seconds. All [Abrosimova] has to do is shoot it. That time-out gave us the opportunity to get the ball to the only player who could get from our foul line to their foul line in two seconds. So we did and it just didn't work out. If Sue doesn't take the timeout, does she come down and take the last shot and make it? I don't know.

"In one sense, in that Tennessee game, there were too many players available. Shea had played great that game. Sue and Sveta are going to make that shot if they take it. We got it right to where we wanted it with the person we wanted. If Sue had had it, she wasn't passing it. Sveta was like, 'We got a lay-up.' Well, no, Tamika was looking for the tip-in."

Auriemma's feud with his Russian star would linger for another week, but it was the only blip on UConn's radar down the stretch of the season. Even in their lone defeat, the Huskies still looked the favorite to claim their second national championship. And Tennessee looked to be the only team capable of preventing it.

If they did meet for a third time in Auriemma's hometown of Philadelphia for the Final Four, they'd have a hard time topping their historic primetime performance.

"I think if you ask most people that followed the series, that game wouldn't even get brought up, but there hasn't been a game in that series any better than that one," Fleser said. "You had three shots in the last minute, Randall hit two and Bird hit one, and Bird had her hand on the last one Randall made. She just muscled it in over her.

"I remember after it was over, he was in the hallway talking to the [UConn media] and I went up to [Auriemma] and said, 'Congratulations on your national championship,' because the [Lady Vols] were not going to beat them again."

No one would beat UConn for the remainder of the regular season, Big East tournament, or early rounds of the NCAA tournament. Tennessee would have similar ease in reaching the First Union Center in Philadelphia for the Final Four. Only Rutgers and Penn State stood in the way of arguably the most anticipated matchup in women's basketball history.

And everyone got their wish. After Tennessee easily handled Rutgers in one semifinal and UConn dispatched Penn State in the other, the dream matchup was set for Sunday, April 1.

No fooling. As in the case of Muhammad Ali and that famous Philly fighter, Joe Frazier, there would be a third heavyweight fight to settle the 2000 score once and for all.

"No two coaches demanded more from their players, and their teams played that way," Fleser said. "The thing that always got me about those games was how ferocious they were. Just two teams that wanted to kill each other. That, more than anything, benefitted the women's game, that two teams could play like this, making great plays and going at each other. It was just fun to watch and people gravitated to that. Who knows where women's basketball would be today if that series hadn't come along, because I know how far along they dragged everybody. They pushed it down the road with those games.

"I know the game was advanced because of that series. It's hard to say how much, but it kicked the can down the road a long way in a very short period of time. The sport needed more opportunity to be on TV and it needed teams that could bring out the best in each other like they did. That was really big."

And in the spirit of the hype and trash talk that defined the Ali-Frazier fights, Auriemma would take the opportunity to throw a smart-alecky, sound bite–worthy shot across Pat Summitt's bow.

On the day before the championship game, Auriemma and his starting five took part in yet another NCAA-sanctioned press conference at the First Union Center. As in 1995, the assembled media throng that day was substantial, and the opportunity for lighthearted questions and answers mixed in with the Xs and Os was at an all-time high. Consider the second question asked of Auriemma:

"Could you please talk about what Sue brings to the team, and could you also discuss the cosmic significance of the fact that the first names of the two coaches in the finals are also the names of the two most famous cheesesteak restaurants in Philadelphia?"

A glint came to Auriemma's eyes and a wry smile crossed his face. Pat's and Geno's. Perfect. Auriemma was truly in his element at this Final Four. He had the best team, was playing in his hometown, and he knew it. Flush with confidence, Auriemma took a playful jab at his coaching counterpart. The joke pretty much wrote itself, and the temptation was too much for the Philly wise guy to resist.

"Yeah, you been down there recently? Pat's is old, beat-up, and dilapidated; Geno's is bigger—you know I noticed that when I was over there. Not that it means anything."

Not that it means anything. The assembled writers and television reporters let out a combination laugh and playful groan, all the while making sure to get that gem of a line down on paper, recorded to tape recorders, and saved to videotape. *Good one, Geno.*

But Geno's playful jab elicited a different reaction behind closed doors in the Tennessee locker room.

"She did not like that," Fleser said. "[Auriemma's] response to the Randall stuff [in 1998], that more or less kind of shocked her, but I don't think she took that personally. But she took the Pat-Geno stuff personally."

It was not the first time, but certainly not the last, that Auriemma's brand of humor ran afoul of Summitt's sense of manners, but the personal nature of the jab would come to define the rivalry over its final seven years.

"They're different people with different backgrounds from different cultures," said *New London Day* columnist Mike DiMauro. "What the wise-ass Northeastern man thinks is funny, as opposed to a Southern woman, the cultures are just different. We do sarcasm up here. I'm sure they do it down there, but not as well. The columnist at the *[Nashville] Tennessean* wrote a piece after that saying how unfunny that thing was. We were falling off our chairs. ESPN thought it was funny. But that just showed the difference in cultures."

But at least in 2000, the game on the court was still bigger than the he-said/she-said games Geno and Pat played. And even before Tennessee took the floor that Sunday night for the title game, Summitt had much, much more to worry about than Auriemma's bad jokes.

On Sunday morning, in the arena empty except for the ESPN production crew setting up for that night's game, Tennessee took part in its usual morning shootaround, a last chance to go over strategy and warm up before the lights came on for real that evening.

And, as per routine, the players limbered up by going through a lay-up line, one side shooting, the other rebounding and passing the ball to the next shooter. At one point Ace Clement, Tennessee's junior guard, drove in for her lay-up as center Michelle Snow cleaned up the rebound of the previous shot.

Suddenly Clement crumpled to the floor, letting out a blood-curdling scream. She had accidentally stepped on Snow's foot as their paths crossed and turned her ankle horribly wrong.

"The biggest thing about that whole game, we were ready," Randall said. "We had prepared, we knew what to expect from Connecticut. We knew they were coming out for revenge based on what we had done to them prior to that [in February]. And mentally we were in a very good place.

"I recall Ace dribbling into the layup line, going in for a layup, and she steps on Michelle Snow's foot and she goes down as if she had torn her ACL with that loud scream, a noise like she's really hurt. This isn't your typical ankle sprain here. This is something serious.

"And at that moment, all our energy went right into her, just thinking, 'Man, is she okay? Is she going to be all right?' I think it caught all the coaches off guard, too. It was like, this can't happen right here. This can't be true."

But it was true, and the Tennessee coaching staff was faced with a double dilemma. Not only was one of their key players seriously injured, there was the matter of the crew from ESPN, their headquarters based just forty-five miles from Storrs. The network had already earned a reputation for being decidedly pro-UConn—Auriemma had even been employed by ESPN as a WNBA game analyst. This development, with Clement still wailing and writhing in pain, was not to be revealed to anyone.

So when a wheelchair was rolled out to take Clement away, a sheet was placed over her to conceal her identity. The bizarre and scary scene was enough to shatter the pre-championship focus of the entire team.

"She's going off in a wheelchair and we go back to the hotel and we're all just sitting around, 'What are we going to do? We have to get ready for this game,' and we just weren't there [mentally]," Randall said. "The first time we stepped out onto the court, we were like zombies out there."

Hours before the game, as the national media gathered at the arena, rumors spread like wildfire that Ace Clement would not be playing. Some were hearing that it was her ankle. Other, darker theories began to spread that the ankle story was a cover; that Clement, from the Philadelphia area, had been out past curfew the night before and was being secretly suspended.

If the ankle story was a ruse, it was certainly an elaborate one. Clement limped to her seat on the bench before walking gingerly to a spot under the basket as the team went through pregame lay-up drills. She would sit on Tennessee's bench throughout the game, staring glumly at the game going on without her.

All of the Lady Vols would be glum before long.

The early minutes were frenetic. Bird's runner and Abrosimova's three-pointer gave UConn a 5–0 lead, while UConn's defense attacked Clement's replacement in the starting lineup, Kyra Elzy. The senior guard committed three turnovers in the first six and a half minutes as UConn built a 15–6 lead.

"I thought they came out with a great plan to really take us out of some things we wanted to do offensively," Summitt said.

By this time Kelly Schumacher had blocked three shots, the last two on successive attempts by Randall and Catchings, who had just been named national player of the year.

It was the crowning achievement for the junior center from Canada, who had earned a place in the Huskies' rotation in midseason with her rebounding and defense. Schumacher, at six-foot-five, would later go on to have a professional career as a volleyball player.

"What's funny about Schuey is that she was like that," said Matt Eagan, who covered the Huskies for the *Hartford Courant* in 2000. "People think of her as elegant, but she would yap at you. [Former Red Sox manager] Don Zimmer would say that Bill Lee didn't have a killer instinct, but Bill Lee would pitch his guts out to win a game and Zimmer never understood that.

"Schuey wasn't Shea Ralph. But in fairness, she's on a team with Shea and Svet and Sue Bird and Tamika Williams and how much of the foreground is she supposed to have? She's on a team with people who can really score. I'm not sure I'm going to dial up a play for Schuey.

"In those games, they only wanted one thing from her. The thing about Schuey, sometimes we try to attribute things to attitude that are simply talent. I don't mean to denigrate her talent, but there's a level. You can't have five players who want the ball all the time. It's just not going to work. So that's what Schuey was."

Something else was happening, too. With 13:46 left in the half, Ralph scored on a perfectly executed back-door cut, taking the pass from Tamika Williams. The play would haunt Tennessee all night.

"We haven't run it all year," Williams said. "They were out denying us, and we just decided to try and do it to them."

At the other end, Tennessee could not buy a basket. They shot 2 for 21 before Catchings connected on her first two field goals to get the Lady Vols back to within 10, 25–15, with 3:31 left.

The half ended with Schumacher getting block number six on Randall (0 for 7), and Bird, despite jammed fingers on her right hand, hitting a flip shot with 11.3 seconds left for a 32–19 lead.

The Lady Vols shot 5 for 27 and their 19 first-half points were the lowest in championship game history.

It only got worse in the second half.

Ralph scored the first 4 points of the second half, and the Huskies added 4 more to take a 40–19 lead with 16:57 left. Ralph scored on a fast-break lay-up to open the half, then double-pumped in the lane, hit the shot, and was fouled by Elzy. Ralph missed the free throw, but UConn rebounded and Schumacher hit a jumper to put the Huskies up by 19.

Ralph then stole a Randall pass and fed Abrosimova for a lay-up. Summitt called time, the partisan UConn crowd erupted, and the Huskies could at last sense ultimate victory. All that remained was for Schumacher to record her NCAA championship game record ninth block in a 71–52 victory.

But as the game ended another bit of ugliness between the coaching staffs unfolded. Perhaps irked by Auriemma's "old and dilapidated" comment, perhaps frustrated by the nature of the blowout loss—or perhaps annoyed that the UConn starters, having long since been removed from the game, started celebrating their title with seconds still remaining on the clock by diving headlong onto the floor en masse, even as the reserves for both teams played the final three seconds—Tennessee assistant coach Al Brown snubbed Auriemma in the postgame handshake line, offering, as Auriemma recounted in his 2006 book, *Geno: In Pursuit of Perfection*, a limp-wristed shake.

"A classic cold fish," Auriemma writes. "He barely looks at me ... so unprofessional, it is unbelievable."

Auriemma was so enraged that he yelled back at the Tennessee coaches as they departed for their own bench and started toward them to confront Brown, even as the celebration of his team's title swirled around him. Associate head coach Chris Dailey then stepped in to grab Auriemma by the face to turn him back the other way.

"She says, to me, 'Geno, we just won the national championship. Let it go.' Sorry, I can't. It's one of the worst cases of poor sportsmanship I can imagine. And I'll tell you one thing—Pat Summitt would never do that. Win, lose, or draw, she understands how it works. I bet she's more disappointed than anyone in the history of basketball when her team loses, but she's never going to show that in public, or belittle the other team's accomplishment by walking down there and acting like some spoiled brat."

The dust-up was quickly forgotten as UConn cut down the nets. Ralph, who made 7 of 8 shots (15 points) to go with 7 assists and 6 steals in twenty-eight minutes, earned Final Four MVP honors, two years removed from her second torn ACL.

"There were moments during the game, I was thinking, this is why I worked so hard," Ralph said. "But when we won, it was just complete elation. The fact that I was with my teammates and coaches and to see them so happy . . . it really wasn't about me. Especially Coach, because he was the reason I was able to achieve and get back [to playing]. He stuck with me and pushed me. Just to see everyone's reaction was really cool.

"And as time went on during the summer, it started sinking in and I thought about how far I had come. And being back on the court after we won, practicing again, just thinking, it's possible we can do this again, we know what has to be done. It starts to sink in."

For the Lady Vols, the sinking feeling came early and never left.

"Connecticut is back-dooring us and Coach Summitt is calling time-outs, getting in our faces, which she needs to, to get us some energy," Randall said. "But our energy and focus was on Ace. She was on the bench and there was no way she could remotely compete. If she could, maybe she would have come out there and maybe given us some life, but we were never into the game.

"We lost the game in shootaround. When that happened, it was over. Not to take anything away from what Connecticut did to us. They did what they were supposed to do, which was kick our tails, and they did it. To this day, I can see it and remember it and feel it.

"Coach Summitt calls me in after we get back from the trip, and I go over to her house and I'm the one that's stuck and have to watch the game over and over, and wondering about the game and how we approached it and I can remember every play, everything we did, what mistakes I made. And I'm sitting there thinking, here comes the back door, here comes a Catchings foul, there's a turnover here, and I can remember Coach Summitt saying, 'My word, I didn't coach this team.'"

On the UConn side, four years of bad breaks and heartbreak were finally behind them. Losses to Tennessee in the 1996 and 1997 NCAA tournaments and early injury-fueled exits in 1998 and 1999 had finally given way to UConn's second national championship. And with virtually the entire team returning in 2001—along with arguably the greatest incoming freshman of all time in Diana Taurasi—fortune was smiling on Auriemma like never before.

"It really is an indescribable feeling when you win something like this," Auriemma said after the game. "The reason you can't describe it is because you really can't put into words what the looks on the kids' faces are and what's going through their minds and their bodies, and that's what this is all about. You know, I've told these kids all year long that every pass we make in practice, every cut, every rebound, you know, pretend like it's the one that's going to win the national championship, and these kids have practiced like this all year long and the night that they had to do it, they did it better than any other time in the season.

"And the fact that we did it against a team as good as Tennessee—it's unfortunate what happened to Kristen [Clement] at practice today, and it's a shame she didn't get a chance to play—but the fact that we did it against a team that's as good and has as much tradition as Tennessee, makes this an accomplishment all the more worthwhile, because I know how hard it is to beat them, how difficult it is to deny them when they are playing for a championship. So I'm really proud of my players and extremely—extremely happy for them."

1. Geno Auriemma and
Pat Summitt exchange
pleasantries before UConn
faces Tennessee in a regular
season game in Hartford
in 2005.

2. UConn All-American
Rebecca Lobo celebrates as
the Huskies complete a
35-0 season by beating
Tennessee in the 2005
NCAA championship game.

3. Tennessee's Abby Conklin looks to make a pass around UConn's
6-foot-7 Kara Wolters to a wide-open Vonda Ward (24) during the 1995
NCAA championship game.

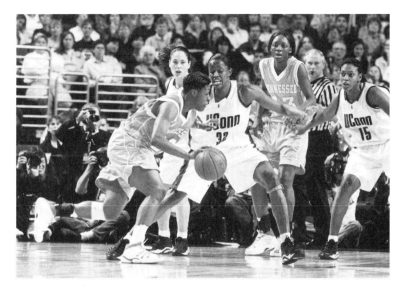

4. Tennessee's Semeka Randall drives against three UConn defenders during the 2000 NCAA championship game in Philadelphia.

5. UConn's Sue Bird dribbles into the path of Tennessee's Michelle Snow during the 2000 NCAA championship game.

6. UConn's Diana Taurasi drives past Tennessee's Shanna Zolman in a 2003 regular season game in Hartford.

7. Diana Taurasi puts up a shot over Tennessee's Tasha Butts in 2003.
Taurasi averaged 22 points in eight career games against the Lady Vols.

8. The last game. UConn's Charde Houston shoots a free throw as Tennessee's Candace Parker (*foreground, right*) gets in position for a rebound in the 2007 regular season game in Hartford.

8

2001

Everybody Hurts

The stands at the First Union Center in Philadelphia were littered with UConn and Tennessee basketball alums the night UConn routed the Lady Vols in the 2000 national championship game, all of them sitting in the sections behind their teams' respective benches.

But perhaps the most intriguing player with a connection to the UConn program was seated on the opposite side of the arena.

Diana Taurasi was in the house for the 71–52 victory, watching the UConn team she would begin playing for later that year.

Taurasi, a six-foot guard who had scored over 3,000 points for Don Lugo High School near her home in Chino, California, was the latest in a long line of freshmen to have an immediate impact on the UConn-Tennessee rivalry—Nykesha Sales in 1995 and Shea Ralph in 1997 for the Huskies, Chamique Holdsclaw in 1996 and Semeka Randall and Tamika Catchings in 1997 for the Lady Vols.

But none entered college with the fanfare and expectations of Taurasi. And none would add fuel to the ever-smoldering dislike between the programs even before playing in her first collegiate game.

Even as she joined a team including six All-American candidates among its upperclassmen, Taurasi was expected to be a game-changer not just for the Huskies, but perhaps for the entire sport. No player in recent memory, not even the other-worldly Holdsclaw, seemed to have the combination of long-distance shooting, clever passing, and desire to make plays in the clutch quite like this freshman.

This is perhaps why, at a rally at the state capitol in Hartford following a victory parade through the heart of the city, that Geno Auriemma boldly predicted the Huskies would repeat as champions in 2001. And this was also perhaps why, just a fort-night before the start of the 2000–2001 season, Taurasi came under withering criticism from a most curious source.

By 2000 Sally Jenkins had already earned herself the deserved reputation as one of the top sportswriters in the country as a columnist for the *Washington Post*. Jenkins also wrote about women's basketball for *ESPN: The Magazine* and the network's evolving website, espn.com, and she had coauthored both of Pat Summitt's autobiographical efforts—*Reach for the Summit* in 1988 and *Raise the Roof* in 1999.

It was the latter entry in Jenkins's resume that raised plenty of eyebrows in Storrs on October 30, when espn.com published her UConn season preview.

In a simple capsule format that ESPN used for all its previews, Jenkins, who had UConn ranked number one, led her piece with the category "Who to watch: Diana Taurasi."

"The freshman guard was the nation's most sought-after recruit," Jenkins wrote. "But she also is giggly, turnover-prone, and lacks a conscience with the ball. Even worse, her ego needs its own zip code. She announced during recruiting that she didn't intend to sit. Really? Then who will? Bird? Don't think so."

Taurasi and the UConn coaching staff were stunned. Jenkins had never met Taurasi, never talked to her on the phone, and almost certainly had never seen her play, be it in high school, AAU, or high school All-America games.

But Taurasi had crossed Tennessee off her recruiting list early, never really had given them a chance. Although the fact was never admitted publicly, it was widely assumed in the offices at Gampel Pavilion that Summitt had planted this bad seed.

"I'd never met the lady," Taurasi said in 2009. "I was taken aback, because for someone that I'd never talked to or met, those were some strong words. Everyone has their own opinion, and she's a Tennessee gal, so it's all good. It only gets to you if it's true. She said that, but it didn't bother me, because I knew it wasn't true. All my teammates, people I had played with, they knew I wasn't like that."

Still, the Jenkins assessment, regardless of its true origin, drove another wedge between the two programs. And while she would never come out and say it, it may have been the catalyst for what would be four years of Taurasi's nonstop torture of the Lady Vols on the court.

The first opportunity would come on December 30 at the Civic Center in Hartford. But, much to the horror of the young freshman from Southern California, Mother Nature had other ideas about the playing of this game.

Weather had been an unwelcome subplot to the UConn-Tennessee rivalry in the past. In 1996 both teams found themselves stranded in Knoxville the day after UConn ended the Lady Vols' sixty-nine-game home winning streak. But that storm didn't arrive until well after the game was played. This time a massive snowstorm threatened to dump over a foot of snow on greater Hartford before, during, and just after the scheduled 4:00 p.m. start time.

The issue was not so much whether the game would be played. Tennessee had arrived in Hartford ahead of the storm, as had the CBS crew that would be televising the game nationally. The real concern was for the sixteen thousand fans expected to descend on the Civic Center at the height of the storm.

But, after all, these were fans of a team nicknamed Huskies, and this was Tennessee. Even the Postal Service would have to be impressed with the fans' determination. Despite a storm that brought rumbles of thunder to the Hartford area less than two hours before tip-off, a near-capacity crowd of 15,500 showed up.

They were not disappointed.

The first time UConn had played at the Civic Center that season, in the State Farm Tip-Off Classic against third-ranked Georgia, the Huskies played nearly flawlessly, bolting to a 29-point lead in the first half before settling for a 99–70 victory. It was in the first half that Taurasi attempted her first shot ever at the Civic Center—and buried a twenty-five-foot three-pointer.

Now, with Svetlana Abrosimova limited to eleven minutes against the Lady Vols because of a back injury, Taurasi had a chance for a more expansive role. By happenstance Sally Jenkins was in the building—not as a writer on press row, but sitting in the section reserved for Tennessee's guests and fans.

Jenkins would get to see close up just what this giggly freshman was really all about.

UConn hit Tennessee with a 19–2 run early in the game and led by as many as 14 in the second half. But just as the Lady Vols had done at Gampel Pavilion almost eleven months earlier, Tennessee hacked away at the large deficit to make a game of it late. And when Tamika Catchings buried a three-pointer with 5:27 left, UConn's lead was sliced to just 2.

Then Taurasi struck. Taking a pass from Bird, Taurasi dribbled up to about thirty feet from the basket. Catchings waited for her next move in a defensive crouch. But Taurasi's move was to quickly pull up and fire. Three points.

"I turned my head at that moment," Summitt said. "I didn't see it."

Summitt didn't have to. The eruption of noise from the crowd around her told Summitt all she needed to know. And she knew it was Taurasi who had done it.

"Was that from downtown Hartford?" Summitt asked.

"No," assistant coach Mickie DeMoss responded. "It was from Storrs."

The shot restored UConn's lead to five. Of Taurasi's 12 points in twenty-two minutes of play, they were the biggest of all.

"Four more years of that?" Summitt lamented after the game. "I don't want to think about it."

There was much for Summitt to think about on that day. Taurasi's three-pointer was a backbreaker, but not a game-ender. A three-pointer by April McDivitt and a drive by Catchings made it 77–74 with 1:04 left. The Lady Vols got the ball back after Taurasi missed from the corner. At the other end Catchings looked to set a screen at the top of the key to free up a teammate. Instead the senior was called for an offensive foul, a moving screen.

With thirty-three seconds left it was a curious call to make, and it proved too much for Tennessee to overcome. UConn escaped with an 81–76 victory. It was hard not to think that the Lady Vols were the victims of a snow job.

After the game, Randy Smith, the late and truly great columnist from the *Manchester (CT) Journal-Inquirer*, asked Summitt a simple question.

"When do you suspect the officiating will catch up to the game?"

Summitt offered only a wink. "You know, I really can't comment on that," she replied, even though she just had.

For Taurasi, it was her first taste of the rivalry and the passion UConn fans brought to the proceedings.

"The weather was horrible," Taurasi said after the game. "We didn't know if many people would show up. Then we went, 'The faithful, they'll show.' It's awesome how much UConn basketball means to everyone around here. Tamika Williams tapped me on the shoulder when we went to the sidelines after our 19–2 run in the first half. It was so loud you could hear the electricity. She said, 'There it is.' That's why I came here."

Auriemma had seen Jenkins sitting in the stands. After Taurasi's clutch performance, he took the time to defend his precocious freshman.

"When I was recruiting Diana, I really felt this is a once in a lifetime kind of kid," Auriemma said. "Her skills are one thing. I wasn't sure if she was a con artist or not. I think she's got more skills than any kid at that age. But what she brings from a personality standpoint is unlike anybody else. A lot of kids have personality and don't have a game. A lot of kids have a game and no personality. She's been blessed with both.

"Nobody has more fun playing basketball than she does. Nobody has more fun doing anything than she does."

That night, the Lady Vols stayed in the Hilton Hotel in downtown Hartford, the lodgings connected to the Civic Center by a sky bridge, allowing the entourage to avoid the storm outside. But dark clouds began following Catchings.

Because many UConn fans—and even some UConn media members who lived no more than ten minutes from the Civic Center—also chose stay at the hotel to ride out the massive blizzard, the Tennessee coaches and managers warned the players to watch their belongings, lest some Husky-fed mischief take place.

Catchings apparently did not get the message. After dinner, as the players retreated to their rooms, it was discovered that Catchings's game jersey had gone missing. Worst of all, Tennessee had a game in New York two days later. Catchings would play it wearing a generic Tennessee jersey.

"I remember our managers running around [the hotel] like crazy," Randall said. "I think Adidas had to send us one."

Replacing Catchings's jersey was one thing. Replacing Catchings? That was the unthinkable horror the Lady Vols were forced to confront two weeks later.

It was Martin Luther King Day once again, and Tennessee, 16-1 and ranked second behind UConn, was back on ESPN, this time playing an SEC rival, Mississippi State, at Thompson-Boling Arena.

With 5:43 left Catchings drove the lane and landed hard on her right knee. Suddenly she collapsed to the floor, grabbing at the knee and crying out in pain. The senior All-American had torn the ACL. Her season—and her Tennessee career—was over.

"We lost our best player and leader by example," Summitt said after their 66–59 victory. "She was injured the way she played the game—all out and hard on every play."

The blow to the Lady Vols was almost incalculable. A preseason All-American for the third time in her career, Catchings entered the Mississippi State game leading the Vols in points and rebounds, averaging 15.1 and 8.6.

She was only the third Tennessee player to score 2,000 points in her career, joining Holdsclaw and Bridgette Gordon. Along with Holdsclaw, Catchings was the only player to have more than 2,000 points and 1,000 rebounds, surpassing the rebound milestone with 13 in her final game, her seventh double-double in 17 games on the season.

"To me, if Joe DiMaggio was a women's basketball player, he'd have been Tamika Catchings," said *New London Day* columnist Mike DiMauro. "You know how he had that elegance about him, that's what I think of with her. I remember when Geno brought in that great class with Sue and Swin and Tamika [Williams], he said he'd trade them all in for Tamika Catchings."

Tennessee did what it could to rally around its fallen leader, even creating the Tamika Catchings Hustle Award, with each game's recipient donning Catchings's trademark blue Adidas headband for the postgame press conference.

The first winner was fellow senior Semeka Randall, who had 20 points, 9 rebounds, and 5 assists in a win over fourth-ranked Georgia just three days after Catchings's injury.

"I'm the first to win it," Randall said. "I'll go down in history. I might win again, but everybody has to compete."

"I challenged her to keep her intensity and leadership up and to have a positive approach," Summitt said. "I thought she did a terrific job. She can make a difference with her attitude. She's also playing a little more under control.

"Our goal is to go to St. Louis and win a championship. I told them, 'We're going to be there in St. Louis.' If they get satisfied, we're going to struggle."

Catchings, who had hoped to make a Kellie Jolly–esque quick

return for the NCAA tournament in March, underwent surgery on February 5, just four days after UConn played Tennessee for the second time that season. And now it would be the Huskies who would be dealt a crushing blow.

When UConn arrived at Thompson-Boling Arena for the in-season rematch on February 1, the Huskies were a team still in search of an identity despite their abundant talent. On the same Martin Luther King Day as Catchings's season-ending injury, UConn had absorbed a wicked beating at the hands of the new number one in the nation, Notre Dame, and were still reeling from that 16-point loss as they traveled down to Knoxville.

Fifth-year senior Shea Ralph had uncharacteristically struggled with her game and fellow senior All-American Svetlana Abrosimova was inconsistent. The junior class of Sue Bird, Swin Cash, Tamika Williams, and Asjha Jones were sometimes brilliant but not entirely certain of their roles during games. And while Taurasi was clearly a star in the making, she was every bit the freshman Sally Jenkins had alluded to back in October.

Was Taurasi giggly? She certainly had fun on the court. Did her ego need its own zip code? She certainly played with enormous confidence. Foul-prone? Yes. Turnover-prone? Yes. Undisciplined? A million times yes.

"I had to learn how to be more disciplined," Taurasi said. "Not always go for the home-run pass. As a freshman I wouldn't even think about making a 50-50 pass. Now, it has to be 80-20. Those are the little things you learn as a freshman, especially with Coach, who wants everything to be perfect.

"I was lucky enough to play under him with USA Basketball a couple months before I got there, so I got a taste of it. He had to be nice to me then."

But once the season was well into January and February, it was no more Mr. Nice Guy.

"There were a lot of battles," Auriemma said in 2009. "With all of her talent and God-given ability and the way she plays the game, it almost was like a young pitcher who throws 98 [miles per hour] and comes into the majors and can't find the strike zone and doesn't care. 'I'm just going to throw it as hard as I can and I don't care where it goes,' just undisciplined and not caring about being disciplined.

"Coaching her was easy and it was hard. It was easy, because she could do things that you didn't have to coach. And it was hard, because you're trying to coach her into understanding there's more to this game than who makes the last three, and how much fun it is, and thinking that winning is easy.

"I've always said, your greatest strength is your greatest weakness. Her greatest strength is her emotion. That's why she'll get hit with a technical, or if her man gets by her, she'll smack 'em in the back of the head, because her passion and emotion just takes over. She's not content to just get a lay-up. She wants to go in and elbow you in the face and make the lay-up, and then get an offensive foul call and scream at the ref."

Before the second game against Tennessee was over, it would be Auriemma screaming at the refs. But at the start of the second-ever primetime UConn-Tennessee game on ESPN, it would be the players who would be gasping for air.

The Huskies and Lady Vols were known for playing scintillating games. On this night they would be remembered most for six extraordinary minutes.

College games are spaced into 10 four-minute segments, with automatic time-outs built in for every stoppage of play after the 16-, 12-, 8-, and 4-minute marks of each half. These are known as "TV time-outs" because they allow for commercials to be played for the benefit of NCAA sponsors. But the time-outs can only be triggered by an actual stoppage in play—a foul, a turnover, a ball out of bounds, an injury. It is rare in any game for play to last continuously for more than sixty to ninety seconds at a time.

Not this night. For the first six minutes the Huskies and Lady Vols traded baskets and fast breaks at a furious and remarkably mistake-free pace. There were no wild passes, no cheap fouls, and no whistles. Even as both coaches sent substitutions to the scorer's table, the starters could get no relief.

To make matters worse, because of the Tennessee tradition of pregame glitz with the players being introduced in a shower of indoor pyrotechnics, a smoky haze lingered at the game's beginning, burning the rapidly emptying lungs of the ten starters.

"I remember telling Birdie, 'Yo, could you just throw it off someone's leg or something?'" Lawson said. "I remember how tired I was. That was the most tired I've ever been in a college game."

But even as the players began to wilt and wheeze under the withering pace, neither side was willing to make the first whistle-inducing mistake. Finally—Finally!–UConn was called for a three-second violation and the first time-out was triggered. Ten exhausted women staggered to their benches with UConn leading, 17–16.

"That was the highest level of women's basketball in the history of the game, the first six minutes of that game," DiMauro said. "It was awesome."

Although there would be no such extended stretches of non-stop play the rest of the game, the furious pace did not relent. Tennessee would finally build a workable 7-point lead in the second half when Taurasi connected on another long-distance three, shooting it literally from nearby Bristol, Tennessee—at least where Bristol was on the long map of the state that was painted to the court at its midpoint. In reality it was a thirty-footer, and when Abrosimova hit her own three with roughly ten minutes to go UConn took a 64–63 lead.

Moments later Taurasi launched another three-pointer but missed. From her vantage point at the foul line, Abrosimova saw that the shot would miss and rushed to the basket to grab the carom. As she tried to elude a Tennessee player on the way to the baseline, Abrosimova made a sudden awkward step and landed hard on her left foot. Grimacing in obvious pain, she fell face-forward to the floor.

A twisted ankle? A sprain? At first, there was no diagnosis, but when the senior All-American tried to retake the floor, it was obvious she could not continue.

As Abrosimova watched in pain from the bench the teams continued to trade baskets, with Tennessee eventually extending its lead to 83–79 with just over a minute remaining. Now it was UConn's turn to have a critical call go against them.

Lawson led Tennessee on a break and drove the lane, where Ralph was waiting to draw a charge. Indeed, Lawson ran over Ralph, but there was no call. Play continued, and Taurasi did pick up the foul, her fifth, trying to deny a Michelle Snow layup. Taurasi had hit six three-pointers and scored 24 points. Now she was gone with 1:02 remaining.

At the UConn bench Auriemma lost control. He rushed up toward midcourt, got the attention of referee June Courteau, and flashed her the choke sign, putting his hands to his throat. That gesture earned Auriemma a technical foul. Tennessee converted the free throws to put the game away, winning 92–88 on the night Chamique Holdsclaw had her number 23 retired.

"I've been to a lot of women's basketball games," Holdsclaw said afterward. "But this is definitely the most exciting game I've ever been to."

And for Connecticut perhaps the most costly. In the short term Auriemma's late outburst drew the most attention. His technical and the resulting two free throws sealed the Huskies' fate.

"I regret that, no question," Auriemma said. "Someone takes a charge and then you end up with the kid that is shooting lights out going out. It was an awful call and I said it."

Auriemma then took one more thinly veiled shot at Sally Jenkins, who was in the interview room as Auriemma and Taurasi sat together at the dais. Whatever battles the coach and player had endured in practice, it was all praise for the freshman now.

"She is a unique player," Auriemma said. "She makes spectacular plays and drives you crazy at the same time. She's the most fearless player we've ever had. And she's managed to keep her ego in check all year, which is really good. She came with a reputation of having a big ego."

Three years earlier, some might have said the same thing about the forward from St. Petersburg, Russia. Certainly Svetlana

Abrosimova was one of the most stubborn players in UConn history. Once, early in her UConn career, she failed to make a pass in practice, as instructed, and shot the ball. "Why should I pass?" she asked Auriemma in all seriousness. "I'm already open."

In 2000 she did pass, instead of shoot, at the end of the classic Tennessee game at Gampel Pavilion, and the coach and player banged heads over it for a week.

But now, with her UConn career entering its final two months, Abrosimova's stubbornness had given way to anguish. An initial diagnosis of a sprained foot would prove to be far too optimistic. Three days later UConn would confirm that Abrosimova had a torn ligament in her foot. Her college career, like Catchings's, was over.

"For Sveta, it was heartbreaking," Ralph said. "As good a player as she was and how important she was to us, it was hard to watch her go through that, but you can't dwell on it. She already feels bad enough, she doesn't need to see us all mopey as well. I knew that from having gone through it myself. That was the worst, to see your teammates upset. You hope they're inspired, because you feel bad as it is.

"It was hard to watch her go down, but I felt a greater sense of responsibility to step it up for her. It is what it is and it's part of the game. You have the cards you're dealt, and that's what you have to deal with. I don't think we were in our own world. It was more about our team and what could we do to help them."

But there would be no helping either team. For only the second time since 1994—but for the second time in three years—neither UConn nor Tennessee would reach the national championship game. Tennessee never could replace the production of Catchings and fell to Xavier in the round of sixteen, Tennessee's earliest loss in seven seasons, ending the careers of both Catchings and Semeka Randall.

"I can teach a lot of things, but I can't teach effort," Summitt barked at the gathered media in Birmingham, Alabama, site of the Mideast Regional. "I'm disappointed. I'm sick. I'm as mad as I've ever been in my life."

Summitt would get madder still. As she wrote in her 2013 memoir, *Sum it Up*: "After our traumatic upset loss to Xavier, someone faxed me a note scribbled in what looked like Geno's handwriting. 'I predicted Tennessee would lose to Xavier, and I also predicted Pat would blame her team instead of herself,' it read. I faxed it to Geno. 'What's this about?' I wrote. He never replied."

There would be payback. During UConn's heroic last-second victory over Notre Dame in the Big East tournament final, with Sue Bird hitting a shot at the buzzer after a full-court rush up the floor, Shea Ralph tore the ACL in her left knee—the third such injury of her college career—and she too was lost for what remained of the season.

But Taurasi, the freshman, was there to fill the void. She dominated the East Regional against North Carolina State and Louisiana Tech, scoring 41 points in the two games and hitting all six of her three-pointers in the regional semifinal against the Wolfpack.

But in the Final Four semifinals in St. Louis, facing top-ranked Notre Dame for a third time in one season instead of the Lady Vols, Taurasi came undone, missing all eleven of her three-point attempts and shooting 1 for 15 overall as the Irish overcame a 17-point first-half deficit to win 90–75.

According to Summitt's book, members of her coaching staff celebrated UConn's demise with a chant from a popular song at the time, "Who let the dogs out?" and the display was communicated back to UConn.

What had begun with Randall's comments about UConn in 1998, and continued with Auriemma's jab at Summitt in Philadelphia in 2000, was turning nasty as the teams prepared for a three-year stretch of Final Four battles.

"I look back on those two coaches, they're from different backgrounds and their delivery is different, but they're actually very similar," Dan Fleser of the *Knoxville News-Sentinel* said. "I think that was part of the problem, that they were so much alike. And they were playing for such high stakes that invariably things were going to get [contentious]. If there had been other rivals, if there had been two or three other teams to diffuse it . . . but I think they both knew that that was the team they have to worry about. So it became something so big, it was almost obsessive. And you bring those two personalities into the thing, maybe it was inevitable that it would get chippy, at the very least."

Back on February 1 at Thompson-Boling Arena, lost in all the pomp for Holdsclaw's retirement ceremony, the petulance of Auriemma's technical foul, and the pathos of Abrosimova's injury, was perhaps the biggest piece of news to come out of that game, the back half of the second home-and-home series between the great rivals.

The news was that there would be no more UConn-Tennessee home-and-home series in the same season. Pat Summitt was pulling the plug. Starting in 2002, there would be just one UConn-Tennessee regular-season game a year.

"The reason I wouldn't want to play this game twice a year is because of where the two programs are right now," Summitt said. "I don't see that changing. Both programs have positioned themselves not only this year, but if you look at recruiting and returning players, obviously Connecticut and Tennessee will be in contention for a national championship in the future.

"Would you want to meet them for a third time each season?"

The primetime games had been a bonanza for ESPN. The 2000 and 2001 games each earned a 0.8 share, a terrific number for a women's basketball regular-season game. In 2000 the game attracted just short of one million viewers, in 2001 a shade under 1.2 million.

But for a rare time in her career, Summitt was putting her team's welfare ahead of the sport.

"I've been in that position before [three games in one season] with Auburn and I never liked it," Summitt said. "You get into that situation with SEC opponents sometimes, but you have a choice with teams outside your conference. ESPN started this game. It's the best thing for women's basketball, but I don't think it's the best thing for Tennessee.

"I'm trying to look at the big picture. Is it in our best interest to play a third time to get to a Final Four, to win a championship? It's not something, if I have a choice, I would favor. I would admit I have thought about it. I've even second-guessed myself. But I'm not changing my mind."

At the time Auriemma said he favored still playing twice a year. But twelve years later Auriemma said he understood where Summitt was coming from.

"It got to be a little bit of overkill, it got to be a bit of a pain in the ass," Auriemma said. "And by that, it's all that anybody talked about. It's as if those were the only two games that existed, then the third one in the NCAA tournament, which came to be seen as inevitable. I think it came to be seen as a pain in the ass for the other coaches in America, the other fans.

"The non–women's fans loved it because it gave them something to look forward to. People who didn't like women's basketball liked watching that game. But I think for everyone else, and even for us and for them, 'Yeah, sure, you're 39-0, but if you don't beat Tennessee and you're 38-1, then you suck.' And I'm sure the same was going on down there. So what started out as innocent and became great, then became really great, became kind of a pain.

"People were putting in the paper what clothes I was wearing, what clothes she was wearing. It just got to be stupid at some point. And they say publicity is great, good and bad. And I think the players loved it. They couldn't wait to play it, because we're really good, they're really good and they want to play someone really good, they don't care who it is. But for the rest of us involved in it, it started to become a real nuisance.

"When we beat them in all four championship games, it started to wear out its welcome. A rivalry is supposed to be where both teams enjoy a certain level of success. And we did. We each had our share. They won 1996–'97–'98. Then we won 2000, 2002–'3–'4. For the longest time, we both enjoyed the benefits of the rivalry and the ups and downs. But when they decided they didn't want to play two times a year, that was the beginning of the end, really."

9

2002

Hitting Something Orange

By 2001, with UConn and Tennessee playing each other twice a season—three times in 2000, including a national championship matchup—there was a grumbling in the women's game that it might be time for someone else to share some of the stage.

Certainly both Geno Auriemma and Pat Summitt were not immune to such talk, and with the relationship between the two coaches showing signs of strain, it was probably no surprise that Summitt balked at continuing the in-season home-and-home matchup.

But for one season anyway there was another natural rival for the Huskies within the Big East Conference, the Notre Dame Fighting Irish, who asserted themselves and slew the giant in much the way UConn had stolen the throne from Tennessee in 1995.

Led by national player of the year Ruth Riley, Notre Dame won two of three matchups against the Huskies in 2001. The final game was the most devastating for UConn, a 90-75 loss in the national semifinals in St. Louis, a game in which the Huskies collapsed in the second half, no longer able to compensate for the season-ending injuries to seniors Svetlana Abrosimova and Shea Ralph.

It was the first time since 1996 that UConn had reached the

Final Four but not advanced to the championship game. That summer Auriemma had begun laying the groundwork for the greatest recruiting class of his career, and in the fall of 1998 Sue Bird, Swin Cash, Tamika Williams, and Asjha Jones had arrived in Storrs, ready to usher in a new era of UConn basketball with the greatest collection of talent in one class.

Now those four freshmen were entering their final season at Connecticut with just one title in their first three seasons to show for their efforts. The loss to Notre Dame a constant memory over the course of that fateful summer of 2001, and with now-sophomore Diana Taurasi also with an incentive to prove her doubters wrong after her 1-for-15 performance in the national semifinal, the Huskies were poised for one of the most dominant seasons in the history of the sport.

The owners of that distinction were the 1997–98 Tennessee Lady Vols, still, for the moment, the only team to go 39-0 in a single season. But now the two great freshmen from that sublime season—Tamika Catchings and Semeka Randall—had moved on to the WNBA. And the players the two "Meeks" had left behind, although certainly talented, even Final Four–worthy, would be in the highly uncharacteristic position of being heavy underdogs to the vengeful Huskies.

But if UConn did have a weakness, an area to be exploited, it would be in the frontcourt. For all their talent, hard work, and chemistry, the trio of Cash, Williams, and Jones all lacked the same key attribute: height. UConn's starting frontcourt ran six feet two, six feet two, six feet two, and Williams, a devastating inside scorer with a shooting percentage upwards of 70 percent, was hampered during her final season by a rare medical condition in her shoulder called thoracic outlet syndrome, which at times limited her ability to play.

And if there was one place the Lady Vols thrived for virtually all of Summitt's tenure in Knoxville, it was in the paint. The 2002 team was no exception, with a pair of six-foot-five stars in Michelle Snow and Ashley Robinson. So when UConn arrived in Knoxville for the teams' annual—and only—meeting in early January, it was anticipated that the action would be at the rim.

"I think the game will be decided on defense and on the boards," Snow said. "Both teams are going to score and get up and down. That's a known fact. But it's going to be who gets on the boards and who plays the best defense."

Interestingly, despite their diminutive stature—relatively speaking, of course—the Huskies had actually been the better rebounding team early in the season, and they agreed that inside play would likely decide things.

"We have to play good defense and rebound," Williams said. "I'm just going to keep saying, 'Rebounding, rebounding, rebounding.' If we don't rebound, they're going to kill us. If we allow them to get second shots, they're going to kill us."

"Right now, they're playing out of their minds," Snow said of the Huskies. "They're rebounding that ball like it's their own child."

But if the first six years of the rivalry had taught anything, it was that for all the talented post players who had graced the UConn-Tennessee stage, it was usually a guard who stole the show: Jennifer Rizzotti in 1995, Michelle Marciniak in 1996, Sue Bird in 2000.

Or Diana Taurasi in 2002.

The only nonsenior in UConn's formidable starting lineup, the sophomore was essentially UConn's version of the Fifth Beatle. But Taurasi was hardly a Pete Best. In terms of overall talent and ability, she was The Best—not just the most dangerous player for UConn, but already a force unlike any other in the nation, with her ability to shoot like Larry Bird and pass like Michael Jordan.

"I've got pretty strong hands, and a lot of girls playing basketball, their hands aren't very strong," Taurasi would explain in 2009. "I think it comes from shooting the basketball and getting a good feel for it, shooting all day, even when you're really tired. And you have to have the confidence to shoot it. Even when I was younger, I would always shoot from really far out. It was second nature to shoot threes. I was probably shooting threes before I was taking lay-ups when I was in third and fourth grade. I was the only one shooting them that far, even the boys."

And the swagger? It was Bird, Magic, and Michael all wrapped into one. In her first game back in Knoxville, after walking off the floor in tears the previous February upon fouling out of a 92–88 loss, she exacted a stunning measure of revenge. With a crowd of 24,611—the largest ever in women's college basketball—awash in orange, Taurasi strutted and smiled amid the sudden silence.

"I really wanted to win this game, because I remember how miserable it was when we lost last year," Taurasi said. "It is a great feeling to win here."

The Lady Vols chased Taurasi all over the floor but were powerless to stop her. The sophomore guard had a career-high 32 points on 11-of-16 shooting, scoring baskets from a variety of spots as the top-ranked Huskies ran away from the second-ranked Vols, leading by as many as 22 late in an 86–72 victory.

"There is a big gap between number one and number two," Summitt said. "We're all chasing Connecticut right now."

Taurasi's 32 were the most points by a UConn player since Shea Ralph had 36 against Boston College in 1999.

"Diana did a lot of things for us today," Auriemma said. "I don't think there is anyone in the country her size that does the things she can do. Her ability to shoot and drive makes her hard to replace."

Taurasi shot and drove at will all afternoon. She hit three three-pointers and scored on three three-point plays. One of them became an instant classic.

With 7:01 remaining and UConn already salting the game away, Taurasi drove the lane, taking the ball directly at the six-foot-five Snow, switched to her left hand for a running one-hander and scored as Snow fouled her. Taurasi then ran right up to the basket support, adorned by a list of Tennessee's championship seasons, and punched it with a lethal right cross.

"I saw orange," Taurasi explained, "and I wanted to hit it."

"The one thing I remember is when she did that [punched the support]," said UConn's redshirt freshman center, Jessica Moore. "It just showed that she is a competitor. It was just Dee being Diana. I think if I was on the other team and I saw Diana do that, I might have gone up to her and set a pretty hard screen, pushed her a little bit and gotten ejected from the game. But for us, when she did that, it lit a fire under everybody. It was an awesome moment. I was loving it."

Tennessee had no answer on this day, other than to give their new tormentor a grudging respect.

"Wow," said Tennessee guard Kara Lawson. "That's all you can say about her. She was incredible. She made shots with people in her face. She took it in the lane and got the [basket] and one. When a player is such a potent offensive weapon, you have to harness her and try to limit her touches and shots. We weren't able to do that.

"She has expanded her offensive game. She had a lot of confidence last year, but she has even more confidence this year. She really looks to be a big-time player."

The victory lifted UConn's record to 16-0, and the wins kept on coming. Only once in the regular season, at Virginia Tech late in the year, were the Huskies even remotely threatened in the second half.

UConn ripped through the Big East tournament, then dominated the first four games of the NCAA tournament, destroying Old Dominion in the regional final by making its first thirteen shots to advance to San Antonio for the Final Four.

And, once again, waiting for them in the semifinals would be Tennessee.

The Lady Vols had recovered nicely from the thrashing they took from Taurasi and the Huskies in early January, crushing defending champion Notre Dame by 39 points in the second round of the Tournament, then edging past SEC rival Vanderbilt to reach the Final Four after a rare absence in 2001.

"I didn't think our defense had much effect on Connecticut at all the last time we played," Summitt said. "Hopefully our intensity will be at the level of the Vanderbilt game and we can generate some transition opportunities. That's the way we want to play—up and down basketball."

Tennessee was getting greater contributions from its freshmen, mainly Michelle Munoz and Brittany Jackson. Snow, who did not start against Vanderbilt, shook herself out of a funk to provide 8 points on 4-for-4 shooting off the bench in the 68–63 victory.

"We're a lot better," Summitt said. "But certainly Connecticut is playing super. I turned on the ODU game last night and I thought, 'I don't need to watch this if I want to sleep.'"

For the first time the women's Final Four was being played inside a dome, the Alamodome, with an expected crowd of thirty thousand for the UConn-Tennessee semifinal on Friday night, another sign of the sport's rapid growth over the past decade. But there was no structure big enough to contain these Huskies. And for the second consecutive time in a Final Four matchup, UConn simply overwhelmed their familiar foe.

The senior class that had been assembled in the wake of consecutive losses to Tennessee in the mid-1990s left an indelible image in the penultimate game of their UConn careers, turning back the Lady Vols with remarkable ease in the national semifinals on their own inexorable march to an undefeated season.

In what would be the most lopsided affair of the entire twenty-two-game series between the great powers, UConn built a 32-point lead in the second half and settled for a 79–56 victory to earn the right to face Oklahoma and match the 1998 Lady Vols with a 39-0 season.

"The funny thing is, they never really backed down, we were just that good tonight," said Sue Bird, who continued her torrid pace in the tournament, scoring 18 points to give her 90 over her past four games. "They never stopped playing. But that's when we play our best, when teams pressure us."

So thorough was the defeat that not a single Tennessee player scored in double figures. Kara Lawson and Courtney McDaniel each scored 9 points.

With 10:57 remaining, the Lady Vols had 36 points. UConn led by 28.

"I looked up at one point, and they had like 36, and I thought, 'Boy, I'll tell ya, to keep them at that number at that time," Auriemma said. "Everything has to go right. It starts with our inside guys having a pretty good understanding of what they're doing. When our guys are focused, it looks like that. And in a game of this magnitude, it has to be like that."

Asjha Jones was once again the anchor. Jones had 18 points and 10 rebounds and rendered Snow a nonfactor, limiting her to 6 points. Jones had the same number of points as Tennessee's starting frontcourt.

"We were not as competitive as I'd anticipated," Summitt said. "They executed so much better, and they knocked down shots. You've got to give Connecticut all the credit. They outplayed us at every position."

The beating was so emphatic, the opponent so gifted, that Summitt was moved to perform a gesture no one on the UConn side could ever remember happening before. On the court, after the final buzzer, Summitt had shared an unusually long moment with Auriemma in the handshake line—a far cry from Al Brown's snub after the 2000 championship game in Philadelphia.

"In San Antonio she got him a little," Dan Fleser said. "There was a little conciliatory interaction between them after that semifinal game. He could have really hammered them. It could have been a lot worse. It was 23 points, but it felt like 40. You could tell in the first five minutes they were going to beat them. And I remember after that game there was a little bit of a truce."

But Summitt would go a step further, entering the Connecticut locker room to address the players and compliment them for their outstanding season. It was a highly gracious gesture, and also a highly surprising one to the celebrating players.

"We were just laughing and talking, we hadn't taken our uniforms off yet, just enjoying the moment, and she just walked in quietly, and one by one, we stopped talking," Moore said. "My jaw was open. It's not every day Pat Summitt comes into your locker room. And she just said, 'I wanted to tell you guys you played a great game, you played awesome.' It was short and quick. She just wanted to say we played awesome, and then she left.

"That was one of the coolest things ever. We were all like, 'Wow,' I can't believe she just did that. You hear stories about Pat being mean and stern and not really saying too much, so for her to come in there and do that . . . we already had great respect for her, but even more so, she is an awesome coach to do that. We were really proud.

"I don't think any of us will ever forget it. It was pretty darn cool. And she never did it again, and I don't think she's done it for anyone else, either."

But while the players were awestruck, even after their lengthy postgame chat on the court Auriemma couldn't help but be suspicious of Summitt's motive. Perhaps it speaks to the deterioration of the relationship between the two coaches in the spring of 2002, but, as Auriemma recounted in *Geno: In Pursuit of Perfection*, he simply couldn't take Summitt's visit at face value.

"She comes into the locker room and tells our guys she admires the way they play the game. She tells them they played like champions," Auriemma wrote. "I'm not around when it happens, so I'm not really sure what context to put it in. People ask me what I think about it, and I don't know what to say. I always wonder when something like that happens. What is the motivation for doing it? Is it for publicity? To gain some kind of edge? I have no idea. I just thought it was a little odd."

Two nights later, any gamesmanship that might have been in play after the Tennessee victory was long forgotten. The best UConn team in program history was forty minutes from perfection, and it would not be denied.

Oklahoma puts up a surprisingly tough challenge, staying within 6 points of the Huskies with ninety seconds to play. That's when Taurasi, the fifth starter but the best player, secured the championship.

Just as when she punched orange in Knoxville, Taurasi used a three-point play to punch UConn's ticket to immortality. Posting up on a rare clear-out called by Auriemma against Oklahoma's All-American Stacey Dales, Taurasi drew a foul and scored the basket, giving UConn a 9-point lead. It ended 82–70, completing the 39-0 season.

"I'm just proud of our team, that we could handle all this adversity, all this pressure, all the questions about the entire season," Bird said. "And then we were finally able to put it all away in the final game and come out on top. It's a very, very fulfilling feeling.

"I was crying, man. I didn't want anybody to see that. There's twenty seconds left, and you're able to dribble out the clock in the national championship game to go undefeated in your senior year. I don't know. What would you do?"

10

2003

. . . .

The Evil Empire

If the pathogen that ultimately sent the great rivalry between UConn and Tennessee into its death spiral could be traced back to an original host, it would not be Geno Auriemma or Pat Summitt, although they would certainly be the most afflicted.

As it happened, the one man most responsible for setting in motion the wheels of the rivalry's destruction not only had never even seen a women's basketball game, he had never—save for the rarest of occasions—been inside the United States.

Jose Contreras was a star right-handed pitcher for the Cuban national baseball team when he defected to the United States in October 2002, making himself available to the highest bidder in Major League Baseball.

In late 2002 the two highest bidders were the New York Yankees, winners of four World Series titles over the previous seven seasons, and the Boston Red Sox, still searching for their first championship since 1918. This was the greatest rivalry in baseball, a blood feud that went back as far as the sale of Babe Ruth by Red Sox owner Harry Frazee some eighty-three years earlier, and it became entirely one-sided as the Yankees racked up twenty-six world championships during that span to the Red Sox's zero.

Nowhere was the Red Sox–Yankees rivalry more keenly felt

than in the state of Connecticut, which served as the land buffer between the feuding cities 250 miles apart. The state was largely divided along geographical lines. South and west toward Middletown, New Haven, Stamford, and Greenwich was largely Yankees country. North and east, including Hartford, Manchester, and the tiny hamlet of Storrs, was annexed into Red Sox Nation.

In many cases fathers rooted for one team, sons for the other. So passionate were the fan bases, so rich was the history, that the state's leading newspaper, the *Hartford Courant*, covered both teams (as well as the football Giants and Patriots) on a full-time basis, home and road, giving equal treatment to both sides. Every move the two teams made was closely followed in a state with split provincial pride.

The move in late 2002 that Boston's newly installed ownership regime—led in part by CEO Larry Lucchino and a twenty-eight-year-old general manager named Theo Epstein—thought could finally turn the winning tide in the Red Sox's favor was the signing of the fireballing Contreras, the newest weapon in an escalating arms race.

The Red Sox made an enormous effort to land the Cuban free agent. But in the end, as was so often the case between the two teams, it was the Yankees who emerged victorious, signing Contreras to a four-year contract just after Christmas.

So upset were the Red Sox that Epstein reportedly trashed the Florida hotel room that had been doubling as the forward command post during the Contreras pursuit. Lucchino took out his frustrations with the Yankees in a more public forum, delivering a memorable quote that reverberated across the Northeast.

"I'll make a comment," Lucchino told the *New York Times* on December 27. "The Evil Empire extends its tentacles even into Latin America."

A week later, the other great rivalry on the twenty-first-century sports landscape renewed itself for its sixteenth installment at the Hartford Civic Center.

As had been the case just before New Year's Eve in the 2000–2001 season, the Lady Vols arrived in Hartford barely ahead of a raging snowstorm. Ranked fifth as they took the floor on the first Saturday of 2003, the Lady Vols were led by Kara Lawson and leading scorer Gwen Jackson (15.7 points per game), now both seniors and still seeking their first national championship, having been twice thwarted in blowout losses to UConn in two previous Final Four appearances.

"I think a senior always remembers their last game against an opponent," Lawson said before the UConn game. "I would like, as a senior, to end this series with a victory, if it's the last time we meet. In the last couple of games against UConn, we haven't been as fortunate as we'd have hoped."

But this was a Tennessee team unlike any that had come before it, and they had Geno Auriemma's best friend to thank.

Harry Perretta, the women's basketball coach at Villanova since 1978, shared Auriemma's Philadelphia roots, staying close to home to lead the small Catholic school's basketball program as a charter member of the Big East Conference.

The two coaches had long been friends, a bond that indirectly led to one of the most controversial moments in the history of women's basketball, a moment that revealed Perretta's willingness to help a fellow coach in need, no matter how unorthodox the situation.

As the 1997–98 season headed to its climax that February, UConn senior All-American Nykesha Sales stood on the precipice of history. Entering the penultimate regular season game against Notre Dame, Sales stood at 2,149 career points, just 28 behind UConn's all-time leading scorer, Kerry Bascom, who had amassed 2,177 points from 1988 to 1991.

Sales, who played a critical role as a freshman on the 1995 championship team and who had made arguably the most memorable shot in UConn women's history to that point, hitting the game-tying three-pointer with the clock running out in regulation against Tennessee in the 1996 national semifinals, had been a victim of her team's great success during her career. Her playing time had been curtailed because of the disproportion-ate number of blowouts the emerging national power partici-pated in over her four seasons.

Although Sales would ultimately play in seventeen more career games than Bascom, largely a function of UConn's deep postseason runs in Sales's first three seasons, she would only accrue fifty-five more career minutes. Had Sales been needed in more of her 137 career games, her overall totals would have been far higher.

Instead Sales, from nearby Bloomfield, Connecticut, took the floor on Senior Day at Gampel Pavilion needing 29 points to overtake Bascom and proceeded to pump home 27 over her first 27 minutes, pulling within a basket of the record.

And that basket appeared in the cards as Sales started a drive to the hoop midway through the second half, when suddenly her right leg gave out and she crumpled to the floor.

In a moment, Sales's college career was over, two points shy of the record. She had torn the Achilles tendon in her right leg and would not be able to play in the upcoming Big East and NCAA tournaments, let alone the regular-season finale at Vil-lanova, scheduled just three days away.

Or would she?

The same evening as Sales's injury, Auriemma reached out to his good friend from Philly. Would Perretta go along with a plan Auriemma was hatching to give Sales a "gift" basket at the start of their upcoming game?

Auriemma planned to allow Sales, despite being on crutches, to begin the game in the starting lineup and stand alone under the Villanova basket. The Villanova players would allow UConn to win the opening tap, guard Rita Williams would dribble the ball up to Sales, and Sales would score the basket, giving her the two points needed to set the UConn scoring record. In turn, UConn would allow Villanova to score an uncontested layup to tie the game at 2–2, take a timeout, remove Sales from the game, and proceed as if the game were starting 0–0.

Perretta wholeheartedly agreed with the plan and Big East

commissioner Mike Tranghese gave it his blessing. No harm, no foul, everybody wins. It might even generate some publicity for the sport, Perretta thought in the days before the game.

On that point Perretta was proven correct. But not in the way anyone intended.

Almost from the moment Sales's basket fell through the net, the roof fell in on Auriemma and Perretta. The "gift" basket was decried from coast to coast, with the *Courant* labeling it "a farce" and ESPN delivering scathing editorials by anchors Dan Patrick and Kenny Mayne at the start of that evening's *SportsCenter*.

But while the media roasted Auriemma, the coaching fraternity came to his defense, including Summitt, who answered in the affirmative when asked if she would have agreed to the plan as Perretta had.

Then Summitt went to bat for Tranghese, who found himself hip-deep in his own controversy while explaining his position on *l'affaire Sales*.

"I have to be candid: If it were two men's teams, I never would have done it," Tranghese told the *New York Daily News*. "It is a women's sport; this was a female player. I am a man. I am not going to pretend to handle decisions on [men and women] exactly the same way."

Summitt helped defuse the mounting backlash by defending Tranghese's position.

"I think women's basketball may be a little different [from men's]," Summitt said. "This is probably a reflection of it. It shows the feelings, the emotions that are in the women's game."

Five years later the emotions of the game would come pouring out at the Final Four in Atlanta, and Perretta would again find himself as Auriemma's unwitting partner in crime. This time there would be no defense from the Tennessee head coach.

After the Huskies blistered Tennessee by 23 points in the national semifinal game in San Antonio in 2002, Summitt looked to make changes to her offense.

It would not be the first time in the wake of a crushing loss to Connecticut on the game's biggest stage that Summitt would seek counsel from fellow coaches about her team's style of play.

After losing by 19 points to UConn in the 2000 national championship game, Summitt began looking for ways to improve her team. She spent time with Don Meyer, one of the winningest coaches in the country at Lipscomb Academy in Nashville; Tennessee men's coach Jerry Green; fellow Hall of Fame member Billie Moore, who coached Summitt on the 1976 Olympic team; and even UCLA legend John Wooden.

"I just want to get better," Summitt told the *Hartford Courant* in 2000. "We're making some changes this year from an offensive standpoint. The senior group [of Tamika Catchings, Semeka Randall, and Ace Clement], they made a tremendous impact on our program. They came in in great fashion and I want them to go out that way."

While attending an AAU game in the summer of 2002, Perretta came upon Summitt and fellow Big East colleague Cathy Inglese, the head coach at Boston College. Inglese introduced Perretta to Summitt and the conversation turned to Villanova's highly successful motion offense.

Summitt asked Perretta if he would be interested in teaching her and the Tennessee staff how to implement it, and the Lady Vols coaches flew up to Philadelphia that June for a tutorial. Perretta brought in some of his former players to run the offense and gave permission to Summitt's staff to videotape the session.

"I think they were in a period there, after the series initially started, they went into an extended period where they were preoccupied with their offense," Dan Fleser said. "'We need to be able to make tough shots in key moments against them and they did it more than we do.' So that was part of it. I think they really wanted to install a motion offense and he was the source. And it became a media circus. It turned into more than they thought it would."

From there a friendship between Summitt and Perretta

blossomed. The coaches would often speak to each other over the phone, sometimes as often as twice a week. Pat would send Harry orange neckties. Perretta would show Summitt diagrams for inbounds plays.

The results, leading up to the UConn game on January 4 at the Hartford Civic Center, were mixed by Tennessee standards. The Lady Vols came to Hartford with a 9-2 record and a fifth-place ranking, but a 21-point loss to Duke around Thanksgiving stuck in Summitt's craw.

"Well, it remains to be seen," Summitt said before the UConn game. "We certainly have, at times, demonstrated strong play with our veterans and our sophomore class is getting better, but I think they need to take their game up a notch to feel like we are nine deep.

"We hope our players go in and compete. It's been hard for our staff to understand when a veteran team doesn't compete hard in a game like this with what happened against Duke this year and Connecticut last year. We expect them to compete and work as a team.

"We're going into a great environment, but as the visiting team, it's a hostile environment. That's where a veteran team has to understand communication. . . . Yes, I'd be a lot more comfortable if I could predict what would happen, but that is why we play the games."

UConn entered the Tennessee game with an 11-0 record, extending the program's overall winning streak to fifty, just four short of Louisiana Tech's all-time record.

But unlike the Huskies of 2002, led by the senior class of Sue Bird, Swin Cash, Tamika Williams, and Asjha Jones, who comprised four of the WNBA's top six first-round picks in that April's draft, the current undefeated edition had just one player with big-game experience.

Following her disastrous showing in the 2001 national semifinal against Notre Dame, Diana Taurasi had re-established her big-game credentials in 2002, dropping 32 points on the Lady Vols in the regular season game in Knoxville, then clinching the national championship and 39-0 season with a three-point play against Oklahoma's All-American (and future NFL Network reporter) Stacey Dales.

But not only was Taurasi the only player on UConn's eleven-woman roster with considerable big-game experience, she was virtually the only player with any experience. Of UConn's ten scholarship players in 2002-3, four were freshmen. Of the remaining five, only junior guard Maria Conlon and two red-shirt sophomores—center Jessica Moore and forward Ashley Battle—had played regular minutes the previous season, and at that only sparingly behind the greatest starting five the women's game had ever known.

Among the top-ranked freshman class that season was Ann Strother, a lanky six-foot-two guard from Castle Rock, Colorado, who had been the national player of the year in 2001-2 at Highlands Ranch High School.

Strother had joined the unique ranks of players recruited by both UConn and Tennessee, including a wildly divergent experience of both.

Her official visit to the Knoxville campus was marked by frivolity, with the hosting players wearing T-shirts featuring the image of Strother as a baby and a mini-blimp inside Thompson-Boling Arena dropping a letter of intent to Strother at midcourt after an "introduction" of Strother as a Lady Vol over the public address system.

Strother's home visit with Auriemma was something else entirely, as it took place during the afternoon of September 11, 2001.

Watching the attack on the World Trade Center unfolding on the television in his Denver hotel room, Auriemma discussed what to do with the Strother family before they all agreed to go ahead with their original plans.

"You know that you're not dealing with ideal circumstances," Auriemma later said. "I would have been okay if it didn't work out. I think everybody was understanding that, hey, it's something that has to be done, and let's go ahead and do it. But it wasn't the easiest of circumstances to be in, believe me."

They tried to make it as normal as possible. They shared a meal at the dinner table. They talked about basketball and college. They even turned off the television.

"It couldn't be as lighthearted as it would have been otherwise," said Jan Strother, Ann's mother. "Neither were as bubbly as they might have been. They were affected by this. That's the kind of people they are. Geno called [before the visit] and said, 'It seems strange talking about basketball.' I don't think it changed things, as far as the recruiting part of it, but it showed another side of them."

Strother would eventually commit to UConn, and the game against Tennessee in her freshman season would be played at the Civic Center under wintry conditions, much the same as the other UConn-Tennessee game she had attended during the recruitment process back in late December 2000.

"The game was at the Hartford Civic Center and a blizzard had hit the night before," Strother said. "The city was shut down, the streets were closed, and the teams needed police escorts just to get to the building. But when I went inside there were thirteen thousand people in the stands. I still don't know how they got there. I remember thinking, 'This is really a big deal.'"

That afternoon Strother watched Taurasi hit a clutch three-pointer in the final minutes to point UConn to an 81-76 victory. Now, two years later, Strother would head into battle at Taurasi's side.

"Just being around her, you get a taste of her leadership," Strother said. "It's hard to explain. It's just a feeling that you get. She's more worried about the team than she is about herself. And because she's like that, everyone's going to listen to what she has to say."

Through the season's first eleven games, Taurasi had been part basketball player, part traffic cop. Often she could be seen and heard directing her teammates to certain areas on the floor.

In particular, Taurasi helped the freshmen—Nicole Wolff, Barbara Turner, Willnett Crockett, and Strother—get assimilated.

"Everybody welcomes it, because she is an extension of Coach out there," Strother said. "She knows the offense so well and she knows how to read things. And the way that she goes about it is, she has everyone's respect because she genuinely cares about everybody. She's going to make an effort to get everyone involved."

Although perhaps not as demonstratively as on the court, Taurasi helped guide the younger players through the non-basketball part of life.

"It's tough coming in as a freshman to a big-time program, knowing you're going to have pressure on you," Taurasi said. "I think it's just the little things that people don't see when you're off the court. We've all tried really hard to incorporate them into everything. Everybody's going to do what they want off the court, and hopefully you can help them make the right decisions. I think with the group we have. They know what to do."

In 2000 Taurasi had joined a veteran team that had seniors Shea Ralph and Svetlana Abrosimova and the junior class that would lead UConn to a perfect record in 2002 as seniors.

Taurasi had learned from her elders. Now she was passing on that knowledge.

"When she came in, she did what she had to do, but she wasn't nearly as intense as she is now," said forward Morgan Valley, who arrived the same season as Taurasi. "She'll yell at people when she needs to. Off the court, it's pretty much the same thing. If people aren't doing what they're supposed to do, she'll tell 'em. She doesn't BS with anybody. She's right up in your face.

"She's definitely the leader on the team. I think the thing the rest of us [upperclassmen] do is when she says something, we have to make sure the younger guys understand what she's saying. Help them through certain situations. We can't let Dee do it alone. Sometimes the younger guys don't understand what she's saying, so we help them out. But she's definitely the leader."

In her previous four games against the Lady Vols Taurasi

averaged 21.3 points, including a career-high 32 in Knoxville the previous year.

But Taurasi, who was averaging 19.3 points entering the Tennessee game, said she didn't plan to punch anything orange, as she did with the basket support at Thompson-Boling Arena.

"If I punch something orange, I'll probably get ejected," Taurasi said.

But if the Huskies were to extend their winning streak to fifty-one games, she was going to have to put a dent in Tennessee's defense.

"Dee's going to win the game," Auriemma said. "All those guys have to do is make sure everything is lined up right, and then let her do her thing. The reason I can say Dee is as good a player as there ever lived is because she has a certain bravado, and she has the game to back it up. That allows us to try to ride her to wherever we're going."

And, as if on cue, Taurasi took the game over and tortured the Lady Vols once again.

Her first bolt of lightning came just before the half. With the score tied at 26–26, Taurasi gathered a Lawson miss with four seconds left, took two dribbles to about sixty-five feet from the UConn basket and let it fly. The ball swished through the net for the longest three-pointer of her career.

"Oh yeah, I knew it was going in," Taurasi said. "I've always wanted to make one of those. It was a lucky play."

In the second half it appeared Tennessee had weathered the storm, inside and out. The fifth-ranked Lady Vols enjoyed a seven-point lead over number-three UConn with 3:51 remaining.

"I thought it was over," Auriemma said. "I didn't know if we had it in us to come back."

But, as Auriemma would say throughout the 2002–3 season, UConn had Diana and no one else did—that was the difference between winning and losing.

Taurasi completed a furious comeback, hitting a three-pointer with 6.6 seconds left to send the game to overtime. Then Taurasi struck again, scoring the game-winning basket in the final seconds as UConn survived a miss at the buzzer by Lawson for a heart-stopping 63–62 victory before a delirious crowd at the Civic Center.

"When you have Diana Taurasi, you're never out of it," Summitt said. "She hits the shot at the end of the half, the shot to send it to overtime . . . she just makes big shots."

UConn had Diana. That afternoon, it also had a deep reservoir of luck.

Consider:

With 2:46 remaining—UConn trails 54–49 as Tennessee's Tasha Butts drives into the lane. Willnett Crockett and Jessica Moore rush to help, leaving Shyra Ely open on the baseline. Butts sees her, and a good pass means a certain lay-up. But the pass is slightly behind Ely, and she has to dribble once to gain control. That's enough time for the freshman Crockett to recover, forcing Ely to take a tough shot. She misses and Crockett rebounds.

At 2:15—At the other end Maria Conlon sees Taurasi make a cut into the lane and forces a lead pass into traffic. As Taurasi and the ball meet on her way to the basket, Ely sets up to draw what should be an offensive foul if Taurasi tries to shoot. But instead Taurasi makes a touch-pass to Moore, then crashes into Ely. The ball gone from Taurasi's hands at the point of contact, no foul is called. But Ely is sent sprawling, which gives Moore an open look. Her bank shot makes it 54–51.

At 1:26—When Taurasi misses in the lane, Tennessee's Loree Moore starts out on the break. The Vols have two great chances to score here and make the score 56–51. Moore can drive herself or throw a long lead pass to Ely, who has raced behind the defense. Moore chooses to drive and it's costly, because Summitt, focused on getting the attention of a referee and not on her team's unfolding fast break, signals for a thirty-second time-out. It takes the officials about three seconds to acknowledge and grant Summitt's wish. Should Moore make the quick pass to Ely, the basket would probably be scored before the whistle blows. Instead, Moore's driving lay-up is waved off.

At 1:01—On the play after the ill-advised timeout, Ashley

Robinson misses and Jessica Moore deflects the ball into the corner. Moore, Conlon, and Ely give chase. It appears that Moore is going to lose the ball out of bounds in her attempt to corral it. But behind her Ely bumps into Conlon and loses her balance. As she tries to regain it, she accidentally kicks the ball away from Moore and out of bounds. UConn ball. On the Huskies' ensuing possession Strother scores on a behind-the-back dribble along the baseline and Tennessee's lead is down to 54–53.

At 0:06.6—Taurasi hits the big-time three-pointer to tie it at 56–56, but she wasn't supposed to get the ball. The play was designed for Conlon, a less likely but still dangerous three-point shooter, with Taurasi throwing the ball in with 11.4 seconds left.

"I figured there's no way they're going to let Dee touch the ball," Auriemma said. "I thought [Ashley Battle] would catch, over to Maria, and Maria would knock it in."

But when Battle cuts to receive the pass, Taurasi sees a Tennessee defender interceding and doesn't pull the trigger. Instead, she finds Jessica Moore at the top of the key, with Ely defending. Now Tennessee has a split-second decision to make. Does Ely foul Moore, a 47 percent free-throw shooter, for a 1 and 1? Or do the Vols let the play unfold, risking the possibility of Taurasi shooting a three?

"We did not discuss it, but I thought about that," Summitt said. "We were trying to play straight-up, one-on-one."

With no orders to do so, Ely doesn't foul. Moore quickly passes to Taurasi. Catch. Shot. Tie ballgame.

"Obviously, that's a pretty tough shot to make right there," Summitt said.

At 0:02.4—Tennessee has another chance. Loree Moore gets the pass and races up the court. Again Jessica Moore steps up in the lane, leaving Ely open behind her. But Loree Moore doesn't see it and blows past Taurasi into the lane. Taurasi reaches and appears to get a fistful of orange jersey as Loree crashes into Jessica, who has perfectly timed the charge.

Offensive foul. Overtime.

At 4:20 (overtime)—Taurasi's bad ankle is bothering her,

and Loree Moore looks to take advantage. With Tennessee leading 58–56 she drives past Taurasi on the right baseline and has a clear path to the basket. But Taurasi makes another savvy, Larry Bird–like play, poking the ball away from behind. It goes right to Conlon, and the Vols are denied a chance to lead by four.

At 1:22—UConn leads 61–60, but Battle can't convert a makeable lay-up and Ely rebounds. At the other end, Tennessee freshman Shanna Zolman gets open at the top of the key. If Zolman's right foot is on the three-point line, it's by a little toe. She hits the shot, and it's ruled a two-pointer. One inch, maybe two, and Tennessee would lead by two instead of one.

At 0:58—Battle is open at the free-throw line but her jumper misses to the right. Loree Moore has position but the taller Jessica Moore is able to get a hand on the ball to knock it away. Strother gets the deflection and passes to Taurasi, who scores in the lane. Who does Taurasi shoot the game-winner over? Ely.

At 0:01.9—UConn's luck runs out with a vengeance. Zolman tracks down a Lawson miss with four seconds left. As she starts to drive, Conlon swipes the ball from behind. It bounces out of bounds, and referee Lisa Mattingly signals Tennessee ball with 1.9 seconds left. Conlon is beside herself. She should be. Replays clearly show the ball was off Zolman's foot.

At 0:00.0—Now Tennessee can win it, and for the final time UConn catches a break. Battle, guarding Lawson, slips while fighting through a Brittany Jackson pick, freeing Lawson to accept the inbound pass. But Lawson's open look at the final shot bounces away. UConn wins.

"I think we're upset about not capitalizing on a great opportunity to win the game," Lawson said. "Any time you're in a top-five matchup and you're on the road and you have a chance to win, it's just disappointing when you can't make that one more play to get the win."

A week later UConn set the NCAA Division I women's record for longest winning streak by beating Georgetown for its fifty-fifth in a row. The streak would reach seventy games before the Huskies faced Perretta's Villanova Wildcats in the Big East tournament final in Piscataway, New Jersey.

Worn down by a season in which their winning streak set expectations much higher than a team with four freshman and a group of role players should have been expected to uphold, and with Taurasi playing with a serious back injury as well as a bad ankle, the Huskies crashed and burned against Perretta's maddening motion offense, scoring a season-low 45 points in a grisly, record-busting loss, a performance so disappointing that Auriemma would famously lash out at a young female reporter for the UConn student newspaper, the *Daily Campus*, just as a worldwide ESPN audience was brought live into the press conference.

"You ask a lot of questions that really piss me off," Auriemma growled at the student.

Auriemma would later apologize for his actions during the first two rounds of the NCAA tournament as his team, having regrouped and been led by Taurasi's virtuoso performance, steamrolled toward the Final Four in Atlanta, where Tennessee would likely greet them in the championship game.

But it was neither of the two titans that garnered the big headlines as the tournament was pared down to its final eight teams. Facing Summitt in the regional final in Knoxville was none other than her new best buddy, Harry Perretta, and his Wildcats. The media was flush with stories about the unlikely relationship between the two coaches, the exchanges of coaching philosophies at summer cookouts—even the gifting of four neckties to Perretta, including an orange tie that Perretta wore in Villanova's Sweet Sixteen victory in Knoxville.

The day before the Villanova-Tennessee matchup, UConn dispatched Boston College in the East Regional semifinal in Dayton, Ohio. UConn would be returning to the Final Four for the fourth year in a row, but that achievement, remarkable for a team not expected to contend after the departure of their four All-American-caliber seniors, was about to take a decided backseat.

It was customary, after making formal remarks at the official postgame press conference—and sometimes informal, as the nation discovered two weeks earlier—for Auriemma to loiter in the hallways of whatever arena they were playing in and engage the media in a more spirited, free-wheeling gaggle. Mostly on the record, sometimes off, and occasionally walking the line in between, Auriemma would riff on whatever topic was lobbed his way, usually game-related, but sometimes veering off on strange tangents.

For instance, on this Sunday afternoon in Dayton *Hartford Courant* columnist Jeff Jacobs asked Auriemma about the apparent traitorous maneuver in his old buddy Perretta's friendship with Summitt, which had become a running story on ESPN during the tournament as Villanova and Tennessee stayed on a collision course for the regional final in Knoxville.

Never one to pass up the opportunity to bust the chops of his best friend from Philly, Auriemma took the cheese—and if Summitt took a little playful shrapnel in the process, all the better.

"It's nauseating," Auriemma deadpanned. "If I see them one more time together on ESPN, I'm going to throw up. Do you see Roy Williams and Gene Keady in the hot tub together going, 'Yo, what do you think, man?' C'mon. There are about twelve kids on Villanova's team that somebody should be talking about. Ask one of them, 'Do you think you'd go to the final eight at Villanova?' Final eight of what? The Big East tournament? Now this kid's forty minutes from the Final Four and she's got to read in the paper and see on ESPN how these two lovebirds are sharing information? Give me a break.

"Give me two guys that hate each other. Two guys who might fight at half court. You don't want a foul tonight and have them go, 'What do you think, Pat?' 'No, Harry, you take it.' 'No, you take it.' Kiss. Kiss. Give me Jim Calhoun and Mike Jarvis. That's what it's all about.

"When I heard about the cookout, the swimming and the lucky tie . . . well, I didn't want to say this, but one of the reasons

BC didn't play so good today was I had Cathy Inglese and all of them over and they were in the hot tub a little too long."

The more Auriemma talked, the more his eyes twinkled, the more he smiled. He was on a major roll now, and he and the reporters all knew it. This is why Auriemma, who just weeks earlier had uncomfortably upbraided a defenseless college student on national television, is given a free pass by the media that cover him. He fills a notebook like no one, not just in women's basketball but in all of sports.

He's funny, clever, and opinionated—the journalistic Triple Crown.

"Geno used to call it 'throwing snowballs' at each other, and I think that's what he thought it was," said *New London Day* columnist Mike DiMauro, also a participant in this Dayton performance. "Here's this great rivalry and it's the only women's game that non-women's fans watch. I think he always saw the opportunity to put on a little bit of a show."

Now, his routine in full swing, Auriemma went for the killshot.

He seized on the fact that Summitt had had Perretta to her house for summer pool parties. A lifelong Philadelphia Phillies fan and a New Englander since 1985 who has adopted the Red Sox as his favorite American League team, Auriemma recalled Larry Lucchino's verbal blast against the Yankees after the Jose Contreras fiasco, applying the rhetoric of that historic rivalry to his own.

Like Rumpelstiltskin, Auriemma wove his thoughts into spun gold.

"I am jealous," Auriemma said. "Harry and I used to be in the hot tub together. He dumped me for the Evil Empire."

Bursts of laughter filled the hallway of the arena. Auriemma kept going, poking more fun at his favorite foil Harry.

"If it was all on the up and up, he wouldn't call me every week to swear to me, 'I don't tell her anything that you and I talk about. Honest.' There's an old French saying: '*Qui s'excuse, s'accuse.'* Those who excuse themselves, accuse themselves. I know he's guilty. Did it ever dawn on anybody that Harry has no friends and that's why he talks to Pat all the time? Nobody in Philadelphia will talk to him. All of his coaching friends have deserted him, now that he has hooked up with the Evil Empire.

"I probably talk to Harry more than she does. The difference is I'm smart enough not to listen to him. Now he figures there's no way Connecticut can win after all their guys graduated. So he gets on the phone with the person he thinks who can win it. 'Here's what you've got to do to beat Connecticut.' I got to give him credit. He's got everybody snookered.

"I want to see when they kiss and hug at the end of the [regional final] if Villanova wins. If Harry liked the house, if he liked the pool, if he liked the barbecue, all he has to do is lose by 40. They win, that's it. He'll have to order barbecue by mail."

Jacobs captured all of it on tape, transcribed it and filed a winner of a column. Back in Connecticut the wisecracking nature of Auriemma's relationship with Perretta is well-known and the column reads fancifully—one friend needling the daylights out of the other as they both sit on the edge of reaching the Final Four.

Of course Auriemma was joking. It would be impossible to miss that.

Wouldn't it?

Geno Auriemma and Pat Summitt are similar in many ways. They are brilliant basketball minds. They are expert motivators of young female athletes. They are visionaries in their sport, with a passion to make it grow. They are driven to succeed and are not afraid of taking on great challenges.

They are winners. They are champions. They are Hall of Famers.

And yet the Italian wise guy from Philadelphia and the proper Southern lady from Henrietta, Tennessee, could not be more different. Certainly they both are fine orators, but they do not speak the same language. And the barrier between them was about to grow higher.

Jacobs's column with Auriemma's jabs at Harry and Pat quickly spread across the nation. They were picked up in other newspapers and by the Associated Press. They were played and replayed on ESPN. It was without question some of Auriemma's finest work on a resume loaded with zingers.

Pat Summitt was not laughing. Evil Empire? He said that about us? About me?

Summitt is not a Red Sox fan. She has not even seen the movie *Star Wars*. And from where she sits, where she's from, there's nothing funny or cute about being called evil.

"The Evil Empire stuff, she honestly did not get that," Fleser said. "It just went right over her head. I tried to explain it to her. I said, 'You're taking it literally. He doesn't mean that.' But she just did not get it.

"All she heard was 'evil,' and it played into some of her worst imagery of him and his banter.

"I tried to explain it to her and she had already made up her mind. I couldn't get her to see it. 'He used an expression that comes from a whole different context. He's not calling you evil. If anything, he's complimenting you.' I might as well have been speaking Greek to her at that point."

Auriemma had always used his sharp tongue as a weapon, but only on behalf of his team. If Auriemma felt the Huskies were vulnerable before a big game, and he wanted to take the pressure off his players, he would say something controversial to the media, let the bull's-eye fix on his back, and let his players just go play.

Six weeks earlier UConn had taken on Duke at Cameron Indoor Stadium in another primetime number one vs. number two battle. But this was a UConn team that was still essentially Diana Taurasi and a bunch of untested players, and Cameron Indoor was perhaps the most intimidating arena in the country for both men's and women's teams.

Before the game Auriemma opined that Duke's graduates

were just as likely to wait on tables as UConn's. The Cameron Crazies had their target. Then UConn went out and built a 28-point lead in a statement victory.

"He was always saying, 'I'm taking the pressure off you guys and putting the focus on me, so you go out and play,'" said Jessica Moore, UConn's redshirt sophomore center in 2003. "You know how coaches are sometimes mysterious and don't tell you what they're thinking. Coach kind of is too, but when he needed to tell us something, he would."

So now, with the same untested UConn team headed to the Final Four and a possible title matchup with Tennessee, here came "The Evil Empire."

"In '03 he did the whole Evil Empire thing," DiMauro said. "You're going into the national championship game with Maria Conlon as your starting point guard. Don't you think you're a little apprehensive? So he said, 'This one is on me, you guys go out and play.' And that's why they always did. Why do you think they're [9]-0 in national championship games?"

The war of words between Auriemma and Summitt was generally one-sided. While Auriemma never met a comment he didn't like, Summitt tended to go the route of self-censorship. For instance, there had been no public rebuke of Auriemma's "old and dilapidated" comment back in 2000. Instead, for her own reasons, she had suffered in silence.

"She always felt it would hurt her in her recruiting to engage him in some of that banter," Fleser said. "He just was a master at pushing her buttons, and no coach had ever dealt with her that way. If anything, most coaches were deferential to her. For someone to go after her like that, she never got the high ground there. I've been around her enough to know, she could be pretty darn sarcastic and bitingly funny if she wants to be. But he always had the high ground on her on that. She just never got the better of him in one of those. Most times she wouldn't engage him, and when she did, she never scored a body blow like he did."

But now, on the day of her regional final matchup against

Perretta and the Wildcats, the Empire struck back. Speaking at a press gathering before the game, Summitt finally went toe to toe with her tormentor.

"It was interesting," Summitt said of Auriemma's jabs. "First, I think I was defensive for Harry. I thought some of Geno's comments were out of line. Harry is not two-faced. He is so genuine. I was bothered for him. Second, I agree with Geno that he is jealous. But I think you could also put paranoid in there. I think you learn more about Geno from this than you do about Pat or Harry.

"It is not worth dwelling on. He made the comment that Harry left him for an older woman. In Philly, he talked about me being old. Well, I think you all need to look at the record. He is just a year behind me [in age]. I'm glad Harry likes me over him."

Then Tennessee went out and buried Villanova to advance to Atlanta, along with UConn. Texas and Duke were there too. Allegedly.

Before the national media could pick the Evil Empire story apart, UConn and Tennessee had to get past their semifinal games at the Georgia Dome. Tennessee had little trouble with Duke, a team many hoped would crack the UConn-Tennessee stranglehold and become a third national power, led by All-American guard Alana Beard. But as had been the case in 2002, Duke was simply not ready for prime time, and Tennessee easily dispatched the Blue Devils to reach the finals.

Texas, coached by another legend, Jody Conradt, who had led her 1986 squad to a 36-0 season, was another matter entirely. At last it appeared that UConn's overachieving season was coming to an end, with Texas leading 66–60 with 3:14 left when the Huskies made their final push.

Taurasi drove across the lane and converted a three-point play to make it 66–63 with 2:56 left. Then Ashley Battle drew a charge with 2:40 to play. Strother was fouled, and she made 1 of 2 free throws to close within 2.

But fellow freshman Willnett Crockett rebounded the second

miss, the first of two critical rebounds off missed UConn free throws, and the ball found its way out to Taurasi.

The national player of the year pulled up straightaway from twenty-two feet and hit the three to give UConn a 67–66 lead with 2:07 left.

"We didn't get rattled," Taurasi said. "We just said, 'Let's get a couple of stops and run it back down.' That's what we did. We got good shots, and we hit them."

With the lead still 1, Battle made another big play, rebounding a Taurasi miss and making two free throws to give UConn a 69–66 lead with 1:18 left.

Taurasi was fouled with forty-six seconds left, but uncharacteristically missed both free throws. However, once again Crockett rebounded the second miss, which led to two Maria Conlon free throws and a 71–66 lead with thirty-six seconds left.

"I just didn't want to go home at all," Crockett said. "I wanted to stay here and help get my team to the championship game."

The Longhorns had one last chance. Jamie Carey hit a three-pointer with 28.2 seconds left to make it 71–69, and after Crockett missed two free throws with 8.2 seconds left Alisha Sare stormed upcourt with the final shot in her hands.

But she never took it. Taurasi stripped the ball as Sare started to shoot from the top of the key, and Moore cradled the loose ball and UConn's entry into the championship game in what was Auriemma's five-hundredth career victory as a head coach, all at UConn.

"I will always remember this one," Auriemma said. "There hasn't been many games in those five hundred that I think I'll remember more than this one."

That was Sunday night. Monday was pretty memorable, too.

Practice day on the eve of the national championship is a chance for the national media to interview all the players and the two head coaches, looking to fill space in newspapers, magazines, and online sites that were increasingly devoting more room to women's basketball, especially when UConn and Tennessee were playing for the title, and especially when the two coaches were having quite the tiff.

Summitt was the first to the meet the press. There were questions about how her team would deal with Taurasi, who was having one of the greatest individual performances in tournament history, but the subject *du jour* was Pat vs. Geno.

"Let's just say, personality-wise, we're very different," Summitt said. "I think we grew up differently, too. If I ever spoke out like Geno's speaking out, my dad would probably whip me today. He'd probably take me out behind the barn and get out the tobacco stick.'

"I think a lot of people have tried to make something out of Geno and Pat's relationship. He is a coach. I'm a coach. I have tremendous respect for Geno's coaching abilities and what he has done at Connecticut. We're not talking on the phone every week. As a matter of fact we don't talk on the phone. But I would just say that I think that's what you have. You have a great rivalry and certainly a coach that I respect tremendously as a basketball coach."

Then it was Geno's turn: "When I first started playing [Tennessee], no, I never brought the needle out," Auriemma said. "That only came along later, because I don't want people to get bothered with us playing Tennessee. So you just try to keep things light and lively, I know how you guys love that stuff. You all love the little sound bites, you know. It would be great, wouldn't it, you know, if we would go out to the game tomorrow and everybody is having, you know, big séances and we are all holding hands and wishing each other luck but that's not what you all want. You just want two people going at it tomorrow, two programs that just hate each other. We want to kill each other. That's not the case either. I was just talking to Pat fifteen minutes ago. Sense of humor is a rare commodity in America today, I'm just trying to do my part.

"I live in Connecticut. I'm a Red Sox fan. If you talk about Tennessee—they are the Yankees and Pat is George Steinbrenner.

We make fun of it. It's just a way to have fun. There is nothing evil about them unless you live in Connecticut. They don't do anything wrong. Her program speaks for itself and her reputation certainly speaks for itself. Throwing snowballs is part of what you do in a tournament. We are just throwing a couple of snowballs at each other.

"What would I want to get from Harry? As far away as possible. He keeps calling me on my cell phone. Pat thinks he is going steady with her. He calls everybody. I mean he called me like five times the other day. I'm trying to tell him it's over, you are out of the tournament, go the hell home. He wants to still be part of it but I'm not going to let him. He is done. He is on his own now. Do you ever see the way he dresses? Why would I want to be seen in public with him? Never shaves, he has no hair, wears a baseball hat, goes to nice restaurants wearing shorts and sneakers. I have an image to uphold."

At one point, Auriemma recounted the fifteen-minute conversation the two had had earlier that morning.

"'You think I'm evil,' she said. I said, 'No, come on. No.' We talked about a lot of things. We did. We talked about a lot of things. Basketball, basketball. Just kids in general. Some of her kids, some of my kids. After you break it all down she can think what she wants about Connecticut. I can think about what I want about Tennessee in our darkest moments, but you can't help but respect each other."

But for all the hard feelings and tough talk between the two coaches, the players tended to stay completely out of the fray. The rivalry on the court was about winning championships but was never personal.

"We didn't really follow it," Lawson said. "It's not like we thought Geno and Pat were best friends, you know? Every time in college when I had an interaction with Geno, or any of the players, to be honest with you, it was positive, good relationship. In fact, a lot of the UConn players I knew prior to them going to UConn. There was a relationship that predated college.

"So when people say, 'Oh well, you don't like these players,' . . .

no. I'd been playing against Sue [Bird] since I was nine. We've known each other since the fourth grade. So, all of a sudden now, I'm supposed to hate her? That doesn't make any sense. Same thing with Tamika Williams. I played against her since the fifth grade. I knew her and her family. My dad and Sue Bird's dad used to talk together all the time. From the players' perspective, it was a lot more blown up. Now, we were competitive. We wanted to win, but it wasn't personal.

"When you're in college, it's really like a bubble. You go to practice and they talk about, the focus needs to be on the team and what we're trying to do, your scouting report. We would sometimes hear it through the media, when they would ask, 'What do you think about Geno saying this?' And we'd be like, 'We didn't know he said that. We didn't hear it.' We didn't get involved in that. There's enough going on, being a student-athlete."

And once Tuesday arrived it was finally all about the players. Or, rather, the player.

Diana Taurasi, who hoisted her novice teammates on her aching back and carried them through the NCAA tournament on one good ankle, did what she seemed predestined to do, scoring 28 points to turn away the Lady Vols again, as UConn won 73–68 to win back-to-back titles for the first time in its history, winning its fourth championship overall.

"To beat Tennessee and to win the national championship with this group is truly one of the more remarkable things that has ever happened," Auriemma said. "Maybe they are a lot better than I thought. Maybe they're tired of listening to, 'We're too young and inexperienced.' But we're tough enough. We really are."

UConn was leading 58–52 with 9:10 left when Taurasi came back in after her only rest of the night. She scored UConn's next 9 points to make it 67–54 with 6:11 left, including a remarkable left-handed scoop shot as she was falling out of bounds.

But Kara Lawson, Tennessee's senior guard, scored 7 straight to make it 67–61 with 4:05 left. Ashley Robinson was fouled with

2:39 left and made the first of two free throws to cut the lead to 5. She missed the second, and Shanna Zolman rebounded for the Lady Vols, but Maria Conlon, who finished with 11 points and 6 assists, stole the ball. Strother scored on a baseline drive to make it 69-62 with 2:08 left.

Gwen Jackson, who had 15 points but just 6 in the second half, put back a missed Lawson three-pointer with 21 seconds left to make it 71-68.

Then the freshman Strother was fouled with 20.4 seconds left and made both free throws for a 73-68 lead. Ashley Battle stole the inbounds pass and the Huskies ran out the clock, with Taurasi throwing the ball into a section of Tennessee fans at the buzzer.

Taurasi, the consensus national player of the year, finished the tournament with 157 points, third-most in Division I history, and had 54 in the Final Four, fourth all-time. The 28 points in the final tied for second-most ever (Sheryl Swoopes had 47 for Texas Tech in 1993). She was an obvious choice for Final Four Most Outstanding Player.

"They all thought we were going to lose, and whenever you tell Dee no, she's going to say yes," said Jessica Moore. "She's always going to bring her best, and even more. Her competitive spirit just helps her rise to the occasion, and you see her play like she's never played before. And that kind of mentality, you can't teach that. You either have it, or you don't. Only the great players, the Michael Jordans, think that way, and Diana is the same way."

2004

End of an Era

After everything that went down between Geno Auriemma and Pat Summitt in the spring of 2003, come the fall it was time to move on.

Going into the preseason before the start of the 2003-4 season, Summitt decided that one year of Harry Perretta's motion offense was enough. After giving the Villanova system a go in the 2002-3 season—resulting in Auriemma's "Evil Empire" routine and all the hard feelings that accompanied it—Summitt scrapped the offense in favor of the triangle system made famous by Phil Jackson and Tex Winter with the Chicago Bulls in the 1990s.

And it appeared, at least for a time, that the UConn-Tennessee rivalry, as both coaches—and many more coaches outside the rivalry—had hoped, was starting to get company on the national scene.

In the 2003 season UConn and Duke had played the first half of a home-and-home series at Cameron Indoor Stadium, and UConn had won easily. Now, in the first week of January in 2004—and for the first time ever, after eight consecutive seasons—CBS broadcast a UConn women's game with someone other than Tennessee as the opponent.

Although Tennessee had scrapped the in-season home-and-home arrangement with UConn after the 2001 season, ESPN was still able to keep the regular-season game, securing the rights to the 2004 game to be played in Knoxville. As it had in 2000 and 2001, ESPN placed that game in the first week of February as part of its annual Rivalry Week.

That left an opening for CBS on its triple-header day, going against the NFL playoffs. And this time the opponent was Duke.

UConn-Duke already had an extremely rich history of scintillating basketball and hot tempers, but it was entirely confined to the men's side. Duke had ended the UConn men's bid for the Final Four on a Christian Laettner buzzer-beater in overtime of the regional final in 1990 and the teams had a memorable scrape (think Randall-Abrosimova '99) in their NCAA tournament rematch in 1991.

But the pinnacle came in 1999, when the underdog Huskies shocked the world and beat Duke 77–74 in the NCAA championship game.

Now it was hoped that the two women's programs could approximate that action and emotion and become the Next Great Rivalry in the game. And it appeared off to a good start. In the seconds after beating Duke in Durham in 2003, Diana Taurasi mocked the Cameron Crazies by pantomiming a phone at her ear and chanting "Call me" as she strutted off the court.

Then Duke answered the call at the Civic Center the next season. With UConn going glam with never-before-worn silver uniforms—think a bad 1950s sci-fi film—for the national audience, Duke rallied from a double-digit deficit and stunned the two-time defending champs with a Jessica Foley three-pointer at the buzzer.

Ah, but nothing is chicken soup for the UConn soul quite like a little Huskies–Lady Vols controversy, and *Sports Illustrated* tried to do its part in mid-January.

To commemorate its fiftieth anniversary in 2004, the magazine conducted a survey of the sports landscape in each of the fifty states over the course of the year. Included with each feature story was a two-page infographic detailing such facts as the state's greatest athletes and greatest moment (UConn women's 1995 title) and a memorable quote.

And there was a fan poll, conducted by Harris Interactive with 416 participants, listing the responses to such questions as favorite pro team (Yankees 28 percent, Red Sox 16 percent).

Of note were the UConn women–related answers. While Ray Allen was the top athlete who played in Connecticut, second, third, and fourth were Rebecca Lobo, Diana Taurasi, and Sue Bird (Gordie Howe was fifth).

And while Red Sox–Yankees easily won best rivalry with 39 percent, UConn-Tennessee was next at 17 percent.

And that probably explained the result in the most intriguing category, Connecticut's Enemy of the State. Garnering 25 percent of the vote? You guessed it: Pat Summitt.

She earned more votes than Yankees owner George Steinbrenner (20 percent) and almost double the total of Patriots owner Bob Kraft (14 percent), who had actually done real damage to the state when he backed out of an agreed-upon deal to move the Patriots to Hartford in 1999.

Summitt took it all in stride. This was, after all, quite a compliment.

"I laughed at that. I thought it was pretty interesting," Summitt said shortly before the resumption of women's basketball's real rivalry in early February. "I would have been disappointed if I hadn't won. As many times as UConn has beaten us as of late, though, I ought to be Miss Popular up there."

Indeed, since the wild 92–88 game in 2001—the last time ESPN had displayed the rivalry in prime time—UConn had won four straight games in the series, the longest winning streak either team had enjoyed over the first seventeen games, giving the Huskies an overall record of 11-6. That mark now included a 3-0 record in NCAA championship games.

And with UConn's entire roster from the 2003 title team back in Storrs and the Huskies the odds-on favorites to join Summitt's 1996–98 squads as the only three-peaters in women's basketball history, Auriemma turned down the volume on his Summitt-centric rhetoric.

Even with the *Sports Illustrated* poll for fresh material, Auriemma chose not to take the bait, although prodded on a national conference call in the leadup to the Tennessee game.

"I don't know who they interviewed to get that response," Auriemma said. "People don't tell you that if 28 percent of the people said Pat was the Enemy of the State, the little-known fact is I got 27 percent. People are funny around here. We've lost two games this year, so if they took the poll again today, she'd be second and I'd be first."

"It's fun for everybody," Auriemma said of *SI*'s state-by-state series. "You look at some of the other states, some of the other stuff. The people Tennessee hates the most are [former Florida football coach] Steve Spurrier, or Alabama or Auburn. It's one of those things that generates a lot of interest and it's good for people to talk about."

But Auriemma was dubious of Summitt's new title. He remembers when she came to Connecticut in 1998 for a book signing, and fans waited in line for upwards of three and a half hours to get her autograph.

"People are two-faced," Auriemma said. "When she came up here to plug her book, they were standing in line, couldn't wait to get her autograph. 'Hi Pat, we love you.' So they'll say one thing to her face, and say another thing behind her back. I wouldn't put too much stock in that Enemy of the State stuff."

Auriemma, of course, could at times be guilty of the same kind of thing. While publicly he sought to smooth over the hard feelings that had developed after the 2003 Final Four, privately he would occasionally air his grievances with the Tennessee program, most of the focus on his perception that Tennessee, despite all its success, would go out of its way to try to one-up the Huskies, such as inflating home attendance figures to ensure that Tennessee ranked ahead of UConn for single-season records.

And when CBS's *60 Minutes* did a piece on Auriemma in March 2004, it aired a clip of the UConn coach addressing his team after a practice the week of the Tennessee game and mocking the Lady Vols' mindset.

"For us, this is just another game," Auriemma was captured saying. "For them, it's 'REVENGE!'"

But Auriemma's little jab wasn't just for effect. If Tennessee's 1997 team lost ten games despite its riches of talent because it lacked a killer instinct, the 2003-4 Huskies were similarly afflicted, losing two games in January after having lost just three regular-season games—two to the Lady Vols—in the previous four seasons combined.

And because of those two January losses—to Duke and Notre Dame—Tennessee took the floor against UConn as the top-ranked team in the nation for the first time since the famous game in 1998 when Semeka Randall had called UConn "scared."

Tennessee entered the game with an 18-1 record, its only loss to Texas, and had beaten the same Duke team that had knocked off UConn just two weeks earlier. But the victory was marred by the loss of junior point guard Loree Moore to a torn ACL. That loss, coupled with the graduation the year before of Kara Lawson and Gwen Jackson, left the Lady Vols vulnerable though still dangerous.

Junior forward Shyra Ely, who led the Vols in scoring (14.5 points) and rebounding (7.8), had become the go-to player. Sophomore guard Shanna Zolman, who played just eleven minutes in the 2003 title game without attempting a shot, was emerging as a consistent three-point shooter, averaging 40.6 percent from beyond the arc, good for 12.1 points per game, complementing the steady play of seniors Tasha Butts and Ashley Robinson.

"I still think right now that our team is better than it has been," Summitt said. "Our front line game is better than it has been. We play the team game the way we should play it. We don't have a [Diana] Taurasi that puts up the numbers that she does. We have to do things collectively."

If Auriemma was concerned about the mental makeup of his team, he got some re-assuring answers in Knoxville. Before a crowd of 20,961, the Huskies broke open a deadlock late the first half and answered every Tennessee challenge in the second half for an 81–67 victory.

UConn saw a 10-point second-half lead twice cut to 4, the last time with 6:28 left, and Diana Taurasi picked up her fourth foul with 8:01 left, fouling out with forty-six seconds left. But the Huskies refused to get frustrated and rode their free-throw shooting to the finish line, making 12 of 14 free throws in the final 6:28, compensating for having one field goal in the same stretch, as they slowly drew away to end Tennessee's eleven-game winning streak.

It was a sharp contrast to the endings of UConn's losses against Duke and Notre Dame in January, when the Huskies had failed to execute in late-game situations.

"We had the lead the whole game, but it wasn't like we were sitting back and being comfortable about it, like we were in the Duke game," Auriemma said. "With about three or four minutes left, I turned around and said to the guys, 'We're not giving this one away, under no circumstances.' And we didn't. Maybe we've grown a little bit since that day."

Most notably, UConn outrebounded Tennessee, 42–39, and held a 17–11 edge on the offensive boards.

"They attacked on both ends of the court," Summitt said. "They were aggressive in their offense. That gave them an edge. I was disappointed we didn't match their intensity. They've got some big-time players that stepped up."

Both teams would emerge from the game with a renewed focus. UConn would lose just one more regular-season game— yet another loss to Villanova in the season's final week—while the Lady Vols would run their regular-season table.

But both programs would hit a bump in their respective conference tournaments. Tennessee, which remarkably had not won an SEC tournament since 2000, continued its drought in 2004, dropping an overtime loss to Georgia in the semifinals.

The Huskies would also lose in the semifinals, with a bit of homegrown drama sprinkled in. After the late loss to Villanova, the Huskies sputtered into the Big East tournament, beating a far-inferior Virginia Tech team 48–34 in the quarterfinals, a game in which Taurasi, coming down to the final stretch of games in her illustrious career, clashed with Auriemma on the sidelines in a rare display of public rancor between the two.

The Big East player of the year had arguably her worst game since the 2001 national semifinals, scoring 4 points in 23 minutes.

With 7:54 left she picked up her third foul. Then, in frustration over that call, Taurasi picked up her fourth foul 17 seconds later.

And when Auriemma barked at her on the bench for her foolish fouling, Taurasi barked right back. Auriemma benched Taurasi for the rest of the game, even as the Hokies cut a 14-point deficit to 9 with 4:51 left.

"Dee hasn't fouled anybody in four years," a visibly annoyed Auriemma said after the game. "She has not been wrong in four years, and I'm just sick of it. You don't sit there and argue with me. Nobody argues with me on the bench. Jen [Rizzotti] never did. Nykesha [Sales] never did. Svetlana [Abrosimova] would never do that, as much as I would bust her chops about it. When they were wrong, those guys knew they were wrong. This kid hasn't been wrong in four years, and it's catching up to her. I'd rather lose than let kids get away with that."

Auriemma's displeasure carried into the interview room. When the first three questions were for Taurasi—non-benching-related—Auriemma cut in.

"How about a question for somebody who actually got something done today," Auriemma said.

Things then went from bad to worse. UConn lost the next night to Boston College in the semifinals, a loss punctuated by several miscues in the final seconds that allowed the Eagles to steal the win.

The next night Auriemma and the coaching staff forced the players attend the championship game—the first UConn had not played in since 1993—in hopes of angering them to the point of refocusing their attention to the upcoming NCAA tournament.

The strategy worked. Playing their first four tournament games inside the state—the first two rounds in Bridgeport and the regionals in Hartford—the Huskies steamrolled their way back to the Final Four for the fifth straight season.

Tennessee had a much more controversial road to New Orleans.

Playing Baylor in the regional semifinals in Norman, Oklahoma, the Lady Vols appeared on the verge of a fantastic finish. With the score tied at 69, Shyra Ely found herself on a breakaway as the clock ticked under five seconds in regulation. But Ely missed the lay-up with two seconds left. Butts was then unable to tap in the putback. In the scramble for the ensuing loose ball, Baylor's Jessika Stratton collided with Butts, and though neither possessed the ball Stratton was called for a foul as the buzzer sounded.

So not only was Baylor whistled for a foul that probably shouldn't have been called in the first place, the officials checked the monitor, put two-tenths of a second back on the clock, and awarded Butts two free throws.

With Baylor coach Kim Mulkey-Robertson having a meltdown at the other end of the floor, Butts made both free throws for a 71–69 victory.

Mulkey-Robertson alternated between being somber and angry at the postgame news conference.

"I don't like to see basketball games end like you all just saw," Mulkey-Robertson said. "I don't think Pat Summitt does either. Didn't she say that?"

Summitt did.

"I hate to see a good game end like that," Summitt said. "Tonight was a situation where there were a lot of calls everybody is on edge about."

Tennessee went on to defeat Stanford to set up a Final Four matchup against LSU, but the talk in New Orleans was still on the bizarre end to the Baylor game.

"That's what makes coaching and playing so incredibly frustrating, that a game that's played that hard and it comes down to that," Auriemma said. "I'm sure there's a rule that covered whatever happened, but common sense has got to say there's got to be a different way to end that game than the way it ended. I mean, I give [Baylor coach] Kim Mulkey[-Robertson] a lot of credit. She had a lot more restraint than I would have had in that situation."

Summitt's main concern was the backlash directed at her team, with critics saying the Lady Vols were not worthy of their place in the Final Four.

"Well, obviously I was upset about it," Summitt said. "But people are entitled to their own opinion. I firmly believe that those people that are professional should be professional and be fair. [The players] were mature, they ignored it. And I was so concerned because I was afraid they wouldn't ignore it."

Tennessee would validate its candidacy in the semifinals with another heart-stopping 2-point victory.

LaToya Davis scored with 1.6 seconds left after LSU's Temeka Johnson lost the ball in the backcourt, giving the Lady Vols a 52–50 victory.

"They have low blood pressure," Summitt said of her team. "My blood pressure right now is not even worth checking. . . . I told them I was really proud of them but I don't know how much more of this I could take."

With the score tied at 50 and the clock running down, Butts again had the chance to win it but missed, giving LSU the ball with 6 seconds left. But Tennessee trapped Johnson in the backcourt, forcing the turnover when Johnson tripped as she tried to advance past Ashley Robinson. Ely came up with the loose ball and quickly fed Davis underneath for an uncontested lay-up.

"I was just in the right place at the right time," Ely said.

UConn's victory over unlikely Final Four participant Minnesota didn't come down to the wire, but wasn't any less tense. The Golden Gophers, who had shocked Duke in the regional finals, played the Huskies tough the entire game before Ann Strother hit a three-pointer with four minutes remaining to give the Huskies a 6-point lead on the way to a 67–58 victory.

Taurasi, in her penultimate college game, scored 18 points,

her spat with Auriemma long forgotten. Now one win away from a third straight title, Taurasi had joined the list of the all-time greats in the history of women's basketball, joining Cheryl Miller, Nancy Lieberman, and Tennessee's Chamique Holdsclaw.

"When I look at Taurasi, she just has great offensive skills and physically so strong and great vision," Summitt said on the eve of the 2004 NCAA tournament. "She finishes unlike anyone we've talked about, particularly when you look at her range. She's the best I've seen from three-point range."

Like Taurasi, Holdsclaw wanted the ball in clutch situations. Even as a freshman she demanded the ball from Summitt.

"You can be talented and versatile, but if you can't compete under pressure, then you're never going to be known as one of the all-time greatest players, and that's what Chamique could do," Summitt said. "She was just a fierce competitor who believed if you give her the ball, she's going to win the game. And more often than not, she would make the play. She wasn't going to be denied. She had the greatest impact on this program of any player I ever coached.

"The confidence that Chamique gave us and that Diana gives her team is powerful. From what I see from both players, they make everybody else better. You never feel like that you're out of any game with players of that caliber.

"I don't know of anybody else in thirty years I've been coaching that has the offensive skills from long range and the ability to make big plays for herself and other people. I just think she's been the best at making the big plays, night in and night out. Impact on the women's game is the way I look at it. And when I look at Diana's impact, it's huge."

As for her own team, a championship victory would have to be a team effort.

"I think it says obviously we don't have the superstar," Summitt said. "And we don't have a player that's going out every night and consistently putting up 25, 30 points a game. But what we recognize is that we do have each other. And we have some players that are very talented on this team. They understand their roles. That's important. I think when Loree went down they just really had to have a self-examination of who they were individually and what they could do individually and how they could be stronger collectively because of it.

"And that's been the beauty of watching this team in that they have all taken one more responsibility, sometimes as a coach you see potential in players that you feel like they don't see in themselves. And we have challenged every individual from our coaching staff, but I think more importantly they have challenged themselves and they're seeing their own potential and then they're playing well together."

Of course, no UConn-Tennessee championship game would be complete without some back-and-forth banter between the coaches. There had been *l'affaire cheesesteak* in Philadelphia in 2000 and, of course, all the Evil Empire talk in Atlanta in 2003.

But in New Orleans in 2004, despite the best efforts of the media to drag it out of them, there was precious little sniping by Summitt and Auriemma to be had.

"We really don't have a relationship," Summitt said. "We coach against each other. As I've said before, I don't have his cellphone number. We don't talk. We speak before and after the games. That's it. But that's the relationship that Geno has worked so hard to create. At one time I thought we had a pretty good relationship. So I don't know why it went south. But that's the way it is."

"People usually don't hate those they beat all the time," Auriemma said. "If they hate me because we win a lot, I'd rather that be the case than they like me because they kick our butt all the time."

There was one question that did manage to steal the show. Trying to find a way to gauge the hostility level between the two, an enterprising reporter posed an interesting scenario: What would Summitt do if she were driving down a dark highway in Tennessee and encountered Auriemma stranded on the side of the road?

"Well, I'd stop and ask if I can help him. Why wouldn't I?" Summitt said. "Reverse the roles."

Auriemma, who clearly had grown tired of such questions and was a bit surly when pressed, answered curtly, "I would walk."

"I hope Pat said, 'That might be the stupidest question I've ever heard,'" Auriemma said. "I'm here to answer questions about my team versus their team. One thing that exists is UConn against Tennessee, five-on-five basketball. Unless you're from *People* magazine and you want a story, well that's different."

Only when asked about the irony of playing for a third straight title against the only other program to have done it, did Auriemma open a window into his feelings toward Tennessee.

"Perhaps this will put all of those stupid questions about us and Tennessee to rest," Auriemma said. "When we started winning championships in 1995 and started to be really, really good, it was like we were the new kids on the block. I remember a specific comment that there had been a lot of newcomers that pretended to be good. Old Dominion, USC, Texas, Virginia, and Stanford all challenged at one time. But only Tennessee had been on top of the mountain forever.

"And there was a sense that after a year or two we'd just go back to Storrs and say, 'Boy, wasn't it great to visit New York City once?' But you know what? A funny thing happened. We kept coming back. And as a result, that's when things began to get a little dicey. It's because we wouldn't go away."

That UConn was the favorite again in this 2004 championship game, unlike the year before, may have also explained Auriemma's reticence to kick the hornet's nest.

"The way I looked at it, he made more noise when he thought Tennessee might beat them," said Dan Fleser of the *Knoxville News-Sentinel*. "He would get into Summitt when he thought he needed to take heat off his team. It was very Spurrier-like. In 2003 Tennessee was playing really well at the end of the year. They were just blistering people in the tournament and I think he thought 'They could beat us,' and he turned the heat up. He waited until the regional final. I think that was part of his thinking and that Final Four was all about the two of them.

"And then the next year [2004], he wanted no part of it, because I think he realized he had the better team and he didn't want to create anything."

On April 6, 2004, UConn and Tennessee took the floor for the final time in a national championship game. In the first three meetings, in 1995, 2000, and 2003, the Huskies had emerged victorious. The outcome would be no different in New Orleans.

Three weeks earlier Auriemma had reflected on the regular season. UConn had lost four games—as many as the team had lost in the previous four seasons combined. It had been a struggle the team had expected to endure in 2003, after their 39-0 season and the loss of four WNBA first-round picks. Instead the hangover came a year late.

"The journey the first time you go to the beach is fun as a kid," Auriemma said. "The next couple of years, you just want to get to the water. You don't want to deal with the car ride."

But the long ride ended at the right destination.

UConn and Tennessee alone would share the distinction of winning three national championships in a row, as the Huskies gutted out a 70-61 victory over the Lady Vols. UConn's fifth national championship put them one behind Tennessee.

"There's a tremendous amount of responsibility that the kids carry around," Auriemma said. "And I think it got to them this year. All we had to do was focus on three weekends in March, because the journey leading up to that was very, very hard. They had to defend it every night. It's hard to do that. It's just remarkable what they were able to do, under the circumstances."

And for one year Storrs could truly proclaim itself the center of the college basketball universe. The night before the women's victory, Jim Calhoun's men defeated Georgia Tech for their second title. The women then secured the first dual basketball titles in the same season in NCAA history.

"It's history," Taurasi said. "I think being from the University of Connecticut, we always think of ourselves as a basketball school, and this year we made a definite impact on how prominent our programs are."

The championship game was the conclusion of Taurasi's unparalleled UConn career, and she went out as Final Four Most Outstanding Player for the second year in a row. She had 17 points to lead the Huskies, kicking the ball into the stands at the final buzzer.

Taurasi ended her career with 2,156 points, third-most all time at UConn, and Tuesday's championship left little doubt as to her place as the greatest player in UConn history.

"It's been amazing," Taurasi said. "Coming in as a freshman, I never expected this at all. I know I speak for [seniors] Maria [Conlon] and Morgan [Valley], it's just unbelievable. Three in a row? You just don't do that."

But the true hero of this championship night was center Jessica Moore, who scored 12 of her 14 points in the second half to prevent UConn from wilting under a furious Tennessee charge.

Moore had come to symbolize what Auriemma referred to earlier in the season as the "girly-girl" mentality of his team. The six-foot-three center from Palmer, Alaska, had always been more of a finesse-type player. But she also possessed a certain mental toughness. She had been the first nonmedical redshirt in program history in 2000–2001, but never wavered in her commitment. Now, in the most important game of her career, she delivered her finest performance.

After UConn had raced to a big early lead Tennessee scored the last 11 points of the first half; then Zolman hit a jumper to open the second half to make it 30–26.

But Moore kept UConn afloat, scoring the Huskies' first 8 points of the half, the last on a pick-and-roll from Conlon that offset a 5-point burst by Zolman to put UConn ahead, 38–33.

Moore then drew a charge on LaToya Davis, and Taurasi cashed in the possession with a three-pointer for an 8-point lead. Summitt later called it the turning point of the game.

"It's one of my most favorite and amazing awesome games I played in, in my life," Moore said. "It was time to turn things on. There's nobody else you have. You have to get it done. Whatever has to get done is going to get done. I remember saying to Dee, 'I'm going to do whatever we have to do to get you this win. Whatever I have to do, you've got me.' She said, 'I know, Jess, I know.' I would always tell her that. I just went somewhere in my head and me and Maria were like Stockton and Malone on the pick-and-roll. We always called ourselves that.

"Something in my head just clicked and I got that angry face on. I don't care who's in front of me, I'm just going to find a way to score. I think they did a great job of seeing where I was and gave me the opportunity to score and I made sure that I finished."

But the Lady Vols, who showed true grit in their previous three games to reach the final, kept coming, closing to 48–45, then 50–48 with 9:51 to go as Taurasi got a rest on the bench.

Moore then scored inside again to put UConn up by 4. Then with UConn leading by 5 with 6:26 left, Moore twisted her right knee grabbing an offensive rebound and had to leave the game for several minutes. But that rebound led to three Strother free throws and an 8-point lead. Tennessee got no closer than 4 the rest of the way.

What no one knew at the time, least of all Moore, was that the center had torn the ACL in her knee. Despite the incredible pain, Moore actually returned to the game in the final minutes to help secure the win.

"I honestly didn't think it was that bad," Moore said. "I thought maybe I had sprained my knee. It just happened so quick. I remember that I was about to travel and I threw it to Ann and it felt like fire was going through there. I went to the bench and the adrenaline started going through my body and the pain just left. I did a couple of jogs and [trainer Rosemary Ragle] was like, 'Do you feel okay?' and Coach came over and said, 'Are you okay?' and I'm like, 'Yeah, I'm okay.' I didn't feel pain until about midnight that night as I was laying in bed. I woke up like, 'Aaah!'

"I was playing with controlled rage. You can hit us any way you want to, but if you want the championship, you have to go through us, and we were not letting them take it, no matter what. I don't care if Ashley Robinson started dunking, we didn't care. We were going to do whatever we needed to. The year before that, it was 'We have Diana and you don't.' But I felt in 2004, she couldn't do it by herself. I felt we all played a significant part in us winning, and that's why it meant so much. That championship meant more than the previous two."

Tennessee came back one final time, cutting it to 62–57 with 2:22 left. But seniors Taurasi and Conlon each hit two free throws on consecutive possessions to put UConn up by 9 with 1:32 left.

The title was theirs.

"They have a toughness about them," Summitt said. "An aggressiveness and obviously a confidence. I think they obviously get that from their coach. I thought Diana brought that as well. I have a lot of respect for Geno and I have a lot of respect for this Connecticut program."

There was, of course, a toughness to Tennessee as well. The Lady Vols lost three key players in Gwen Jackson, Kara Lawson, and Loree Moore yet survived, however controversially, a pair of 2-point games to reach the final.

"I told them I hope when they reflect on the year they'll know how they grew as a team," Summitt said. "They were one of the grittiest, most tenacious teams I've ever had in a long time. When I think of them this summer, I won't think they've failed. I think that by most people's standards they overachieved. But by my standards they found a way to win and are champions in that regard."

But the result was still there. Tennessee had now lost six straight games to UConn and was 0-4 against them in championship games.

"I would never say anyone was a better coach than Pat Summitt, but I think Geno prepared his teams for that moment better than she did," said Mike DiMauro of the *New London Day*.

"I think Tennessee won a lot of games with tough, physical defense and getting every rebound, which is a great way to play. But I thought Geno's offense was a lot of read and react. There really are very few set plays. I always thought in those games, the offense took what it was given and just played a very relaxed style, because this is what we do.

"Except for the Randall-Catchings group, I always thought Geno had better basketball players. I thought Pat may have had more physical, sometimes tougher players. But Geno usually had the more skilled kids."

No one was more skilled than Taurasi, who finished her career by going 7-1 against the Lady Vols, averaging 21.8 points per game against them.

"I don't think it's anything complicated. You look back at her career, and other than the semifinal game in 2001 against Notre Dame her freshman year, I don't remember her ever playing poorly in a big game at Connecticut," Auriemma said. "I think the bigger the stage, the better the opposition, the more pressure, the better Diana played. You don't become the legend she's become by getting 30 against Seton Hall and playing lousy against Tennessee. That's not what legends do. They have their best performances in the biggest games against the best teams. And whether it was Tennessee or anyone else, and they were the other 'best' team. That's why those performances stood out so much: the quality of the competition and the bigness of the game."

When the game ended, Auriemma and Summitt engaged in a long embrace at half court. For the past four years, the atmosphere between the two had been icy at best. But the glow of UConn's third straight championship had led to a thaw.

In the handshake line, Auriemma tried to put the bad blood behind them.

"'Don't listen to all this crap you hear and read,'" Auriemma said. "'Sometimes I just stay things for fun. It's not meant to be at your expense. I have tremendous respect for what you've done, and how you do it, and that will always be true.' She says, 'I really appreciate that.'"

"It was a cordial conversation," Summitt said. "I'll leave it up to him if he wants to tell you. Good luck getting it out of him. But I think he has established himself as one of the very best teachers and coaches in the women's game. . . . So I have a lot of respect for Geno and . . . for his program."

One thing the two coaches could certainly agree on in 2004 is that their rivalry had been, as Summitt told ESPN's Carol Stiff back in 1995, "good for the game."

The 2004 national championship game drew a record women's basketball rating of 4.3. That was the equivalent of 3.8 million households, the most-watched college game, men's or women's, in ESPN's first twenty-five years.

"I would imagine people who are emotionally invested in the sport would have hoped it would create other rivalries, but nothing has approached that series," Fleser said. "The powers that be in the sport were probably hoping that would happen, but I don't see that it's happened.

"But that game captured an audience that the women's game hadn't touched before. Casual fans knew about that game. They might not know all the particulars and the history, but they had a fundamental knowledge of that series and those two teams, two really high-profile, successful coaches, and this was really worth watching. This was good theater. I don't think any other women's game, it had its audience, but this one put a whole lot more people into the tent."

12

2005-7

Moore Trouble Ahead

A ripple of boos rained down on the Michigan State coaches and players as they emerged from the tunnel before the start of their game against UConn at the Hartford Civic Center in late December 2004.

Booing Michigan State? Really?

Ah, but there was a reason. She wasn't wearing number 21 in orange anymore, but the eagle-eyed Husky fans knew that face when they saw it.

Semeka Randall was back in town.

"Boooooooo!"

Randall had traded in her sneakers for a nice pair of shoes and was now an assistant coach on Joanne P. McCallie's staff with the Spartans. Also on the Michigan State staff was Auriemma's good buddy Al Brown. Tennessee wasn't due back at the Civic Center for another ten days, so this was like a mini-preview with the two former Lady Vols in town.

But resuming the rivalry was the last thing on UConn's mind that night. It was bad enough that, in the wake of Diana Taurasi's departure for the WNBA, the Huskies were ranked eleventh in the nation, their lowest ranking in a decade. Now, with Randall and Brown looking on, the Huskies were handled fairly easily by the Spartans, losing 67–51.

That same night, Tennessee lost by 14 to Rutgers.

At long last, the parity that so many had hoped would finally become commonplace in the women's game, with new programs ready and able to challenge the Huskies and Lady Vols for a championship, had apparently arrived.

"The biggest difference I see, if I turn on a UConn or a Tennessee game now, is when the other team steps between lines, it isn't an automatic 8- to 10-point spot," ESPN analyst Doris Burke told the *Courant* after the twin upsets. "It's what's happened on the men's side. A jersey doesn't cause people to be intimidated anymore."

Burke pointed to the UConn-Xavier game in the second round of the 1999 NCAA tournament. Xavier led by 6 with 2:17 left but lost by 2.

"Xavier had them on the ropes at Gampel and they couldn't complete it," Burke said. "That's the difference this year: People are playing UConn and Tennessee like they're any other team."

When UConn had defeated Tennessee in the 2004 national championship game just seven months earlier and Taurasi had left the stage for the final time, there was a sense that the golden era of the UConn-Tennessee rivalry, which had just ended its tenth season, had gone with her.

With Tennessee's incoming freshman sensation Candace Parker out for the year after a pair of surgeries before the season had even begun, UConn and Tennessee would find themselves just another pair of teams trying to survive the season and get to the Final Four. For the first time since 1986–87—and the only time between 1988 and 2013—neither UConn nor Tennessee would have a player represented on the WBCA (formerly Kodak) All-American team for the 2004–5 season.

So it was with a little less fanfare in early January 2005 that UConn and Tennessee met in Hartford for the twentieth game in the history of the rivalry.

But no one in blue or orange was talking Final Four this time. Instead both coaches were singing the same sad song: *can't sustain offense; spotty guard play; relying too much on freshmen; early-season losses; frustration to last a lifetime.*

"I've seen Tennessee play some great basketball this year and some really awful basketball," Auriemma said. "And I look at my team and feel the exact same way. It's like we're a mirror image of each other."

Tennessee was 9-3 and ranked tenth. UConn was 8-3—the quickest to three losses since 1992–93—and ranked fifteenth. Never in the ten years of the rivalry had the two met when ranked so low. Auriemma and Summitt tried in vain to mold their teams in the image of their big-game predecessors. Both had gone to extremes. Auriemma had banned his players from their cushy locker room and lounge. Summitt made her team wear their practice jerseys inside out, covering up "Tennessee."

They met at the Civic Center in what amounted to an episode of *Survivor* much more than *Clash of the Titans*. UConn had won the last six meetings and led the series, 13–6, but the teams that took the floor had little resemblance to those the CBS audience was accustomed to. A lack of household names was another tie that bound them.

"When they had [Chamique] Holdsclaw and [Tamika] Catchings, they had a little bit of an edge," Auriemma said. "When those guys graduated and we got Diana [Taurasi], we had the edge. And now that Dee's gone, I don't know who has the edge. Maybe neither of us do."

What they had instead were issues, and lots of them. Auriemma joked on a conference call that he had a ready-made excuse. Not long before the game, Auriemma had had his five championship rings stolen from his car.

"When we look like we never practiced before and my guys can't get a shot off against Tennessee, it's because my playbook was stolen," Auriemma said.

Tennessee was also struggling, averaging 65.8 points, almost 4 fewer than UConn. The week before the game was the first time Summitt had a full complement of players in practice.

The injuries, coupled with the graduation of Tasha Butts, Ashley Robinson, and LaToya Davis, had left a leadership void just as UConn was adjusting to life without Taurasi.

"You lose a player like [Taurasi] and it is incredibly different," Summitt said. "I can tell you that just by the leadership we lost in Tasha Butts out on the perimeter. You know it is going to be different and a change, but not that drastic. I thought that Tasha and Ashley's leadership was some of the best in my career, and that is three decades of coaching. As much as our staff and I appreciated them then, we appreciate it even more today.

"You just do not replace that overnight. With us, it has been such a struggle from a leadership standpoint at times, but I think both teams will come together."

Both teams did rally to make UConn-Tennessee XX a spirited and dramatic contest.

"Everyone thinks we might curl up and die, both programs," Summitt said. "I don't think it's going to happen, so put away your hankies."

In the end, however, the Huskies were again reduced to tears by their own mistakes.

The game had a little of everything. There were big plays in big runs. There were bizarre calls and bad decisions. There were improbable clutch shots made by improbable shooters.

And with 3.9 seconds left, there was Ann Strother, the player UConn wanted, on the line with three shots to win the game.

The Huskies had survived everything Tennessee had thrown at them—and their own mistakes—in a furious second half. Now, trailing by 2, they had the ball in Strother's hands after Strother, a 61.9 percent free-throw shooter, had been fouled by freshman Alexis Hornbuckle on a three-point attempt from the corner.

But the Huskies were left to comprehend what happened next. Strother made the first free throw, cutting the deficit to 1. But she missed the second. And then she missed the third. And that was it.

Tye'sha Fluker hurled the rebound to half court, the buzzer sounded, and tenth-ranked Tennessee danced off the Civic

Center court with a 68–67 victory before 16,294. It was Tennessee's first victory over UConn in seven tries dating back to 2001.

"At the end of the game, I really did want the ball," said Strother. "I just wish it ended differently."

Despite the loss the Huskies showed life, and it would carry them through the end of the regular season and to a Big East tournament title, their first in three years. But the season would end short of the Final Four for the first time in six years, as Stanford knocked the Huskies out in the Round of Sixteen in Kansas City.

Tennessee would also find success beyond Hartford, reaching the Final Four for the fourth consecutive year and ninth time in the past eleven seasons. But Michigan State, which had knocked off UConn in December with old pals Randall and Brown on the bench, now took out the Lady Vols, 68–64, in the national semifinals. That cleared the door for Baylor, a year removed from the highly controversial loss to Tennessee in the regional semifinals, to claim the program's first national championship.

Parity 1, UConn-Tennessee 0. And 2005 was just the beginning.

After a year of waiting, in 2006 Candace Parker was finally ready to show off her skills. One of her most impressive talents would have to wait still longer, however. Parker, the heir to Diana Taurasi as the game's best player before even taking the court for her first game, had burst onto the national scene in high school, but not for being a two-time Naismith player of the year, although this had made her the envy of every college coach in America except Summitt, who landed her to play at Tennessee.

No, what impressed the masses most was that the six-foot-eight-inch Parker, who could play guard as well as forward or center like a female LeBron James, was winning a dunk contest at the 2004 McDonald's All-America High School Game.

Against boys.

But now, at Tennessee, a no-dunk edict was in place. Not because Summitt had a problem with a women's player dunking, unlike Auriemma, who prohibited his players from dunking because he didn't believe it had a place in the women's game. In fact Summitt encouraged it to the point of trying to set them up for Michelle Snow back in 2000.

Parker's cease-and-desist order was put in place for health reasons. Parker had blown out her knee in the summer of 2004 and had undergone three subsequent surgeries to correct the problem, forcing her to redshirt her freshman season.

Then, in late December of her first season on the court in 2005–6, Parker sprained her ankle.

"I'm not about to have her dunk," Summitt said. "That's not the top priority. Just knock down that fifteen-footer."

That was okay with Parker, whose all-around game didn't need to rely on a gimmick.

"If it's a two-point game, I'm not going to dunk," Parker said. "The way I look at it, people know I can dunk. If the opportunity presents itself, then, yeah. I'm not out to prove anything."

Leading into the UConn-Tennessee game in January 2006, Parker was proving her worth as the game's newest sensation. She was second on the top-ranked Lady Vols in scoring with 14.3 points per game and led the team in rebounding (8.9) and blocks (2.4).

She could run the floor, start fast breaks, handle the ball, hit teammates with behind-the-back passes (34 assists), and create turnovers (26 steals).

"I don't think you really realize what you got into with her until you step on the court," said sophomore Alexis Hornbuckle. "She's a big presence, she's hard to go around, and it's hard to guard her. She's hard to match up against."

Summitt has seen some of the best college players grace her court. But not since the days of Chamique Holdsclaw and Tamika Catchings had Summitt coached a player like this.

"She has the potential to be one of the best ever because of her size, her skills, her knowledge," Summitt said. "She's got a good feel for the game. She's gotten better even in the last week. She gets up for big games. Obviously, the challenge is to maintain the intensity at both ends and be able to sustain that.

"She's putting up some good numbers, but I think she should be a dominant rebounder at both ends of the floor, just instinctively going there all the time."

But when the Huskies took the floor at Thompson-Boling Arena, Parker was not the star of the show. Instead it was Sidney Spencer, as UConn cheated off her to double-team Parker and the more prolific offensive threats. Spencer made UConn pay, hitting a career-high five three-pointers and scoring a career-high 21 points in an 89–80 victory, Tennessee's second in a row over UConn after six straight defeats.

"This was the first time that we had played them on 'The Summitt,'" Shanna Zolman said of the floor recently named for coach Pat Summitt. "We didn't want to lose on our floor."

Zolman had 13 points, as did Parker, playing in her first UConn-Tennessee game.

For the Huskies Ann Strother had 25 points, her season high, but again could not make the big play needed to turn back the Lady Vols. After missing two clutch free throws that could have won the Tennessee game the year before, Strother had three cracks at a three-pointer with less than four minutes remaining and UConn trailing by two.

But Strother, who attempted a school-record fifteen three-pointers and made five for a third straight game, missed two open threes on the same possession, then couldn't handle Renee Montgomery's pass on the possession's third chance, resulting in two Spencer free throws with 2:03 left. Spencer hit two more free throws with 1:38 left to finally put the Huskies down.

It was a discouraging loss, coming just weeks after the worst home loss of Auriemma's career—a 23-point wipeout in Hartford against North Carolina.

And though UConn would reach the regional finals in Bridgeport in March, thanks to a last-second fall-away three-pointer by senior Barbara Turner, the Huskies would lose to Duke in overtime of the regional final, missing out on the Final Four for the second straight season.

Tennessee would also be sent home early by North Carolina in the regional finals, as three ACC schools—Duke, Maryland, and North Carolina—would join LSU in Boston for the Final Four.

It was the first and only time in the thirteen seasons of the rivalry that neither UConn nor Tennessee would reach the Final Four. How much had parity taken over? The absence of UConn and Tennessee was not mentioned once in any of the press conferences during Final Four weekend.

Maryland went on to win the 2006 championship, the second year in a row a school had won its first title. But this was no time to get comfortable. The queen would be back on the throne soon enough.

The offseason of 2006 was a good one for Geno Auriemma. In April he landed the top recruit in the nation, Maya Moore from outside Atlanta, his answer to Candace Parker.

Later that same month Auriemma was celebrated in Knoxville—you read that correctly—as the newest member of the Women's Basketball Hall of Fame.

But the biggest honor came in September, when Auriemma joined Pat Summitt in the ultimate shrine to the game. The UConn coach was inducted into the Basketball Hall of Fame in Springfield, Massachusetts.

When Summitt was enshrined in 2000, Auriemma greeted the news with more of his playful banter.

"What I'm happy about in this great run they've had the past thirty-two years she has been there, what I most enjoy, is the fact we have made her a little nervous."

In 2007, as the competition between the two teams headed into its thirteenth season and twenty-second game, Auriemma and Summitt had become the caretakers of the most important rivalry in the history of women's team sports, one perhaps second among women's rivalries only to the one between tennis legends Chris Evert and Martina Navratilova.

"You don't want it to be the Pat and Geno show, you'd rather have it be about the teams," Summitt said before Auriemma's induction. "But sometimes things are said, within the media, and the rivalry has generated a lot of interest. It's been a rivalry that's been good for women's basketball. Our personalities are quite different. At first, I had never been in a situation like that with a coaching colleague, some of the comments that led in to our games. I understand him a little more now. It's just Geno.

"He has this system and what makes him so good is that he sticks to it. They're well-drilled, competitive, and have a certain toughness about them. You always know he's going to have a team every year that's going to be one of the top teams in the country. Expectations are very high. There are a lot of similarities in our programs, which has made for such a great rivalry."

That rivalry was renewed again on January 6, 2007, at the Hartford Civic Center. It was a truly bizarre day in Hartford. Instead of the usual wintry weather that seemed to always accompany the UConn-Tennessee games in Hartford, temperatures outside were practically summerlike, with temperatures in the 60s.

This would be the twenty-second game of the rivalry, which UConn led 13–8, including four victories in national championship games. But neither team had been to the finals in either of the previous two seasons.

"In some sense, a small sense, it's still the Red Sox and the Yankees. It still is," Auriemma said. "But there's still a lot more good things going on in college basketball now. That's just the reality of it."

But led by the sensational Candace Parker, the two teams showed one more time why their game mattered more than any other.

In what was the greatest single-game performance by a Tennessee player against the Huskies in the history of the rivalry, Parker scored 30 points, grabbed 12 rebounds, and blocked 6 shots.

She got her last block on a Kalana Greene shot in the closing seconds to secure a 70–64 victory, Tennessee's third straight over UConn after six consecutive losses.

But that was hardly Parker's most impressive sequence.

In a one-minute span early in the second half, Parker completely took over the game at both ends in a devastating display of talent, power, and teamwork.

Driving through the lane, she rose up for a jumper with her left hand, knocking down the shot. Then Sidney Spencer stole the ball from Mel Thomas and sent a pass ahead to Parker. There was nobody between Parker and the basket, and there were no more bans on dunking either. Parker rose again and fired the ball through the basket as the Tennessee bench exploded.

"I had a chance to dunk on Connecticut's court and I did," said Parker, on the sixth dunk of her college career.

She wasn't finished. Back down at the other end Parker blocked a shot by Charde Houston, grabbed the loose ball, dribbled upcourt, and fed Nicky Anosike for a lay-up.

Four points, a block, an assist, and a dunk. Tennessee's 12-point lead ballooned to 18. Ballgame.

"Cheryl Miller was big enough to do those type of things back in the day," Auriemma said. "But I think the time Candace spent with the U.S. team [in the world championships], being around them, gaining that experience, I just think her intensity level and her concentration is so much better than before. All the skills she has are more evident now.

"It's like when we had Diana. What's the answer? Guess what? There is no answer. Sometimes you just got to hope she has a bad game."

What no one knew at the time, except perhaps Summitt herself, was that Parker's virtuoso performance would be the final highlight of the UConn-Tennessee series.

The Lady Vols would go on in April to win their seventh national championship. But for the only game that really mattered, the show would not go on.

13

2007–13

Unrivaled

On the night of April 3, 2007, Tennessee finally climbed back atop the Summitt. For the first time since capturing its third consecutive title in 1998, the Lady Vols were once again cutting down the nets, winning the program's seventh championship with a 59–46 victory over Rutgers in Cleveland. Candace Parker scored 17 points in the victory, Tennessee's first in a championship game in its last six Final Four appearances.

"We were a team that didn't want to be denied," Summitt said. "We weren't going to leave here without a championship."

But the next day the championship game became embroiled in an ugly controversy when New York's WFAN-AM host Don Imus, arguably the most well-known morning radio host in the country—in no small measure because the show was simulcast nationally on MSNBC—jokingly referred to the Rutgers team, with its predominantly African American roster, as "nappy-headed hoes."

The comments drew an immediate national backlash and ultimately led to Imus's dismissal from the radio station and from MSNBC.

But in the Big East offices, where Rutgers was a member, another crisis was brewing on the women's basketball landscape, one that would make the Imus imbroglio seem wholly minor in comparison.

The day after *Imus in the Morning* was pulled off the air in New York, a roast was held in Plantsville, Connecticut. The honoree was Geno Auriemma, and many former players and fellow coaches came to pay their respects to the fifty-three-year-old coach. One who was not there was Pat Summitt, but her spirit was present thanks to Central Connecticut State University men's coach Howie Dickenman, a former UConn assistant and longtime friend of Auriemma's, who came bearing gifts, orange ones—bright orange ones that could come only from Lady Vol–land.

For a nanosecond Auriemma placed one of the gifts—a Lady Vols cap—on his perfectly coiffed head, quickly throwing it to the ground before any incriminating snapshots could be taken.

Meanwhile word was continuing to circulate that Tennessee was giving serious consideration to a blockbuster decision. After UConn and Tennessee had played that January, the contract between the two schools had come to an end and needed to be renewed. There was no hesitation on UConn's part, especially with their highly touted freshman, Maya Moore, joining the team in the fall.

Moore, from outside Atlanta, was easily the most talented incoming freshman that UConn had recruited since Diana Taurasi signed on in 1999. Unlike Taurasi, Moore was also recruited by Tennessee, and she made her decision in April 2006 at the end of her junior season at Hill High in Suwanee, Georgia, where she won the first of two Naismith Awards as national high school player of the year.

While most basketball recruits send their official letters after picking a college, Moore had fired off unofficial versions to college coaches while still in middle school, sending what amounted to a basketball resume.

"When I was younger, my mom instilled in me that I needed to be proactive in the recruiting process and tell the coaches where I'm at," Moore said on the day of her decision. "I wanted to keep my name in the back of their minds."

"I really like the way the [Huskies] play, and they've put out some amazing talent the past few years," Moore said. "Connecticut women's basketball is extremely popular in the North. It's something I'll look forward to, that love for basketball, just like I have. I can see myself doing a lot of good things at the university, both academically and athletically."

What Moore didn't look forward to was explaining her decision to Summitt, who saw Moore as the bridge to her next generation of title winners, following Parker, who was likely to leave for the WNBA after the 2008 season, despite being eligible for another season at Tennessee.

"Saying no [to the other coaches] was very tough for me because I was so used to saying yes to everyone that was asked of me, like, 'Yes I will visit, yes I am interested, things like that,'" Moore told the *Hartford Courant* in 2011. "But saying no to Tennessee was the hardest for me because I likely had the most contact with Tennessee. I probably visited there the most and I wasn't looking forward to my conversation with Coach Summitt. It wasn't a long conversation, probably a minute long at the most. I think she was disappointed obviously, but I don't remember it being rude."

However cordial Summitt might have been with Moore, the decision exacerbated her feelings toward Auriemma beyond repair.

In late July 2006, three months after Moore committed to UConn, SEC commissioner Mike Slive received a letter from Tennessee women's athletic director Joan Cronan. In it Cronan wrote, "From time to time we have encountered situations related to the University of Connecticut's women's basketball program that would seem to be a violation of the rules."

The letter detailed what the school said was a subtle but systematic effort by UConn to influence recruits through the use of fans, media, and alumni. Tennessee cited as many as eight incidents it saw as violations of eleven NCAA rules in 2005–6.

Six of the incidents allegedly came out of UConn's 2005 Super Show, an annual women's exhibition, akin to Midnight Madness, that routinely includes former and prospective players. The incidents detailed in Cronan's letter included:

UConn alums Diana Taurasi and Sue Bird served as recruiters for the team.

The media interviewed the [recruiting] prospects at the practice.

Fans had signs directed at the prospects, clearly aware who would be present.

Fans gave prospects' parents the signs they had made for their daughters.

Bird and Taurasi allegedly served as hostesses for the prospects.

A prospective student-athlete [whose name was not disclosed but was believed to be Caroline Doty] told her AAU coach that Taurasi and Bird met her at the door upon arrival and escorted her to the coaches' office.

The letter also stated that "reportedly former UConn players are allowed to practice with the team on a regular, rather than occasional basis . . . when asked about this issue, the UConn compliance staff has repeatedly either denied or failed to respond as to how this is allowed."

But the most serious allegation in the report stated that a "prospective student athlete had a visit to ESPN—arranged by UConn—to talk about the possibility of an internship at ESPN. It appears as if no one at UConn provided transportation for the ESPN visit, but the prospective student-athlete did not know anyone at ESPN prior to the visit."

The student-athlete in question? Maya Moore, who had been joined by her mother for a tour of the ESPN campus in October 2005 while visiting Connecticut as part of her recruitment.

"It would appear that the following NCAA Bylaws may have

been violated," the letter continued, citing eleven bylaws including "employment arrangement, offers and inducements and boosters involved in recruiting."

The letter came with thirty-two pages of supporting documents, what Tennessee said was "information that supports the belief that the fans and former elite student-athletes at Connecticut continue to be involved in the recruiting process."

The NCAA began looking into the complaints, but word of the letter did not leak to the media, and wouldn't, save for a very brief, ambiguous mention in the Connecticut media around the time of the regular-season game in January 2007.

But by that spring it was becoming increasingly clear behind the scenes that Summitt, not satisfied merely with filing the complaint with the SEC, was going to take the matter into her own hands. And that meant taking her ball and going home. She was preparing to announce that, after thirteen seasons and twenty-two games, she was going to cancel the series with Connecticut.

"Over the course of about a year, I became increasingly upset with a couple of UConn's tactics in recruiting," Summitt wrote in her 2013 memoir, *Sum It Up*. "I went through the appropriate channels and that's how it will stay. I made my concerns known to UConn through our athletic director, Joan Cronan, and the Southeastern Conference. UConn responded that they saw nothing wrong with what they were doing. I made my concerns known again. Same response.

"I was finished. I didn't see any other choice. 'I'm not putting up with this anymore,' I told my staff. I met with Joan and our university president, Dr. John Petersen, and outlined my reasons for wanting to discontinue the series: the lack of response from UConn and the personal negativity convinced me it was no longer in our best interest. I thought we needed to send a message that we didn't want a game that wasn't played in the right spirit. The administration agreed, and we declined to renew the series."

But before doing so Summitt confronted Auriemma for a final time in May 2007. In a phone call at her home, Summitt and Auriemma let twelve years of frustration and anger come pouring out, long distance.

"I know before they officially didn't renew the contract, he called her at her home and they had it out pretty good and she laid her cards out, 'I don't think we're playing by the same rules,'" said Dan Fleser. "And I think he said something about, when she first started at Tennessee, there were a lot of players who transferred in to play for her and they created the transfer rule, that you have to sit out a year, and he brought that up. Where is that coming from? They really went at it. [Summitt's son] Tyler closed the door because it got really loud. It was done after that."

The news broke on June 8, a Friday afternoon, typically the time and day news is released when the party releasing it knows it's bad and wants the weekend to avoid answering for it. It was now official and it was a shocker.

"Tennessee has elected not to renew its series with the University of Connecticut," Cronan said in a statement. "The Lady Vol basketball team will continue to enjoy its rivalry games with teams from the Big East, the ACC, the Big 12, the Pac-10 and other conferences. Year in and year out, we pride ourselves on the strength of schedule we play and our RPI."

Summitt did not return an avalanche of phone calls from media in Knoxville, Connecticut, and across the nation. Auriemma chose not to comment, but UConn athletics director Jeff Hathaway issued his own statement.

"We are disappointed for UConn fans, Tennessee fans and women's basketball fans in general who look forward to this annual event featuring the greatest women's basketball rivalry in the nation," Hathaway said.

The news stunned every corner of the women's basketball world. In Bristol, Connecticut, where the 2005 tour of Maya Moore had apparently played a significant role in Summitt's decision, there was near panic. The 2004 UConn-Tennessee championship game remained the most-watched college basketball game in the network's history—men's or women's—and ESPN was due to broadcast the regular-season game that upcoming season. Not only was the plan to air it in prime time, but ESPN was planning to make Thompson-Boling Arena the setting for their first-ever "College Gameday" for a women's game. (UConn–Notre Dame in Storrs in 2010 would ultimately earn that distinction.)

"I can't remember where I was, but I thought it was crazy and I flew down to Knoxville to meet with [Summitt] and talk to her about it," said ESPN's Carol Stiff, who had created the series back in 1994. "I remember hearing some grumblings about recruiting and the [ESPN] tour and I just asked her not to do it. 'Don't do this.' And they had their reasons and they stuck to them. So I flew down to meet with Pat and we went for a drive around Knoxville and there was no changing her mind."

After a media blackout that Friday, the *Hartford Courant* made contact with Summitt that Saturday.

"It was a decision made by the University of Tennessee— Joan Cronan, Dr. Petersen and myself," Summitt said. "It was the University of Tennessee that made the announcement and made the decision."

But Summitt refused to say why Tennessee discontinued the rivalry and tried to downplay the significance of the game after twelve years.

"It's been a great series," Summitt said. "There's more to women's basketball than just this game. If you look at the growth of our game, this has been a big part of it. But this past year, you had Duke, North Carolina, Maryland, and all those ACC matchups. I think women's basketball is in a whole different state, in a positive way. You've got a lot of quality teams and quality games."

It was not an answer that anyone was buying. Summitt immediately came under heavy criticism for the decision, which reeked of sour grapes after not landing Moore, who was attending UConn that fall.

Hartford Courant columnist Jeff Jacobs called Summitt

"selfish" and "a coward," and his were among the nicer descriptions in the immediate aftermath.

"No matter who they schedule to fill that spot, it's not going to matter," said Rebecca Lobo, UConn's star of the original 1995 games and now an ESPN analyst. "I'm tremendously disappointed, as somebody who was part of the start of it, as a fan, as someone who's had a chance to cover it. It's bad for the game that it's not being played anymore. It's the one game casual sports fans were attracted to. It's a shame all the way around. I don't know what the reasons are, but whatever they are, they're not good ones."

Finally, after two weeks, some answers. To anyone wanting to see a resumption of the series, they were not good ones.

The *New London Day* was the first to report, on June 22, about the existence of the July 2006 letter to the SEC, which detailed alleged recruiting violations, including Moore's tour of ESPN. The *Day* article also detailed a new allegation: that Sue Bird and Diana Taurasi gave Moore a ride to the Naismith Awards in 2006, when Moore had won the first of her two national honors.

There was only one problem with that accusation: Both Bird and Taurasi were playing in Russia at the time of the Naismith Awards. The two former UConn stars would be required to provide documentation that they had, in fact, been in Russia at the relevant time, which they did.

When reached two weeks later, Taurasi was clearly looking to hit something orange.

"As ridiculous as that theory is, it's also not true," Taurasi said. "Sue and I were in Moscow at the time [playing in the European championships with their Russian team, Dynamo Moscow]. . . . If you are going to make allegations like that, you might want to make sure the people [you are accusing] are in the same place at the same time. It's irresponsible to say something like that. It wasn't humanly possible, either. We weren't in the same continent. We offered a written response about our location. We provided witnesses [to vouch for their location]. It's ridiculous to do something like that.

"All these reasons are ridiculous. If you are going to blame Coach Auriemma for having players who love him and come back to see him, then it's just too bad. When I visit him, and I try to do so as often as I can because of all his family did for me when I was there, the only people I talk to are the current players."

But in the story detailing the Bird-Taurasi allegation, a source told the *Courant* not to focus solely on the Moore angle.

"It's the body of work," said the source. "Take recruiting out of the equation. Look at everything else by itself. Don't even put recruiting in there. That should give you your answers."

But answers remained elusive over the summer of 2007. The first of the two coaches to blink was Auriemma in late September.

Speaking a few minutes before his charity golf tournament for the Connecticut Children's Medical Center, Auriemma finally decided he'd had enough of the talk about what led to Summitt's decision.

"I think she should just come out and say she's not playing us because she hates my guts," Auriemma told the *Courant*. "And I think people would buy that. Then everyone [who seeks a reason] would be happy. She should just say that [Geno is] a dope, a smart-ass, and then everyone could say that they agree with her."

Without revealing their contentious phone call in May, Auriemma said he didn't plan to call Summitt to ask her to reconsider.

"I just won't do it," Auriemma said. "And I don't think she ever would call me. I understand why she feels she can't say publicly why she made her decision. If she did, she would be put into the situation of backing it up.

"But what bothers me is how she keeps changing the story [through the rumor mill]. First it was the recruitment of Maya Moore. Then it wasn't. Then it was something about my principles. Then [a source close to the situation] said that we should all consider his body of work [as reason for the cancellation].

"Well, my response to that is, what does [Summitt] mean by that? Why didn't anyone ask her? There are a lot of unanswered questions out there. But my feeling all along has been, we had a signed contract [to play in 2007] and [Summitt] does not want to play for her own reasons."

Apprised of Auriemma's comments, Summitt finally responded that same night. She said that there was no signed contract for 2007.

She also said that Auriemma knew why the series was canceled and that if he wanted to talk about it he could.

She acknowledged that she spoke to Auriemma when she decided to end the series and that the athletic directors of the two schools had spoken.

"I'm not going to tell you the reasons—that should be between UConn and Tennessee," she said. "If he wants to tell it, he can tell it.

"I'm perplexed by his comments. Clearly, Geno knows exactly why I canceled the series. I articulated that to him in a phone conversation. I was very upfront and straightforward with him. I think that it was something that needed to be discussed with Geno and no one else. That's why I chose not to comment [publicly]."

Summitt said she knew her decision would not be popular, but added, "I'm not trying to win a popularity contest."

She also reiterated her respect for Auriemma as a coach and for the UConn fans.

"He's made me a better coach," she said. "And the series was, for the most part, enjoyable."

So why did Summitt cancel the series? Recruiting? Something deeper, darker? Or had she simply had enough of Auriemma's shtick?

According to sources close to both programs, when Tennessee lodged their complaints in the summer of 2006 with the SEC—who in turn sent their letter to the NCAA regarding eleven potential recruiting violations against UConn—they hoped that an NCAA investigation into these relatively minor issues, including Moore's 2005 tour of ESPN, would lead investigators to chase down the trail of a much more serious violation in the recruitment of Moore that Tennessee suspected had occurred but could not prove.

According to the sources, Tennessee harbored deep suspicions that Moore's mother, Kathryn, had sought and received benefits from UConn in exchange for Maya's decision to attend the school.

"They thought something in regards to Maya's mother," said a source who spoke on the condition of anonymity. "They thought something happened there. They didn't know what, but there were all sorts of rumors in the AAU circles about her mother having her hand out [for illegal benefits].

"I think what they were trying to do, 'We'll give [the NCAA] these bread crumbs,' and they were hoping that they would take a harder look at things. Well, no, they didn't give them anything. They thought it was an issue, but they didn't know anything, couldn't prove anything, but they had a strong suspicion something happened there."

And, perhaps, when Kathryn Moore moved to Connecticut shortly after Maya graduated from high school in the spring of 2007, as innocent as it may have been—Kathryn was raising Maya as a single parent and the two had moved together in the past—Tennessee might have felt their suspicions had finally been justified, leading to the final decision, on June 8, to end the UConn-Tennessee series.

But, ultimately, Tennessee had no tangible evidence to back their suspicions. Their hope was to open the door of what they suspected were a pattern of UConn recruiting shenanigans with the letter to the SEC, then let the investigators take it from there.

But when the NCAA ruled in March 2008 that only the ESPN tour was evidence of any wrongdoing and classified it a secondary violation, which was essentially a wrist-slap, Tennessee, in trying to defend its actions, was left in an intractable position and suffered the consequences of it in the media.

"They took the total PR hit for this thing," a source close to the Tennessee program said. "Everyone saw what they turned in. It was all secondary stuff. You're going to cancel a series like this over that? I think she got sick of the back-and-forth. But it looked like she just took her ball and went home and you can't undo that."

As of late 2013 no evidence—or even an allegation—has ever surfaced that UConn did anything improper in the recruitment of Maya Moore.

"I think [Moore's recruitment] was totally innocent," said Mike DiMauro of the *New London Day*. "Geno doesn't have to cheat. Good players want to go there, and if one player doesn't want to there, fifteen others do. You can say a lot of things about him, but cheater isn't one of them. But I know he was legitimately mad at that. He might have been tweaked when Semeka Randall said they were scared. He'll get over that one. But don't call him a cheater. That's when everything went off the rails.

"My guess is she was sick and tired of the barbs over the years and they really weren't all that successful against them. The Maya thing became a convenient excuse for them to say, 'We don't like the way you go about your business, so we don't want to play you anymore.' I think that's what that was."

The series was officially over, with UConn winning thirteen of the twenty-two games, including all four in the national championship finals. But that hardly meant that they couldn't ever play each other again. ESPN and CBS couldn't force them to do it, but the NCAA tournament could.

And when the NCAA tournament began in March 2008 there was good reason to think the grudge match to end all grudge matches just might happen in the most spectacular fashion possible.

"I was disappointed for us [when it was canceled], because we were going to miss out on a good number [for the regular-season game], a good rating at the right time of year," Stiff said. "And for the game. Everyone circled it on the calendar. But I knew we had the NCAA tournament, so my disappointment turned into my wish that they would align the bracket."

It appeared that Stiff and the fans of the rivalry were going to get their wish. The NCAA tournament committee placed Tennessee, with Candace Parker, in her final season, on one side of the bracket and UConn, with Moore already becoming a star as a freshman, on the other.

If the two teams could navigate their way to the Final Four and win their semifinal matchups, the sport would be rewarded with the most anticipated game in its history, and with it the most anticipated two pre-finals press conferences in the sport's history.

Everyone almost got their wish. In St. Petersburg, Florida, Tennessee won yet another Final Four thriller over LSU—shades of 2004—when Alexis Hornbuckle rebounded a missed shot and dropped in a layup with 0.7 seconds left to bail out the Lady Vols after LSU's Erica White hit two free throws with seven seconds left, to give Tennessee a 47–46 win.

But UConn could not seal the deal, losing 82–73 to Stanford and their star, Candice Wiggins, who dominated the Huskies with 25 points—including several huge baskets in the second half—and 13 rebounds.

So it was only Summitt who appeared at the *St. Pete Times Forum* on Monday for the pre-championship press conference. Naturally she was asked about the possibility of playing UConn sometime in the future.

"I hadn't really thought about it," Summitt said. "At this point I really don't see it happening."

When asked if there was anything UConn coach Geno Auriemma could do to help the situation, Summitt said, "Not now."

Summitt still resisted questions on why she had cancelled the series.

"I didn't want any of that to be a distraction," Summitt said. "It's not about the coaches. It's all about the players. And, unfortunately, some of the media folks out there have wanted to make this about Pat and Geno, and it's all about the players.

"I think it's fair to say that because of the unknown that's still out there, that this would still be a story that has people digging and interested and writing about it. I can respect that from the media, but it doesn't mean that I'm going to reveal anything."

And there things seemed to stand. The next night Tennessee went out and beat Stanford easily for its second straight national championship and eighth overall in program history. Parker, who was named Final Four MVP, left the stage as one of the greatest players ever in women's basketball history, the next level in the individual growth of the game, bracketed between UConn stars Taurasi and Moore.

And with Moore now a sophomore at UConn and Parker off to the WNBA, the pendulum swung back in UConn's favor. In 2008–9, the Huskies embarked on the greatest two-season stretch in the history of women's basketball, becoming the first team to go undefeated in consecutive seasons to win the sixth and seventh championships in UConn history, leaving Auriemma one championship behind Summitt.

While the Huskies cruised to a championship in 2009, defeating Louisville in St. Louis—the site of their 2001 Final Four semifinal disappointment against Notre Dame—Tennessee endured arguably the most difficult season of Summitt's career. Having lost Parker to the WNBA and playing with seven freshmen, the Lady Vols had lost ten games entering the NCAA tournament. But unlike the team that accomplished the thrilling title run in 1997, the 2009 team became the first in Summitt's career to fall in the first round, losing by 16 to Ball State in Tennessee's first loss in the first or second round after forty-two consecutive victories in Summitt's previous twenty-one tournament appearances.

But there was one moment of pure joy for Summitt and the Lady Vols in 2009. On February 5 at Thompson-Boling Arena, Tennessee defeated SEC rival Georgia to clinch Summitt's thousandth career victory, making her the first Division I coach, men's or women's, to reach that milestone.

"It's a time to reflect on a number of things, the administration saying yes to women's basketball and giving us an opportunity to play on the biggest stage in the women's game. I appreciate that," Summitt said. "I feel like I've been extremely blessed, and I thank God for the many opportunities I've had to be your coach and work with these young ladies, and so I want to thank all of you. I want to thank every person who's been a part of my staff. . . . They gave their absolute best."

Things then improved greatly for Tennessee in the 2009–10 season, the team going 30-2 and capturing the SEC tournament title, earning the Lady Vols a number-one seed in the NCAA tournament and giving rise once again to the notion that UConn, in the midst of its second straight undefeated season, might meet Tennessee in the Final Four.

It was a possibility that even crossed the mind of President Barack Obama. During his presidency Obama recognized the unofficial national holiday called March Madness by filling out men's and women's tournament brackets for ESPN.

In 2010 he picked UConn and Tennessee to meet in the national semifinals, his selections monitored in the Oval Office by ESPN's lead women's analyst, Doris Burke.

"It is interesting. Doris, you've got to tell me the story, why is it that they don't schedule a game during the regular season against each other since they're the two top programs?" President Obama asked Burke at one point.

"I think they care for each other as much as Republicans and Democrats," Burke replied.

The media sideshow that a semifinal reunion would create was not something that Auriemma was buying into.

"Man, oh man," Auriemma said on the eve of the tournament. "If that game is ever played in that format it would be a disservice to all the players. The game format will be disrespected, the players will be disrespected. What can I tell you? It might even be the one time I'd be happy to talk about how many in a row we've won."

Auriemma needn't have worried. Much to the disappointment—yet again—of fans and media alike, this time it was Tennessee that lost too soon, falling to Baylor and its freshman sensation Brittney Griner in the regional semifinals. UConn would take down Stanford in the final for its seventh title and seventy-eighth consecutive victory.

Then, in December 2010, UConn broke one of the most treasured records in all of college basketball, winning its eighty-ninth consecutive game to snap the UCLA men's streak of eighty-eight in a row for the longest winning streak, men's or women's, in Division I basketball history.

But before the Huskies opened the 2010–11 season to capture the final eleven victories needed to break that record, the feud between Summitt and Auriemma flared one final time, ironically coming on the same day a source had indicated to the *Hartford Courant* that efforts were under way to bring the UConn-Tennessee game back to life.

In the summer of 2008 Bruce Pearl, the Tennessee men's basketball coach, hosted a cookout at his home. Unlike Harry Perretta's enjoyment of a few hot dogs at Pat Summitt's place in 2003, this cookout had sinister overtones for Pearl and the Tennessee men's program. Pearl had invited a recruit to attend the cookout, a clear violation of NCAA rules, and compounded the infraction by instructing the attendees, including the recruit's father, to lie to investigators about the incident.

It all became public in September 2010 and would eventually lead to Pearl's dismissal by the school. Summitt and Pearl had been good friends during their tenure together—Summitt once famously dressed and performed as a cheerleader at one of the Tennessee men's home games.

But now, as the SEC women's basketball teams gathered for their media day in late October, Summitt offered her thoughts on committing recruiting violations and their consequences.

"For me, I've never compromised at all, and I wouldn't," Summitt said. "And if I did they should fire me."

The comment raised eyebrows in Tennessee. Pearl was still only under investigation. It seemed a harsh comment for one Tennessee coach to make about another.

So when, shortly afterward, Jimmy Hyams of Knoxville radio

station WNML-AM asked Summitt why she made those comments about Pearl, Summitt had a startling response.

"I wasn't even talking about Bruce Pearl," Summitt said. "It never entered my mind. . . . By me saying that, I was talking about the women's game. Seldom do you see [recruiting violations in women's basketball]. I didn't have Bruce Pearl on my mind. I probably had Connecticut on my mind. There's a reason we don't play them."

And there, for the first time, Summitt had accused Auriemma directly of cheating. In Connecticut, anyway, the comments were a bombshell. And any efforts to resurrect the series were quickly shelved.

"I don't have anything to say about that," Auriemma said. "All I can tell you is that we don't have any problems getting games or players. Since the series ended [before the 2007–8 season], we've done okay, I would say."

UConn would go back to the Final Four in 2011, but, in what was emerging as the new great rivalry in the game, Notre Dame and star guard Skylar Diggins took down Maya Moore in her final collegiate game in the national semifinals in Indianapolis.

Before beating UConn, Notre Dame also took out Tennessee, denying a UConn-Tennessee Final Four for the third time in a span of four seasons. But more troubling for the Lady Vols was the unmistakable sense that something was not entirely right with Summitt. Usually a master at in-game adjustments, she seemed to be making fewer in 2011. Her demeanor on the sidelines seemed less intense, less focused.

And then, on August 23, 2011, the world found out why.

Summitt had been diagnosed with early onset dementia.

Alzheimer's disease.

Summitt was only fifty-nine.

"There's not going to be any pity party and I'll make sure of that," Summitt told Dan Fleser of the *Knoxville News-Sentinel* and Sally Jenkins of the *Washington Post* in an interview in her home the night of August 22. "I feel better just knowing what I'm dealing with. And as far as I'm concerned it's not going to keep me from living my life, not going to keep me from coaching."

The outpouring of sympathy and support came from every corner of the sporting world, including Storrs, Connecticut.

"I was shocked and saddened to hear about the news regarding Pat Summitt's diagnosis," Auriemma said in a statement from Italy, where the Huskies were touring and playing exhibition games. "You don't necessarily associate dementia with people our age, so this announcement really put things in perspective.

"Pat has great support from her family, friends and staff and I know they will help her immensely. There is no doubt in my mind that Pat will take on this challenge as she has all others during her Hall of Fame career—head on. I wish her all the best."

For Rebecca Lobo, who played against her, then worked with her as a broadcaster for CBS and ESPN, the news was devastating.

"I think the world of Coach Summitt," Lobo said in 2013. "She was always tremendous to me. Just a class act. When I was covering games, and I did a fair amount of UConn-Tennessee games, she always let me watch practice, she always let me watch shootaround, she was very professional with me, where there have been other coaches where there was a distrust there, like I was going to go back and tell UConn their secrets. But Pat couldn't have been better and I think the world of her. I think people in Connecticut, they might not like her because she was the coach of Tennessee, but I think, for the most part, the fans really respected her."

For sixteen years Auriemma and Summitt had battled on the court, in recruiting and through the media. For the past eight years, and certainly in the aftermath of Summitt's decision to cancel the UConn-Tennessee series in 2007, the relationship had been frosty at best, vicious and contemptuous at worst.

Now none of it mattered. It was, after all, just a game. This was a life hanging in the balance. The time for petty differences was over. Forever.

"When what happened with Summitt, I didn't think it through, as far as the ripple effect," Fleser said. "But that was one of side developments that I never considered: 'Oh my gosh, now this thing is over with now.' It went with her old self."

As she detailed in her 2013 memoir, *Sum It Up*, Summitt revealed that even before her public announcement Auriemma had gotten word of her health concerns and written her a note saying that she was in his thoughts.

And when, soon after her announcement, Summitt created the Pat Summitt Foundation to fight Alzheimer's with the help of Danielle Donehew, Summitt's friend and associate commissioner of the Big East, Donehew asked Geno if he wanted to be the first contributor. Auriemma didn't hesitate, writing out a check for $10,000.

Then, just before Summitt finally stepped down as head coach at Tennessee, while at the Final Four at the Pepsi Center in Denver, where the Huskies were preparing to face Notre Dame in the semifinals for the second year in a row, Summitt walked through the arena during UConn's practice session.

Auriemma spotted her, walked off the court where his team was practicing, and chatted with his former enemy, now his friend.

And when they finished talking, they hugged.

"It wasn't until she got sick that everybody realized, hey, this is just a game," DiMauro said. "I'll never forget, one of the most powerful things I've ever seen live, was Pat walking into the Pepsi Center at the 2012 Final Four and everybody knew she was sick and Geno saw her and they just hugged. It's the day before the game when they have the practices and if you could have just seen the number of [camera] phones that were going off to capture this moment. And ever since then, I think the relationship has been better.

"I think he probably regrets some of the things he said. When they hugged that day, now you start thinking about how much they've meant to the game, and the other stuff is meaningless."

Two weeks later it became official. Summitt would no longer be the head coach at Tennessee. On April 18, 2012, the winningest coach in Division I basketball history stepped down. Summitt was given the title of head coach emeritus, with longtime assistant head coach Holly Warlick replacing her on the sidelines.

"I've loved being the head coach at Tennessee for 38 years, but I recognize that the time has come to move into the future and to step into a new role," Summitt said in a statement. "I support Holly Warlick being named the next head coach, and I want to help ensure the stability of the program going forward. I would like to emphasize that I fully intend to continue working as head coach emeritus, mentoring and teaching life skills to our players, and I will continue my active role as a spokesperson in the fight against Alzheimer's through the Pat Summitt Foundation Fund."

In his own statement, Auriemma offered praise for Summitt's career.

"Pat's vision for the game of women's basketball and her relentless drive pushed the game to a new level and made it possible for the rest of us to accomplish what we did," he said. "In her new role, I'm sure she will continue to make significant impacts on the University of Tennessee and on the game of women's basketball as a whole."

Two days later President Obama announced that Summitt would receive the Presidential Medal of Freedom, the highest civilian award in the United States.

In April 2013 the bond between Auriemma and Summitt got as close as it had ever been in the record books as well. Against Louisville in the national championship game in New Orleans— the site of UConn's first Final Four in 1991, the site of the last UConn-Tennessee final in 2004—freshman Breanna Stewart, the newest heir to the throne of "Best Player Ever" at Connecticut, led the Huskies to a blowout victory, giving Auriemma his eighth national championship and tying him with Summitt for most titles ever by a women's coach.

When it was over, Geno paid his respects to his great adversary.

"Tying Pat Summitt's record puts me in the category of the

greatest women's basketball coach who ever lived," Auriemma said. "On ESPN, they put up a list of John Wooden, Pat Summitt, Geno Auriemma, Mike Krzyzewski, Adolph Rupp. I'm like that's not the way it works. I never beat Coach K in a game. I never coached against coach Wooden. The only person I compare myself to is Pat Summitt. And to be there in that spot with her means a lot to me."

That same evening Tyler Summitt released a statement on behalf of his mother.

"Congratulations to Geno Auriemma and the Connecticut Huskies on a remarkable season and an eighth national title," Pat Summitt said. "Geno is a proven champion and a leader in our game. My best to him, his family, his team and his staff."

And as 2013 came to a close, and the Huskies were once again on the hunt for a national championship, one that would put Auriemma alone with a ninth title, there was talk, developing into a steady drumbeat, that UConn and Tennessee were in the process of arranging for a resumption of the series. Most likely, it seemed, there would be a charity game, perhaps as early as 2015—the twentieth anniversary of the first-ever UConn-Tennessee game—to benefit Summitt's foundation.

But even if UConn and Tennessee were to take the floor again, even if the series were resumed, it could never recapture what took place over thirteen seasons and twenty-two games between 1995 and 2007. The UConn-Tennessee rivalry was the greatest show in women's basketball history, a drama that lifted the sport to unprecedented heights of popularity, and perhaps more important, legitimacy.

"There was this feeling that we helped women's basketball become what it has become. People understand where the sport was before this," said Lobo, the star of UConn-Tennessee I on that Martin Luther King Day in January 1995. "There was no rivalry that mattered. I don't even know now if there is such a game. If you asked me [in 2013] what is the rivalry that matters, I don't know what the answer should be."

"At different times, we had amazing products to put out there," said Kellie Jolly, the point guard on Tennessee's three-peat in 1996–98. "This wasn't an average game. This was the best. And you can turn on the television and watch great athletes playing against each other, and it was women's basketball. I think that rivalry was really good for the game and to get people excited about watching it. This was a much broader rivalry than just our teams. This was communities and states, not just us playing against each other."

"All of a sudden, there was big-city media there," DiMauro said. "Women's basketball was on the front of the sports section of major metropolitan dailies. That never happened. That's why we sensed things were starting to change. Who ever thought this? Connecticut was shifting it, but in that process, you had to recognize the [New York] Yankees of the sport were in Knoxville. You always have to measure yourself against them, because they had been the best team forever.

"And then the whole game started to get framed around it. When are they playing this year? What are the dates? When are we going to Knoxville? And in those years when they played twice, that was great.

"There's never been a good story ever written that didn't have a villain in it. They were the villain. And I'm sure UConn was to them. It was the perfect storm, the perfect story. You had the establishment vs. the upstarts, the Hall of Fame coach vs. the soon-to-be Hall of Fame coach, and the bigness of the Northeast media vs. the expanse of all that freaking orange. And that's what made it great. It's the best the game has ever been."

Afterword

When I was eleven years old, Pat Summitt called me.

I don't mean she called my house looking for Dad, or called home by mistake in search of an office phone. No. This was a deliberate phone call, by Pat Summitt, looking for me. "Hello, Alysa, this is Pat Summitt from Tennessee." Verbatim.

I was *eleven*. We had just started our rivalry with Tennessee. To say I was terrified of Pat Summitt is understating the point. She is an icon of the sport. She's naturally terrifying because of her intensity, her drive, her winning history . . . it's *Pat Summitt*. I mean, cripes!

And I say this as a kid who had spent the past four years on a bus with Rebecca Lobo, so I tend to be unfazed by athlete superstars. This was a whole different kettle of fish.

This is also coming from a girl who spent the *entire* very first UConn-Tennessee game on January 16, 1995, in the Gampel student lounge playing SuperMunchers on a Compaq computer. So if this nerd was freaked out by Pat Summitt, it was a very, very, very big deal.

She had heard, I'm assuming from my father, that I had been saying to people that the University of Tennessee looked like a really good place to go to school. I knew this information from two sources—the games I had seen on television of the Lady Vols playing, and the media guides I had stolen from press rooms when I snuck back there during games to hunt for food or Diet Coke.[1]

I had watched our game tape of the 1995 national championship about 29,347 times. I thought Michelle Marciniak was terrifying. I thought Dana Johnson could rip me in half. And I was particularly drawn in to the replay of Laurie Milligan's turnaround jumper at the foul line near the close of the first half. I will not lie: I spent hours on my basketball court attempting to perfect that jumper. "Milligan fakes, spins, gonna put it up from the free-throw line—good! Milligan hits! Connecticut brings it up and they're not gonna get a shot off, Laurie Milligan with the clock rolling down, to bring Tennessee into the locker room, leading 38–32."[2]

When I heard that famous drawl on the answering machine, I started screaming and could not stop. My mom, listening in the next room, howled with laughter. I was paralyzed with fright, not because of Pat but because of the implications.

I thought Dad would garrote me. I felt *guilty* that she called me. I mean, this was *Pat Summitt*! Tennessee! The supposed antithesis of everything we were at the University of Connecticut, our "mortal enemy," was on my answering machine, addressing me by name, saying in a quite cheerful voice, "I hear you like orange!"

Benedict Arnold didn't have anything on me. I began picturing my funeral.

Thankfully, my dad thought the entire situation was absolutely hilarious and kind of cool. I figured that was the end of it. I'm positive I was so freaked out I never returned her call.

---

1 Some kids collect stamps, I collected media guides of women's basketball programs and tried to memorize the school mascots of every single Division 1 program. It became a huge game with the team to see if they could stump me. I could not be defeated.

2 That is *verbatim* what the announcer said on the highlights video I have in my mom's basement. And yet I wondered why I didn't get a real boyfriend until I was twenty-three.

A few weeks later, during the 1997 Dayton Regionals I ended up *meeting* Coach Summitt. I'm not sure if it's inappropriate to call her "Pat" so I'll stick with "Coach Summitt" out of respect. I don't remember how this meeting came about, but I think we were due to play them in a few days for the NCAA tournament.

I was shaking the entire time. Knowing that I was very young, and *very* aware of Coach Summitt's history and her legacy, I made sure I was polite and didn't say anything too ridiculous. In fact, I don't think I really said much of anything. I think I gaped. She was gracious and welcoming. I can't recall what we talked about but she definitely shook my hand and looked me dead in the eye, which made me feel important.

I'm positive this meeting wasn't because she saw me as a potential recruit, considering that I was, well, the biggest little dork on the face of God's green earth. I was wearing a gigantic Nike shirt that probably could have doubled as a nightgown with a Nancy Drew book tucked under my arm, blinking behind oversized metallic purple-rimmed glasses my sister had stepped on once during a game of one-on-one in the Seton Hall gym, so one lens stuck out and the other pushed into my cheek. My hair was probably unbrushed and I had a unibrow that looked like a caterpillar taking a vacation on my face.

I actually spent most of that afternoon hanging around the gym with my brother and Coach Summit's son Tyler, whom I recall as being an outgoing and energetic kid. I didn't meet her then-husband R.B., but he was around I'm sure. We lost to Tennessee that year in the Dayton regional final—the year we lost Shea to that horrific ACL tear, the sad first of many sad firsts and ends in her career—and flew home, and that was that. I haven't seen or spoken to her since. But I will never forget that.

Let me just clear this up right away. Pat Summitt is a titan of women's basketball. She practically *is* women's basketball.

I know. I'm the daughter of Geno Auriemma. I've met Barack Obama twice. I've been in the Hall of Fame to watch my father inducted alongside Charles Barkley and Dominique Wilkins. Tennessee is the grits-and-gravy-soaked Evil Empire and we're the cool Yankee rivals with good posture and Katharine Hepburn houses on our coastline. I should be stoned for even suggesting a compliment for Pat Summitt.

I would be the world's most ungrateful, insipid, spoiled, solipsistic idiot if I didn't recognize the importance of this woman to the women's rights movement and to the game of basketball as a whole. Women's basketball as an institution would be *nothing* without that woman, and I don't think hyperboles exist in this situation.

Everything my father has done in the world of women's basketball Pat Summitt did first. It's like that episode of *South Park*: "Simpsons Already Did It." Pat Summitt is *The Simpsons* in this corollary. (Sentences I never thought I'd say.) She got a 39-0 season before UConn did, she got a championship three-peat before UConn did, she got the best recruits before UConn did. And she did it with grace and a sense of dignity with which you cannot argue. I won't try to argue with it. I am General Disarray, to keep up the *South Park* comparison. Pat Summitt Already Did It.

Pat Summitt has a gold medal, and more championship trophies, and 1,000+ wins. Whether you like it or not, she is the number-one reason my father was able to do even half of what he's done. And if I can give her those kinds of props, you can, too. She is the standard to which we should all aspire in terms of grit, clout, proficiency, success, and determination. And she did it without dropping nearly as many f-bombs as my dad does. So . . . she's probably a little classier, but Southern people just tend to sound classier than Philadelphia people do in general. I think it's the accent.

When I read of her diagnosis of early-onset Alzheimer's, I was heartbroken for her and her family. Watching the games was too upsetting, because she wasn't the same coach I remember from all of those years seeing her patrol the sidelines like a lioness.

When I read of her retirement this May I was saddened but not surprised, and wished her Godspeed.

When I read the reaction of the Connecticut newspapers,

read everyone's references to the UConn-Tennessee rivalry and the "disappointment" that Pat and Dad didn't "settle their differences or have another UConn-Tennessee showdown before Pat stepped down," I was *enraged*.

Why can't you celebrate the stuff that happened *before* my dad even got into the picture? Hell, before Gampel Pavilion even existed? The gold medal, the national championships, the grand tradition, the countless record-breaking crowds? Pat was winning championships before Dad even coached one game of women's basketball.

And all of these stories about how it's "such a shame" that Dad and Pat didn't "kiss and make up" are forgetting one piece of the puzzle. They had a great conversation and hug in Denver during Dad's open practice at the Final Four. When I read the recap by Mike DiMauro in the *New London Day*, I had to walk off to a private area because it was raining on my face. Not because I missed my dad and thought it was a lovely example of his class, something I really don't think he displays enough (and more people should be aware of the kind of person he is that has nothing to do with snarky comments or side jabs). Nor did I cry because I was thinking, "Oh, look at that, the conflict is over! Maybe we'll play them next year!?"

I cried because of a monument to the women's game who is currently battling a major, major disease that I would be far too weak to deal with. I cried because the person with that disease, that horrible memory-leeching illness, could have easily been one of my parents, and I would not have the guts to endure that. I don't know if I could have nearly the strength that Tyler has to watch his mother fight this battle every day. To lose your memory is to lose a very deep part of yourself. Memories constitute most of your identity. They are a major signifier of self and personhood. To lose your memories can be conflated with losing yourself.

I cried because some things are just much bigger, and more important, than stones in your shoes. You can take your shoe off and let those stones go now.

Pat Summitt's identity splashes over every part of the University of Tennessee, the city of Knoxville, women's basketball, and the triumph of women in sports in general.

I will treasure all of those memories that she has given our state as well, preserved forever on tape and DVD in the state of those epic matches in the tournament and regular season.

But I will mostly remember that this multiple-championship-winning coach, on her way to another championship in 1997, called me on the phone, remembered my name, and looked me in the eye as an eleven-year-old with gnarled hair with a gaze that said, "You are on my level."

But no one is on her level.

She's at the Rocky Top.

Alysa Auriemma
JULY 2012

APPENDIX

OFFICIAL NCAA B. KETBALL BOX SCORE   Date Jan. 16, 1995   Site Harry Gampel Pavilion

VISITOR (Indicate starters by position or with an asterisk)   *** FINAL ***

No.	TENNESSEE (16-1)	FG	FGA	3pt FG	3pt FGA	FT	FTA	Off	Def	Total	PF	TP	A	TO	BLK	S	MIN
23	NIKKI McCRAY	2	10	0	1	6	10	5	2	7	2	10	1	8	0	1	37
53	DANA JOHNSON	6	13	0	0	2	4	5	3	8	4	14	0	2	0	1	29
4	TIFFANI JOHNSON	6	10	0	0	2	2	1	4	5	2	14	0	3	1	3	32
3	MICHELLE MARCINIAK	5	14	2	8	0	0	0	3	3	4	12	4	3	0	2	30
5	LATINA DAVIS	4	10	1	1	1	2	2	2	4	3	10	3	4	0	1	22
24	VondA WArd	0	2	0	0	0	0	1	3	4	4	0	0	3	0	0	12
11	Laurie Milligan	0	2	0	6	0	0	0	1	1	1	0	4	1	0	0	10
00	Michelle Johnson	1	3	1	2	0	0	0	2	2	0	3	1	0	0	1	20
52	Abby Conklin	1	4	1	4	0	0	0	3	3	1	3	0	1	0	0	8
	TEAM REBOUNDS (Included in Totals)							3	3	6							
	TOTALS	25	68	5	16	11	18	7	26	43	23	66	13	25	0	9	200

TOTAL FG% 1st half 12-34 35.3% 2nd half 13-34 38.2% Game 25-68=36.3% OT ____ %   DEADBALL REBOUNDS 3
3-Pt FG% 1st half 2-8 25.0% 2nd half 3-8 =37.5 % Game 5-16=31.3 % OT ____ %
FT% 1st half 7-10 70.0% 2nd half 4-8 =50 % Game 18-18=61.1 % OT ____ %
Shooting Outside Paint: 9-29 =31.6 % Pts. in the Paint: 32   Pts. Off Fastbreak: 10   2nd Chance Pts.: 7   Pts. Off Turnovers: 12

HOME (Indicate starters by position or with an asterisk)

No.	CONNECTICUT (13-0)	FG	FGA	3pt FG	3pt FGA	FT	FTA	Off	Def	Total	PF	TP	A	TO	BLK	S	MIN
33	JAMELLE ELLIOTT	4	11	0	3	4	5	3	3	6	2	12	4	2	0	0	37
50	REBECCA LOBO	5	11	1	2	2	2	4	4	8	5	13	4	5	5	2	27
52	KARA WOLTERS	7	14	0	0	4	5	1	3	4	2	18	2	2	1	1	34
21	JENNIFER RIZZOTTI	6	12	2	5	3	4	0	4	4	3	17	4	3	0	5	39
32	PAM WEBBER	0	0	0	0	0	1	2	2	4	0	0	3	2	0	0	10
42	Nykesha Sales	5	10	2	4	0	1	1	2	3	0	12	3	4	0	2	29
31	CallA Belube	2	4	0	0	1	4	1	2	3	3	5	1	2	0	1	21
5	Kim Better	0	0	0	0	0	0	2	0	2	0	0	0	0	0	0	3
	TEAM REBOUNDS (Included in Totals)							0	9	9							
	TOTALS	29	62	5	16	14	22	14	29	43	15	77	20	20	0	11	200

TOTAL FG% 1st half 16-33 48.0% 2nd half 13-29=44.8% Game 29-62=46.8% OT ____ %   DEADBALL REBOUNDS 2
3-Pt FG% 1st half 3-9 33.3% 2nd half 2-7=28.6% Game 5-16=31.3% OT ____ %
FT% 1st half 6-8 75.0% 2nd half 8-14=57.1% Game 14-22=63.6% OT ____ %
Shooting Outside Paint: 18-24 =33.3 % Pts. in the Paint: 44   Pts. Off Fastbreak: 16   2nd Chance Pts.: 12   Pts. Off Turnovers: 21

Technical Fouls:
Attendance: 8,241 (advance sellout)
Officials: Yvette McKinney, Frank Gieselman, Angie Sanseviro

SCORE BY PERIODS	1st Half	2nd Half	OT	OT	FINAL
TENNESSEE	33	33			66
CONNECTICUT	41	36			77

FOR (indicate starters by position or with an asterisk) Starting Time 2:55 p.m. City, State Minneapolis, Minnesota

No.	TENNESSEE (34-3)		FG	FGA	FG	FGA	FT	FTA	Off	Def	Tot	PF	TP	A	TO	BLK	S	MIN
23	Nikki McCray	F	3	12	0	1	1	2	3	2	5	2	7	4	3	0	1	31
44	Pashen Thompson	F	1	1	0	0	2	2	3	0	3	2	4	1	1	0	0	10
53	Dana Johnson	C	3	11	0	0	3	3	3	7	10	2	9	0	1	0	2	33
5	Latina Davis	G	5	12	1	4	0	1	3	2	5	4	11	1	1	0	1	31
3	Michelle Marciniak	G	3	11	1	6	1	3	0	0	0	3	8	5	3	0	2	30
00	Michelle Johnson		2	3	1	2	0	0	0	3	3	2	5	1	0	0	0	13
4	Tiffani Johnson		3	7	0	0	1	1	2	3	5	3	7	1	2	1	0	21
10	Tiffany Woosley	DNP — Did not dress																
11	Laurie Milligan		1	3	0	0	2	2	0	0	0	0	4	2	1	0	0	10
24	Vonda Ward		2	5	0	0	2	2	1	1	2	3	6	1	0	0	0	16
25	Tanika Smith	DNP - CD																
31	Brynae Laxton	DNP - CD																
52	Abby Conklin		1	1	1	1	0	0	1	0	1	1	3	0	2	0	0	5
	TEAM REBOUNDS (Included in Totals)								1	2	3							
	TOTALS		24	66	4	14	12	16	17	20	37	22	64	16	14	1	6	200

TOTAL FG%: 1st half 13/33 39.4% 2nd half 11/33 33.3% Game 24/66 36.4% Deadball
3-Pt. FG%: 1st half 2/5 40.0% 2nd half 2/9 22.2% Game 4/14 28.6% rebounds 1
FT%: 1st half 10/13 76.9% 2nd half 2/3 66.7% Game 12/16 75.0%

HOME (Indicate starters by position or with an asterisk)

No.	CONNECTICUT (35-0)		FG	FGA	FG	FGA	FT	FTA	Off	Def	Tot	PF	TP	A	TO	BLK	S	MIN
33	Jamelle Elliott	F	5	7	0	0	3	4	2	5	7	3	13	3	5	0	1	39
50	Rebecca Lobo	F	5	10	0	2	7	8	2	6	8	4	17	2	2	2	0	28
52	Kara Wolters	C	4	9	0	0	2	4	1	2	3	4	10	0	1	2	0	31
21	Jennifer Rizzotti	G	6	8	1	2	2	2	0	3	3	3	15	3	4	0	3	32
32	Pam Webber	G	0	1	0	1	0	0	1	0	1	1	0	2	0	0	0	17
5	Kim Better	DNP-CD																
10	Missy Rose	DNP-CD																
25	Brenda Marquis	DNP-CD																
31	Carla Berube		1	6	0	1	3	5	2	1	3	0	5	2	3	0	0	20
34	Kelley Hunt	DNP-CD																
40	Jill Geltenbien	DNP-CD																
42	Nykesha Sales		4	12	1	4	1	4	2	4	6	3	10	3	1	0	3	33
	TEAM REBOUNDS (Included in Totals)								5	7	12			2				
	TOTALS		25	53	2	10	18	27	15	23	43	18	70	15	18	4	7	200

TOTAL FG%: 1st half 12/27 44.4% 2nd half 13/26 50.0% Game 25/53 47.2% Deadball
3-Pt. FG%: 1st half 1/7 14.3% 2nd half 1/3 33.3% Game 2/10 20.0% rebounds 2
FT%: 1st half 7/12 58.3% 2nd half 11/15 73.3% Game 18/27 66.7%

Technical fouls:
Attendance: 18,038
Officials: Dee Kantner, Larry Sheppard

SCORE BY PERIODS	1st H.	2nd H.	OT	OT	FINAL
TENNESSEE	38	26			64
CONNECTICUT	32	38			70

NCAA 9477-8/93

1/06/1996 Thompson-Boling Arena, Knoxville, Tenn.
fficials: Sally Bell, John Morningstar, Art Bomengen

Time of Game: 1:54
Attendance: 10,584

ISITOR: Connecticut Huskies

O PLAYER		FG	FGA	3P	3PA	FT	FTA	OR	DR	TOT	PF	PTS	A	TO	BS	ST	MIN
1 Carla BERUBE	F	2	3	0	1	1	1	0	1	1	1	5	3	1	0	1	25
3 Jamelle ELLIOTT	F	2	7	0	2	4	5	3	3	6	3	8	0	6	0	1	38
2 Kara WOLTERS	C	6	11	0	0	0	0	1	9	10	2	12	3	7	3	1	36
1 Jennifer RIZZOTTI	G	6	11	1	3	5	5	0	1	1	4	18	5	6	0	3	37
2 Nykesha SALES	G	2	8	0	1	0	0	1	7	8	2	4	2	2	0	0	31
3 Rita WILLIAMS		3	5	0	1	0	0	0	4	4	0	6	1	3	0	0	18
4 Kelley HUNT		0	1	0	0	0	0	1	0	1	0	0	0	1	0	0	4
2 Amy DURAN		1	3	1	2	3	4	0	2	2	0	6	0	0	0	0	10
5 Brenda MARQUIS		0	0	0	0	0	0	0	0	0	0	0	0	0	0	0	1
3 Tammy ARNOLD	DNP																
5 Kim BETTER	DNP																
2 Courtney GAINE	DNP																
4 Amy HUGHES	DNP																
4 Sarah NORTHWAY	DNP																
0 Missy ROSE	DNP																
Team								4	5	9				0			
TOTALS:		22	49	2	10	13	15	10	32	42	12	59	14	26	3	6	200

Dead Ball Rebounds : 0   Opponent's pts off TO : 15

PERCENTAGES	Game:	FG: 22/49 (44.9%)	3PT: 2/10 (20.0%)	FT: 13/15 (86.7%)
	1st Half:	11/23 (47.8%)	1/ 5 (20.0%)	4/ 4 (100.0%)
	2nd Half:	11/26 (42.3%)	1/ 5 (20.0%)	9/11 (81.8%)

HOME: TENNESSEE LADY VOLS

NO PLAYER		FG	FGA	3P	3PA	FT	FTA	OR	DR	TOT	PF	PTS	A	TO	BS	ST	MIN
04 Tiffani JOHNSON	F	6	7	0	0	0	0	1	5	6	4	12	0	3	1	1	33
23 Chamique HOLDSC	F	6	14	0	2	3	4	4	1	5	3	15	2	3	1	2	32
44 Pashen THOMPSON	C	0	3	0	0	1	2	0	4	4	4	1	1	1	0	2	22
33 Michelle MARCINIAK	G	5	11	0	3	0	0	0	4	4	1	10	4	6	0	4	33
05 Latina DAVIS	G	3	11	0	1	0	0	2	1	3	2	6	2	0	0	1	31
52 Abby CONKLIN		3	14	2	7	1	2	2	2	4	4	9	1	0	1	2	28
14 Kellie JOLLY		0	4	0	3	0	0	0	1	1	0	0	2	0	0	0	9
11 Laurie MILLIGAN		0	1	0	0	0	0	0	1	1	0	0	0	0	0	1	9
10 Kim SMALLWOOD		0	0	0	0	0	0	0	0	0	0	0	0	1	0	0	3
13 Misty GREENE	DNP																
31 Brynae LAXTON	DNP																
Team								1	2	3				0			
TOTALS:		23	65	2	16	5	8	10	21	31	18	53	12	14	3	13	200

Dead Ball Rebounds : 1   Opponent's pts off TO : 10

PERCENTAGES	Game:	FG: 23/65 (35.4%)	3PT: 2/16 (12.5%)	FT: 5/ 8 (62.5%)
	1st Half:	14/33 (42.4%)	2/ 6 (33.3%)	1/ 2 (50.0%)
	2nd Half:	9/32 (28.1%)	0/10 (00.0%)	4/ 6 (66.7%)

SCORE BY PERIODS	1	2	TOTAL
Huskies	27	32	59
LADY VOLS	31	22	53

Points in the Paint: Huskies 40, LADY VOLS 24
Second Chance Points: Huskies 2, LADY VOLS 11
Fast Break Points: Huskies 4, LADY VOLS 2

−NCAA National Women's Semifinal   Game #1

OFFICIAL NCAA BASKETBALL BOX SCORE   Date 3/29/96   Site Charlotte, N.C.

VISITORS (Last name, first) (Indicate starters with an asterisk)

No.	CONNECTICUT (34-4)	Total FG FG	FGA	3-point FG	FGA	FT	FTA	Reb Off.	Def.	Tot.	PF	TP	A	TO	BLK	S	MIN
3	ARNOLD, Tammy	0	0	0	0	0	0	0	0	0	0	0	0	1	0	0	3
4	HUGHES, Amy	DNP															
10	ROSE, Missy	DNP															
21	RIZZOTTI, Jennifer G	5	11	2	7	5	5	0	3	3	3	17	9	4	0	1	45
22	DURAN, Amy	1	4	0	1	2	2	0	2	2	2	4	1	0	0	0	21
23	WILLIAMS, Rita	0	0	0	0	0	0	0	0	0	0	0	0	0	0	0	1
25	MARQUIS, Brenda	DNP															
31	BERUBE, Carla F	5	14	0	1	3	3	0	1	1	3	13	2	2	0	1	41
32	GAINE, Courtney	DNP															
33	ELLIOTT, Jamelle (:03)F	2	4	1	1	3	4	2	6	8	5	8	2	0	1	0	40
34	HUNT, Kelley	0	0	0	0	0	0	0	0	0	1	0	0	0	0	0	1
42	SALES, Nykesha G	11	23	4	5	2	2	3	3	6	4	28	5	3	0	2	42
44	NORTHWAY, Sarah	DNP															
52	WOLTERS, Kara (1:19)C	6	10	0	0	1	3	3	7	10	5	13	0	3	6	0	31
	TEAM REBOUNDS (included in Totals)							1	4	5							
	TOTALS	30	66	7	15	16	19	9	26	35	23	83	19	13	7	4	225

TOTAL FG%: 1st half 37.9   2nd half 53.3   Game 45.5   Deadball
3-Pt. FG%: 1st half 57.1   2nd half 42.9   Game 46.7   rebounds 0
FT%: 1st half 100.0   2nd half 76.9   Game 84.2

HOME (Last name, first) (Indicate starters with an asterisk)

No.	TENNESSEE (31-4)	Total FG FG	FGA	3-point FG	FGA	FT	FTA	Reb Off.	Def.	Tot.	PF	TP	A	TO	BLK	S	MIN
3	MARCINIAK, Michelle G	5	8	2	3	9	12	1	6	7	0	21	6	3	0	3	41
4	JOHNSON, Tiffani C	6	11	0	0	1	2	3	6	9	3	13	1	1	1	0	33
5	DAVIS, Latina G	6	11	0	0	4	5	2	2	4	3	16	1	2	0	0	40
10	SMALLWOOD, Kim	DNP															
11	MILLIGAN, Laurie	0	0	0	0	0	0	0	0	0	0	0	0	0	0	0	1
13	GREENE, Misty	DNP															
14	JOLLY, Kellie	1	2	0	0	0	0	2	0	2	0	2	3	0	0	0	8
23	HOLDSCLAW, Chamique F	5	15	0	0	3	4	2	4	6	4	13	2	1	0	0	31
31	LAXTON, Brynae	1	1	0	0	2	3	0	0	0	0	4	1	1	0	0	12
44	THOMPSON, Pashen	4	8	0	0	0	1	2	4	6	3	8	0	2	0	0	25
52	CONKLIN, Abby F	4	11	0	1	3	3	1	5	6	0	11	0	1	1	0	34
	TEAM REBOUNDS (included in Totals)							3	3	6							
	TOTALS	32	67	2	4	22	30	16	30	46	13	88	14	13	2	3	225

TOTAL FG%: 1st half 46.7   2nd half 45.5   Game 47.8   Deadball
3-Pt. FG%: 1st half 50.0   2nd half 50.0   Game 50.0   rebounds 1
FT%: 1st half 83.3   2nd half 62.5   Game 73.3

Technical fouls: None
Attendance:
Officials: Bob Trammell, Doug Cloud, Scott Yarborough

SCORE BY PERIODS	1st H.	2nd H.	OT	OT	FINAL
Connecticut	30	45	8		83
Tennessee	34	41	13		88

NCAA 6649-8/89

216 · APPENDIX

```
OFFICIAL BASKETBALL BOX SCORE -- G A M E   T O T A L S
TENNESSEE vs CONNECTICUT
01/05/97 2:00 p.m. at Hartford, CT
-----------------------------------------------------------------------------
VISITORS: TENNESSEE (10-5)
                          TOT-FG  3-PT         REBOUNDS
No.    N A M E            FG FGA  FG FGA FT FTA OF DE TOT PF  TP  A TO BLK S MIN
23 Holdsclaw, Chamique f   9  23   1   2  4   6  4  8  12  2  23  2  6   1 4  38
52 Conklin, Abby       f   1   9   0   5  0   0  1  2   3  3   2  0  1   1 1  23
44 Thompson, Pashen    c   2   5   0   0  0   0  7  7  14  2   4  0  6   0 0  30
11 Milligan, Laurie    g   1   9   0   7  0   0  1  1   2  3   2  6  6   0 2  32
31 Laxton, Brynae      g   1   7   0   0  0   0  3  1   4  2   2  0  1   0 0  17
04 Johnson, Tiffani        5  11   0   0  1   2  9  2  11  2  11  0  1   0 0  26
05 Elzy, Kyra              0   1   0   0  0   0  0  0   0  0   0  1  3   0 0   5
13 Greene, Misty           3   9   3   6  2   2  0  1   1  0  11  0  0   0 2  24
34 Stephens, LaShonda      1   1   0   0  0   0  1  0   1  0   2  0  0   0 0   5
TEAM REBOUNDS.............................  2  1   3
TOTALS                    23  75   4  20  7  10 28 23  51 14  57  9 24   2 9 200

TOTAL FG% 1st Half:  8-35   .229   2nd Half: 15-40  .375    Game:  .307    DEADBALL
3-Pt. FG% 1st Half:  0- 5   .000   2nd Half:  0- 7  .267    Game:  .200    REBOUNDS
F Throw % 1st Half:  0- 0   .000   2nd Half:  7-10  .700    Game:  .700       1, 1

-----------------------------------------------------------------------------
HOME TEAM: CONNECTICUT (11-0)
                          TOT-FG  3-PT         REBOUNDS
No.    N A M E            FG FGA  FG FGA FT FTA OF DE TOT PF  TP  A TO BLK S MIN
31 Berube, Carla       f   7  10   0   0  1   1  3  5   8  1  15  4  4   0 3  29
42 Sales, Nykesha      f   8  20   0   3  6   7  3  7  10  2  22  3  3   0 4  35
52 Wolters, Kara       c   5  12   0   0  0   0  2  3   5  1  10  1  2   5 2  37
22 Duran, Amy          g   3   5   0   1  0   0  0  1   1  0   6  0  2   0 0  24
23 Williams, Rita      g   1   4   0   1  1   3  0  1   1  3   3  0  4   1 1  31
20 Hansmeyer, Stacy        1   1   0   0  0   0  0  0   0  0   2  0  0   0 0   2
33 Ralph, Shea             5  10   0   2  4   4  2  4   6  5  14  2  2   0 3  30
41 Sauer, Paige            0   2   0   0  0   0  0  2   2  2   0  0  1   0 0  12
TEAM REBOUNDS.............................  2  2   4
TOTALS                    30  64   0   7 12  15 12 25  37 14  72 10 18   6 13 200

TOTAL FG% 1st Half: 11-29   .379   2nd Half: 19-35  .543    Game:  .469    DEADBALL
3-Pt. FG% 1st Half:  0- 5   .000   2nd Half:  0- 2  .000    Game:  .000    REBOUNDS
F Throw % 1st Half:  6- 7   .857   2nd Half:  6- 8  .750    Game:  .800       1, 1

-----------------------------------------------------------------------------
OFFICIALS:  Yvette McKinney, Patty Broderick, Sally Bell
TECHNICAL FOULS:
TENNESSEE       -  none
CONNECTICUT     -  none
ATTENDANCE:  16,294
SCORE BY PERIODS:      1st   2nd  OT1  OT2  OT3  OT4    TOTAL
TENNESSEE               16    41                          57
CONNECTICUT             28    44                          72
COMMENTS:  ADVANCE SELLOUT
```

Miscellaneous Statistics

Connecticut		Tennessee
50	Pts. in the Paint	32
12	Pts. Off Fastbreak	0
13	2nd Chance Pts.	20
22	Pts. Off Turnovers	12

VISITORS: Tennessee 27-10

NO PLAYER		FG	FGA	3P	3PA	FT	FTA	OR	DR	TOT	PF	PTS	A	TO	BLK	S	MIN
23 Chamique Holdsclaw	F	8	15	0	0	5	6	3	8	11	4	21	3	2	0	2	33
52 Abby Conklin	F	5	10	1	2	3	4	3	3	6	3	14	2	2	0	0	26
44 Pashen Thompson	C	3	5	0	0	9	12	5	4	9	2	15	3	0	3	3	29
05 Kyra Elzy	G	3	8	1	1	1	2	1	3	4	1	8	1	0	0	1	29
14 Kellie Jolly	G	6	11	2	4	5	8	0	0	0	3	19	3	3	0	0	35
04 Tiffani Johnson		3	5	0	0	1	3	3	8	11	5	7	0	6	1	2	25
03 Niya Butts		0	1	0	0	1	2	0	0	0	0	1	0	0	0	0	2
13 Misty Greene		2	4	1	2	0	0	0	1	1	1	5	1	2	0	0	15
31 Brynae Laxton		0	2	0	0	1	2	0	0	0	1	1	1	1	0	0	5
34 LaShonda Stephens		0	0	0	0	0	0	0	0	0	0	0	0	0	0	0	1
11 Laurie Milligan	DNP-																
TEAM								1	0	1				0			
TOTALS		30	61	5	9	26	39	16	27	43	20	91	14	16	4	8	200

FG 1st (17/ 34) 50.0 2nd (13/ 27) 48.1 OT   Game (30/ 61) 49.2 DEADBALL
3PT 1st (3/ 7) 42.9 2nd (2/ 2) 100.0 OT   Game (5/ 9) 55.6 REBOUNDS 3
FT 1st (8/ 11) 72.7 2nd (18/ 28) 64.3 OT   Game (26/ 39) 66.7

HOME: Connecticut 33-1

NO PLAYER		FG	FGA	3P	3PA	FT	FTA	OR	DR	TOT	PF	PTS	A	TO	BLK	S	MIN
31 Carla Berube	F	4	8	1	2	1	3	2	2	4	4	10	4	1	0	0	35
42 Nykesha Sales	F	11	21	2	6	2	2	5	9	14	4	26	2	3	2	3	31
52 Kara Wolters	C	7	10	0	0	3	6	7	4	11	3	17	1	3	1	1	25
22 Amy Duran	G	2	11	1	5	0	2	3	1	4	5	5	0	4	0	0	32
23 Rita Williams	G	4	16	0	3	6	8	1	2	3	4	14	4	4	1	5	38
41 Paige Sauer		1	2	0	0	1	3	0	4	4	2	3	0	1	0	0	17
20 Stacy Hansmeyer		3	6	0	0	0	3	4	1	5	3	6	0	1	0	0	20
10 Missy Rose		0	0	0	0	0	0	0	1	1	2	0	1	0	0	1	2
03 Tammy Arnold	DNP-																
34 Kelley Hunt	DNP-																
44 Sarah Northway	DNP-																
32 Courtney Gaine	DNP-																
TEAM								1	1	2				0			
TOTALS		32	74	4	16	13	27	23	25	48	27	81	12	17	4	10	200

FG 1st (13/ 32) 40.6 2nd (19/ 42) 45.2 OT   Game (32/ 74) 43.2 DEADBALL
3PT 1st (1/ 6) 16.7 2nd (3/ 10) 30.0 OT   Game (4/ 16) 25.0 REBOUNDS 6
FT 1st (6/ 11) 54.5 2nd (7/ 16) 43.8 OT   Game (13/ 27) 48.1

Attendance: 4,257

OFFICIALS	SCORE BY PERIODS	1	2	OT	OT	OT	FINAL
#0- John Morningsta	Tennessee	45	46				91
#0- Jack Riordan	Connecticut	33	48				81
#0- Lisa Mattingly							

TECHNICAL FOULS: NONE

NCAA BASKETBAI

01/03/1998 Thompson-Boling Arena - Knoxville, Tenn

VISITOR: Connecticut Huskies

NO PLAYER		FG	FGA	3P	3PA	FT	FTA	OR	DR	TOT	PF	PTS	A	TO	BS	ST	MIN
20 Stacy HANSMEYER	F	1	3	0	0	2	5	1	0	1	3	4	0	3	0	0	19
42 Nykesha SALES	F	6	16	0	4	0	0	1	7	8	4	12	2	4	0	1	37
41 Paige SAUER	C	5	7	0	0	2	3	1	0	1	3	12	2	4	5	0	27
22 Amy DURAN	G	4	8	1	4	4	4	1	1	2	3	13	2	2	0	0	30
23 Rita WILLIAMS	G	4	5	0	0	1	2	1	4	5	4	9	1	5	0	0	34
25 Svetlana ABROSIM		6	11	0	0	2	3	0	2	2	5	14	1	8	0	4	26
11 Kelly SCHUMACHE		0	0	0	0	3	5	1	1	2	1	3	0	0	0	1	16
34 Kelley HUNT		1	1	0	0	0	0	2	1	3	2	2	3	1	0	0	13
12 Marci GLENNEY		0	0	0	0	0	0	0	0	0	0	0	0	0	0	0	1
04 Tihana ABRLIC	DNP																
45 Jean CLARK	DNP																
35 Marci CZEL	DNP																
32 Courtney GAINE	DNP																
33 Shea RALPH	DNP																
Team								1	3	4				0			
TOTALS:		**27**	**51**	**1**	**8**	**14**	**22**	**9**	**19**	**28**	**25**	**69**	**11**	**27**	**5**	**8**	**200**

Dead Ball Rebounds : 2

Opponent's pts off TO : 22

PERCENTAGES Game: FG: 27/51 (52.9%)   3PT: 1/8 (12.5%)   FT: 14/22 (63.6%)
1st Half: 11/24 (45.8%)   1/3 (33.3%)   5/11 (45.5%)
2nd Half: 16/27 (59.3%)   0/5 (00.0%)   9/11 (81.8%)

HOME: TENNESSEE LADY VOLS

NO PLAYER		FG	FGA	3P	3PA	FT	FTA	OR	DR	TOT	PF	PTS	A	TO	BS	ST	MIN
23 Chamique HOLDSCLAW	F	9	19	0	1	7	7	3	2	5	2	25	4	3	1	6	35
24 Tamika CATCHINGS	F	4	5	2	3	7	8	4	5	9	4	17	3	5	3	2	33
34 LaShonda STEPHENS	C	0	4	0	0	0	0	1	0	1	3	0	0	2	1	0	13
05 Kyra ELZY	G	4	8	0	0	1	2	4	0	4	2	9	1	1	0	0	18
14 Kellie JOLLY	G	1	6	1	5	0	0	0	2	2	2	3	2	0	0	1	34
21 Semeka RANDALL		8	12	0	0	7	8	3	7	10	1	23	1	4	0	2	30
40 Teresa GETER		2	7	0	0	1	3	2	4	6	5	5	0	2	3	1	27
33 Kristen CLEMENT		0	3	0	2	2	2	1	0	1	2	2	2	6	0	3	10
03 Niya BUTTS	DNP																
13 Misty GREENE	DNP																
31 Brynae LAXTON	DNP																
11 Laurie MILLIGAN	DNP																
Team								2	1	3				0			
TOTALS:		**28**	**64**	**3**	**11**	**25**	**30**	**20**	**21**	**41**	**21**	**84**	**13**	**23**	**8**	**15**	**200**

Dead Ball Rebounds : 2

Opponent's pts off TO : 2

PERCENTAGES Game: FG: 28/64 (43.8%)   3PT: 3/11 (27.3%)   FT: 25/30 (83.3%)
1st Half: 16/34 (47.1%)   2/8 (25.0%)   8/10 (80.0%)
2nd Half: 12/30 (40.0%)   1/3 (33.3%)   17/20 (85.0%)

SCORE BY QUARTERS	1	2	3	4	TOTAL
CONNECTICUT	17	11	20	21	69
TENNESSEE	23	19	14	28	84

Points in the Paint: Huskies 48, LADY VOLS 38
Second Chance Points: Huskies 11, LADY VOLS 11
Fast Break Points: Huskies 8, LADY VOLS 14

MEMO: End of 1st Quarter: UT 23-17
MEMO: Officials: Sally Bell, Patty Broderick, John Morningstar
MEMO: Today's Attendance: 24,597 (New collegiate record)
MEMO: End of 3rd Quarter: UT 56-48

```
OFFICIAL BASKETBALL BOX SCORE -- G A M E   T O T A L S
TENNESSEE vs CONNECTICUT
1/10/99 4:00 p.m. at Storrs, CT
----------------------------------------------------------------------
VISITORS: TENNESSEE 13-1
                          TOT-FG  3-PT          REBOUNDS
No.    N A M E            FG FGA FG FGA FT FTA OF DE TOT PF  TP   A TO BLK S MIN
23 Holdsclaw, Chamique  f 12 17  0  1   1  2   5  4   9   4  25   4  4  1  0  30
24 Catchings, Tamika    f  6  9  2  3   4  6   1  5   6   4  18   1  1  0  0  25
00 Snow, Michelle       c  0  2  0  0   0  2   1  5   6   2   0   0  2  0  1  21
14 Jolly, Kellie        g  2  9  0  2   2  3   0  6   6   2   6   7  4  0  2  38
21 Randall, Semeka      g 10 18  0  1   5  5   4  3   7   0  25   1  4  0  0  33
03 Butts, Niya             0  0  0  0   0  0   0  0   0   0   0   0  0  0  0   2
33 Clement, Kristen        3  6  0  3   1  2   0  2   2   3   7   0  3  0  1  20
40 Geter, Teresa           3  7  0  0   3  4   1  3   4   2   9   0  2  1  0  22
50 Pillow, Shalon          1  1  0  0   0  0   0  0   0   1   2   0  1  0  0   9
TEAM ..................................   6  1   7
TOTALS                    37 69  2 10  16 24  18 29  47  18  92  13 21  2  4 200

TOTAL FG% 1st Half: 20-37  .541   2nd Half: 17-32  .531   Game:  .536   DEADBALL
3-Pt. FG% 1st Half:  0- 2  .000   2nd Half:  2- 8  .250   Game:  .200   REBOUNDS
F Throw % 1st Half:  2- 5  .400   2nd Half: 14-19  .737   Game:  .667      6
----------------------------------------------------------------------
HOME TEAM: CONNECTICUT 13-1
                          TOT-FG  3-PT          REBOUNDS
No.    N A M E            FG FGA FG FGA FT FTA OF DE TOT PF  TP   A TO BLK S MIN
23 Cash, Swin           f  8 11  0  0   3  4   4  2   6   1  19   0  1  0  0  19
25 Abrosimova, Svetlana f  3 12  0  1   5  6   1  3   4   5  11   7  2  0  1  37
41 Sauer, Paige         c  4  8  0  1   2  2   0  1   1   3  10   0  1  0  1  20
14 Walters, Keirsten    g  3 14  3 11   0  2   1  0   1   3   9   4  3  0  2  34
22 Duran, Amy           g  1  3  1  2   0  0   1  0   1   1   3   1  1  0  1  13
15 Jones, Asjha            4 11  0  0   2  3   4  3   7   3  10   2  1  1  0  21
20 Hansmeyer, Stacy        2  3  0  1   0  0   0  0   0   1   4   0  0  0  0  12
33 Ralph, Shea             4  9  1  2   2  2   1  1   2   4  11   2  3  0  0  22
34 Williams, Tamika        1  2  0  0   2  3   1  3   4   2   4   1  1  1  1  22
TEAM ..................................   3  3   6
TOTALS                    30 73  5 18  16 22  16 16  32  23  81  17 13  2  6 200

TOTAL FG% 1st Half: 16-43  .372   2nd Half: 14-30  .467   Game:  .411   DEADBALL
3-Pt. FG% 1st Half:  1- 9  .111   2nd Half:  4- 9  .444   Game:  .278   REBOUNDS
F Throw % 1st Half:  3- 4  .750   2nd Half: 13-18  .722   Game:  .727      4
----------------------------------------------------------------------
OFFICIALS:   Sally Bell, Art Bomengen, Dennis DeMayo
TECHNICAL FOULS:
TENNESSEE           -  none
CONNECTICUT         -  none
ATTENDANCE:  10,027
SCORE BY PERIODS:            1st   2nd  OT1  OT2  OT3  OT4    TOTAL
TENNESSEE                    42    50                          92
CONNECTICUT                  36    45                          81
```

Miscellaneous Statistics

Connecticut		Tennessee
44	Pts. In the Paint	48
17	Pts. Off Fastbreak	20
12	2nd Chance Pts.	17
15	Pts. Off Turnovers	21

SKETBALL

,000 Thompson-Boling Arena
als: Wesley Dean, Patty Broderick, John Morningstar

Time of Game: 2:10
Attendance: 23,385

VISITOR: Connecticut Huskies (12-0, 0-0)

NO PLAYER		FG	FGA	3P	3PA	FT	FTA	OR	DR	TOT	PF	PTS	A	TO	BS	ST	MIN
25 S. ABROSIMOVA	F	5	10	1	2	3	4	0	2	2	4	14	2	6	0	1	35
32 Swin CASH	F	3	7	0	0	0	0	0	3	3	4	6	0	4	0	0	30
41 Paige SAUER	C	2	5	0	0	1	2	2	4	6	5	5	2	1	1	0	19
10 Sue BIRD	G	8	10	2	3	7	8	0	2	2	2	25	2	4	0	4	32
33 Shea RALPH	G	4	10	1	1	4	4	2	6	8	4	13	5	3	0	3	31
11 K. SCHUMACHER		1	5	0	0	0	0	1	5	6	3	2	0	1	0	1	16
13 Marci CZEL	DNP																
15 Ashja JONES		3	5	0	0	0	5	1	1	2	2	6	0	2	0	1	12
20 S. HANSMEYER		0	0	0	0	0	0	0	0	0	1	0	0	0	0	0	1
23 K. JOHNSON		1	5	0	1	1	2	1	2	3	1	3	2	1	1	3	19
24 T. WILLIAMS		0	1	0	0	0	0	1	2	3	1	0	0	1	0	0	5
4 C. RIGBY	DNP																
Team								2	2	4				0			
TOTALS:		27	58	4	7	16	25	10	29	39	27	74	13	23	2	13	200

Dead Ball Rebounds: 7   Opponent's pts off TO: 13

PERCENTAGES	Game:	FG: 27/58 (46.6%)	3PT: 4/7 (57.1%)	FT: 16/25 (64.0%)
	1st:	18/32 (56.3%)	0/2 (00.0%)	7/14 (50.0%)
	2nd:	9/26 (34.6%)	4/5 (80.0%)	9/11 (81.8%)

HOME: TENNESSEE LADY VOLS (11-2, 0-0)

NO PLAYER		FG	FGA	3P	3PA	FT	FTA	OR	DR	TOT	PF	PTS	A	TO	BS	ST	MIN
0 Kara LAWSON	F	2	6	1	3	2	4	2	1	3	3	7	1	1	1	0	27
4 Tamika CATCHINGS	F	3	9	0	3	2	4	1	4	5	4	8	3	3	1	4	36
0 Michelle SNOW	C	8	20	0	0	5	9	4	8	12	3	21	2	3	1	2	31
1 Semeka RANDALL	G	5	14	1	3	9	10	2	2	4	2	20	1	2	0	1	35
3 Kristen CLEMENT	G	0	2	0	1	0	1	1	3	4	3	0	2	7	0	0	29
3 Niya BUTTS	DNP																
5 Kyra ELZY		3	5	1	1	1	3	0	4	4	2	8	0	0	0	3	14
0 April MCDIVITT		1	6	1	4	0	0	1	1	2	3	3	3	1	0	3	15
1 Amanda CANON	DNP																
2 Tashelka MORRIS	DNP																
1 Gwen JACKSON		0	3	0	0	0	2	3	1	4	2	0	0	2	1	0	13
Sarah EDWARDS	DNP																
L. STEPHENS	DNP																
Shalon PILLOW	DNP																
Team								3	2	5				0			
TOTALS:		22	65	4	15	19	33	17	26	43	22	67	12	19	4	13	200

Dead Ball Rebounds: 8   Opponent's pts off TO: 21

PERCENTAGES	Game:	FG: 22/65 (33.8%)	3PT: 4/15 (26.7%)	FT: 19/33 (57.6%)
	1st:	12/30 (40.0%)	3/7 (42.9%)	10/20 (50.0%)
	2nd:	10/35 (28.6%)	1/8 (12.5%)	9/13 (69.2%)

SCORE BY PERIODS	1st	2nd	FINAL
Huskies	43	31	74
LADY VOLS	37	30	67

Technical Fouls - Individual
  Huskies: NONE
  LADY VOLS (1): 3:33 2nd M. Snow

Points in the Paint: Huskies 46, LADY VOLS 36
Second Chance Points: Huskies 10, LADY VOLS 7
Fast Break Points: Huskies 6, LADY VOLS 4

MO: Sold: 23,385 Turnstile: 20,789

OFFICIAL BASKET ̣LL BOX SCORE -- G A M E   T O T A L S
TENNESSEE vs COⵏNECTICUT
02/02/00 7:00 p.m. at Harry A. Gampel Pavilion, Storrs, CT

VISITORS: TENNESSEE 17-3

No.	N A M E		FG	TOT-FG FGA	3-PT FG	FGA	FT	FTA	REBOUNDS OF	DE	TOT	PF	TP	A	TO	BLK	S	MIN
24	Catchings, Tamika	f	5	13	2	4	7	9	5	8	13	3	19	2	1	2	1	38
00	Snow, Michelle	c	5	6	0	0	3	5	4	4	8	3	13	0	3	0	1	28
20	Lawson, Kara	g	4	12	1	7	0	0	1	0	1	3	9	1	2	0	1	27
21	Randall, Semeka	g	8	18	0	2	1	2	3	0	3	3	17	1	1	0	0	31
33	Clement, Kristin	g	2	8	0	1	3	3	3	1	4	0	7	3	1	0	2	32
05	Elzy, Kyra		0	2	0	0	0	0	0	1	1	0	0	1	0	0	0	10
10	McDivitt, April		0	1	0	1	0	0	0	0	0	1	0	1	0	0	1	9
13	Jackson, Gwen		2	2	1	1	0	0	1	1	2	0	5	0	2	0	1	13
50	Pillow, Shalon		1	1	0	0	0	0	0	0	0	3	2	0	0	0	0	12
	TEAM								3	1	4				1			
	TOTALS		27	63	4	16	14	19	20	16	36	16	72	9	11	2	7	200

TOT-FG 1stH: 10-31 32.3%   2ndH: 17-32 53.1%   OT: 0-0 00.0%   Game: 42.9% Deadbl
3pt-FG 1stH: 2-10 20.0%   2ndH: 2-6 33.3%   OT: 0-0 00.0%   Game: 25.0% Rebs
FThrow 1stH: 6-9 66.7%   2ndH: 8-10 80.0%   OT: 0-0 00.0%   Game: 73.7%   0

HOME TEAM: CONNECTICUT 19-1

No.	N A M E		FG	TOT-FG FGA	3-PT FG	FGA	FT	FTA	REBOUNDS OF	DE	TOT	PF	TP	A	TO	BLK	S	MIN
25	Abrosimova, Svetlana	f	3	11	1	4	4	5	1	4	5	3	11	6	5	0	2	35
32	Cash, Swintayla	f	2	2	0	0	2	2	1	2	3	4	6	0	3	1	1	23
41	Sauer, Paige	c	1	4	0	0	0	1	3	4	7	3	2	0	0	0	0	10
10	Bird, Sue	g	6	12	3	6	0	0	0	2	2	1	15	8	2	0	0	36
33	Ralph, Shea	g	6	8	3	5	1	2	4	1	5	3	16	3	3	0	1	34
11	Schumacher, Kelly		0	1	0	0	0	0	2	1	3	3	0	0	1	0	0	7
15	Jones, Asjha		1	3	0	0	0	0	2	2	4	2	2	1	0	0	0	11
23	Johnson, Kennitra		0	4	0	2	0	0	0	1	1	0	0	0	1	0	1	19
34	Williams, Tamika		8	10	0	0	3	3	1	2	3	1	19	0	1	0	0	25
	TEAM								1	2	3							
	TOTALS		27	55	7	17	10	13	15	21	36	20	71	18	16	1	5	200

TOT-FG 1stH: 11-27 40.7%   2ndH: 16-28 57.1%   OT: 0-0 00.0%   Game: 49.1% Deadbl
3pt-FG 1stH: 3-10 30.0%   2ndH: 4-7 57.1%   OT: 0-0 00.0%   Game: 41.2% Rebs
FThrow 1stH: 9-12 75.0%   2ndH: 1-1 100.%   OT: 0-0 00.0%   Game: 76.9%   0

OFFICIALS: Sally Bell, Dennis DeMayo, Angela Lewis
TECHNICAL FOULS:
TENNESSEE   - none
CONNECTICUT   - none
ATTENDANCE: 10,027

SCORE BY PERIODS:	1st	2nd	OT1	OT2	OT3	OT4	TOTAL
TENNESSEE	28	44					72
CONNECTICUT	34	37					71

Miscellaneous Statistics

Connecticut		Tennessee
30	Pts. in the Paint	22
2	Pts. Off Fastbreak	7
15	2nd Chance Pts.	20
5	Pts. Off Turnovers	11

222 · APPENDIX

```
OFFICIAL NCAA BASKETBALL BOX SCORE    04-02-00   Philadelphia, PA
Licensed To: University of Arkansas                                    FINAL BOX
VISITORS: Tennessee 33-4
NO PLAYER              FG FGA  3P 3PA   FT FTA   OR DR TOT   PF PTS   A TO BLK  S  MIN
-------------------------------------------------------------------------------------
21 Semeka Randall       1  11   0   0    4   6    4  4   8    1   6   2  6   0  1   35
24 Tamika Catchings     4   6   3   3    5  10    2  2   4    4  16   1  7   0  2   36
00 Michelle Snow        2   9   0   0    1   2    4  0   4    4   5   0  1   2  1   26
05 Kyra Elzy            3   5   0   0    2   2    2  3   5    2   8   0  6   0  0   19
20 Kara Lawson          3  13   0   2    0   0    0  6   6    2   6   3  1   0  2   35

10 April McDivitt       1   2   1   2    2   2    0  0   0    2   5   0  1   0  0   21
13 Gwen Jackson         2   4   0   0    0   0    2  5   7    0   4   0  2   1  1   12
50 Shalon Pillow        0   1   0   0    2   2    1  1   2    1   2   0  1   0  0   11
03 Niya Butts           0   0   0   0    0   0    0  0   0    1   0   0  0   0  0    5
31 Sarah Edwards        DNP-
33 Kristen Clement      DNP-
34 LaShonda Stephens    DNP-
12 Tasheika Morris      DNP-
11 Amanda Canon         DNP-
   TEAM                                           2  1   3    0            1
-------------------------------------------------------------------------------------
   TOTALS              16  51   4   7   16  24   17 22  39   17  52   6 26   3  7  200

FG  1st ( 5/ 27)  18.5  2nd (11/ 24)   45.8  OT      Game (16/ 51)   31.4 DEADBALL
3PT 1st ( 1/  1) 100.0  2nd ( 3/  6)   50.0  OT      Game ( 4/  7)   57.1 REBOUNDS  5
FT  1st ( 8/ 12)  66.7  2nd ( 8/ 12)   66.7  OT      Game (16/ 24)   66.7

HOME:    Connecticut 36-1
NO PLAYER              FG FGA  3P 3PA   FT FTA   OR DR TOT   PF PTS   A TO BLK  S  MIN
-------------------------------------------------------------------------------------
25 Svetlana Abrosimova  5   9   1   3    3   4    1  4   5    2  14   2  5   0  1   28
32 Swintalya Cash       4   8   0   0    1   2    1  2   3    4   9   0  1   0  2   18
11 Kelly Schumacher     3   4   0   0    0   0    2  4   6    2   6   0  1   9  1   20
10 Sue Bird             2   8   0   3    0   0    1  2   3    1   4   4  0   0  0   35
33 Shea Ralph           7   8   0   0    1   2    1  2   3    3  15   7  1   1  6   28

34 Tamika Williams      3   4   0   0    0   0    2  0   2    4   6   2  3   0  1   14
15 Asjha Jones          5  14   0   0    2   3    4  4   8    1  12   2  0   1  0   22
23 Kennitra Johnson     1   3   0   2    1   2    0  1   1    2   3   3  1   0  1   23
20 Stacey Hansmeyer     0   1   0   1    0   2    0  0   0    1   0   1  1   0  0    5
41 Paige Sauer          1   1   0   0    0   0    0  1   1    0   2   0  0   0  0    3
13 Marci Czel           0   0   0   0    0   0    0  0   0    0   0   0  1   0  0    2
44 Christine Rigby      0   1   0   0    0   0    0  0   0    0   0   0  0   0  0    2
   TEAM                                           1  1   2    0            1
-------------------------------------------------------------------------------------
   TOTALS              31  61   1   9    8  15   13 21  34   20  71  21 15  11 12  200

FG  1st (15/ 34)  44.1  2nd (16/ 27)   59.3  OT      Game (31/ 61)   50.8 DEADBALL
3PT 1st ( 1/  6)  16.7  2nd ( 0/  3)    0.0  OT      Game ( 1/  9)   11.1 REBOUNDS  2
FT  1st ( 1/  1) 100.0  2nd ( 7/ 14)   50.0  OT      Game ( 8/ 15)   53.3

Attendance: 20,060
OFFICIALS                   SCORE BY PERIODS    1    2   OT  OT  OT   FINAL
#1- Sally Bell              Tennessee          19   33                  52
#2- Art Bomengen            Connecticut        32   39                  71
#3- Dennis DeMayo

TECHNICAL FOULS: NONE


NCAA Division I Women's Championship

             This report produced by @game(tm) Basketball DOS 6.01.164.FWNSCH
       55 Technology Drive, Lowell, MA 01851 Tel: (978) 275-0200 Fax: (978) 275-0202
```

Official Basketball Box Score -- GAME TOTALS -- FINAL STATISTICS
TENNESSEE vs CONNECTICUT
12/30/00 4:00 PM at Hartford Civic Center, Hartford, CT

VISITORS: TENNESSEE 11-1

## Player Name		TOT-FG FG-FGA	3-PT FG-FGA	FT-FTA	REBOUNDS OF	DE	TOT	PF	TP	A	TO	BLK	S	MIN
13 Jackson, Gwen.......	f	5-9	1-3	0-1	4	2	6	2	11	0	2	1	0	31
24 Catchings, Tamika...	f	4-11	1-6	8-10	4	1	5	3	17	1	4	2	2	34
00 Snow, Michelle......	c	5-9	0-0	2-5	2	3	5	2	12	0	5	2	0	26
20 Lawson, Kara........	g	6-10	1-3	0-0	1	2	3	2	13	5	4	0	1	33
33 Clement, Kristen....	g	0-4	0-1	0-0	0	5	5	2	0	4	2	0	1	20
03 Butts, Tasha........		0-1	0-0	0-0	0	0	0	0	0	0	0	0	0	3
05 Elzy, Kyra..........		0-1	0-1	0-0	0	0	0	0	0	1	0	0	1	3
10 McDivitt, April.....		2-2	2-2	0-0	0	0	0	0	6	0	1	0	0	5
21 Randall, Semeka.....		5-17	0-1	2-2	5	3	8	2	12	2	2	0	2	26
42 McDaniel, Courtney..		1-1	0-0	0-0	0	0	0	1	2	0	1	0	0	1
43 Robinson, Ashley....		1-4	0-0	1-2	0	3	3	5	3	0	1	0	0	18
TEAM...............					4	3	7							
Totals.............		29-69	5-17	13-20	20	22	42	19	76	13	22	5	7	200

TOTAL FG% 1st Half: 13-28 46.4%   2nd Half: 16-41 39.0%   Game: 42.0%   DEADB
3-Pt. FG% 1st Half: 1-6 16.7%   2nd Half: 4-11 36.4%   Game: 29.4%   REBS
F Throw % 1st Half: 7-8 87.5%   2nd Half: 6-12 50.0%   Game: 65.0%   4

HOME TEAM: CONNECTICUT 9-0

## Player Name		TOT-FG FG-FGA	3-PT FG-FGA	FT-FTA	REBOUNDS OF	DE	TOT	PF	TP	A	TO	BLK	S	MIN
25 Abrosimova, Svetlana	f	0-3	0-1	4-4	2	2	4	2	4	2	0	0	0	11
32 Cash, Swin..........	f	6-9	0-0	2-2	1	2	3	4	14	2	2	1	0	29
15 Jones, Asjha........	c	2-10	0-0	2-4	0	2	2	4	6	1	1	1	2	23
10 Bird, Sue..........	g	5-9	1-3	4-4	1	1	2	1	15	6	6	0	1	37
33 Ralph, Shea.........	g	7-9	0-0	1-1	3	2	5	3	15	2	0	0	2	37
03 Taurasi, Diana......		5-11	2-6	0-0	0	4	4	4	12	1	3	0	1	22
11 Schumacher, Kelly...		0-2	0-0	2-2	0	1	1	0	2	2	1	0	0	4
23 Johnson, Kennitra...		1-4	1-3	0-0	0	1	1	1	3	2	2	0	1	10
34 Williams, Tamika....		2-2	0-0	6-8	1	6	7	1	10	2	2	0	3	27
TEAM...............					1	2	3							
Totals.............		28-59	4-13	21-25	9	23	32	20	81	20	17	2	10	200

TOTAL FG% 1st Half: 17-35 48.6%   2nd Half: 11-24 45.8%   Game: 47.5%   DEADB
3-Pt. FG% 1st Half: 2-8 25.0%   2nd Half: 2-5 40.0%   Game: 30.8%   REBS
F Throw % 1st Half: 8-11 72.7%   2nd Half: 13-14 92.9%   Game: 84.0%   4

Officials: Patty Broderick, John Morningstar, Wesley Dean
Technical fouls: TENNESSEE-None. CONNECTICUT-None.
Attendance: 16294

Score by Periods	1st	2nd	Total
TENNESSEE....................	34	42 -	76
CONNECTICUT..................	44	37 -	81

Points in the paint-TENN 32,UCONN 40. Points off turnovers-TENN 26,UCONN 24.
2nd chance points-TENN 23,UCONN 10. Fast break points-TENN 21,UCONN 17.
Bench points-TENN 23,UCONN 27. Score tied-1 time. Lead changes-3 times.

NCAA BASKETBALL

BOXSCORE
FINAL BOX

02/01/2001 Thompson-Boling Arena
Officials: June Courteau, Bob Trammell, Lisa Mattingly

Time of Game: 2:14
Attendance: Not Counted Yet

VISITOR: Connecticut Huskies (17-2, 0-0)

NO PLAYER		FG	FGA	3P	3PA	FT	FTA	OR	DR	TOT	PF	PTS	A	TO	BS	ST	MIN
25 S. ABROSIMOVA	F	7	12	3	4	1	2	3	5	8	2	18	1	0	0	3	25
32 Swin CASH	F	2	7	0	0	1	3	0	8	8	4	5	3	3	1	1	36
11 K. SCHUMACHER	C	0	3	0	0	0	0	1	0	1	2	0	0	1	0	0	5
10 Sue BIRD	G	4	12	2	7	4	4	1	0	1	4	14	7	2	0	0	28
33 Shea RALPH	G	1	6	0	2	2	2	1	3	4	3	4	6	3	0	0	30
03 Diana TAURASI		9	16	6	9	0	0	1	1	2	5	24	1	3	0	0	27
05 Maria CONLON		DNP															
13 Marci CZEL		DNP															
15 Asjha JONES		0	1	0	0	0	0	1	1	2	5	0	0	3	0	0	6
20 Morgan VALLEY		DNP															
22 Ashley BATTLE		DNP															
23 K. JOHNSON		0	1	0	1	0	0	0	3	3	1	0	0	2	0	1	10
31 Jessica MOORE		DNP															
34 Tamika WILLIAMS		10	13	0	0	3	4	4	6	10	3	23	1	3	0	0	33
44 Christine RIGBY		DNP															
Team								5	3	8				0			
TOTALS:		33	71	11	23	11	15	17	30	47	29	88	19	20	1	5	200

Dead Ball Rebounds: 0   Opponent's pts off TO: 25

PERCENTAGES	Game:	FG: 33/71 (46.5%)	3PT: 11/23 (47.8%)	FT: 11/15 (73.3%)
	1st:	17/35 (48.6%)	5/10 (50.0%)	5/6 (83.3%)
	2nd:	16/36 (44.4%)	6/13 (46.2%)	6/9 (66.7%)

HOME: TENNESSEE LADY VOLS (22-1, 0-0)

NO PLAYER		FG	FGA	3P	3PA	FT	FTA	OR	DR	TOT	PF	PTS	A	TO	BS	ST	MIN
13 Gwen JACKSON	F	12	15	1	1	3	3	6	8	14	1	28	0	3	5	2	37
21 Semeka RANDALL	F	3	8	0	0	2	5	3	3	6	5	8	2	2	0	3	25
00 Michelle SNOW	C	2	4	0	0	5	6	0	1	1	0	9	1	1	3	1	22
20 Kara LAWSON	G	7	17	2	8	7	9	0	6	6	2	23	4	1	1	0	36
33 Kristen CLEMENT	G	3	9	0	0	4	6	0	3	3	3	10	4	3	0	4	28
03 Tasha BUTTS		0	3	0	1	0	0	1	0	1	1	0	0	0	0	0	5
04 LaToya DAVIS		0	0	0	0	0	0	0	0	0	0	0	0	0	0	0	2
05 Kyra ELZY		DNP															
10 April MCDIVITT		2	4	1	3	4	6	0	1	1	2	9	1	1	0	1	24
11 Amanda CANON		DNP															
24 Tamika CATCHINGS		DNP - Injured															
31 Sarah EDWARDS		DNP															
42 Court. MCDANIEL		DNP															
43 Ashley ROBINSON		1	5	0	0	3	5	2	0	2	4	5	0	0	2	0	19
50 Shalon PILLOW		0	0	0	0	0	0	0	0	0	1	0	0	0	0	0	2
Team								2	2	4				0			
TOTALS:		30	65	4	13	28	40	14	24	38	19	92	12	11	11	11	200

Dead Ball Rebounds: 4   Opponent's pts off TO: 11

PERCENTAGES	Game:	FG: 30/65 (46.2%)	3PT: 4/13 (30.8%)	FT: 28/40 (70.0%)
	1st:	17/39 (43.6%)	3/7 (42.9%)	8/11 (72.7%)
	2nd:	13/26 (50.0%)	1/6 (16.7%)	20/29 (69.0%)

SCORE BY PERIODS	1st	2nd	FINAL
Huskies	44	44	88
LADY VOLS	45	47	92

Technical Fouls - Individual
  Huskies (1): 1:09 2nd UConn Bench
  LADY VOLS: NONE

```
OFFICIAL BASKETBALL BOX SCORE -- G A M E   T O T A L S
#1 Connecticut vs #2 Tennessee
01/05/02 4:00 p.m. at Thompson-Boling Arena; Knoxville, Tenn.
-----------------------------------------------------------------------------
VISITORS: #1 Connecticut 16-0, 2-0 BE
                    TOT-FG  3-PT         REBOUNDS
No.    N A M E      FG-FGA FG-FGA FT-FTA OF DE TOT PF  TP  A TO BLK S MIN
32 CASH, Swin      f  7-12  0-0   2-4    3  7  10  4  16  0  6  0  0  33
34 WILLIAMS, Tamika f 5-7   0-0   3-5    3 12  15  0  13  0  3  0  4  32
15 JONES, Asjha    c  4-7   1-1   0-0    0  6   6  5   9  0  1  1  1  24
03 TAURASI, Diana  g 11-16  3-6`  7-8    0  2   2  2  32  2  3  1  0  38
10 BIRD, Sue       g  3-11  2-4   4-4    1  4   5  0  12  8  4  0  1  39
02 VALLEY, Ashley     0-0   0-0   0-0    0  0   0  0   0  0  0  0  0   1
05 CONLON, Maria      0-0   0-0   0-0    0  0   0  0   0  0  0  0  0   1
20 VALLEY, Morgan     0-0   0-0   0-0    0  0   0  0   0  0  0  0  0   1
22 BATTLE, Ashley     1-2   0-0   0-0    0  1   1  1   2  0  0  0  0   9
31 MOORE, Jessica     1-1   0-0   0-0    0  1   1  3   2  2  0  0  0  22
TEAM ...................................   0  1   1
TOTALS               32-56  6-11 16-21   7 34  41 15  86 12 17  2  6 200

TOT-FG 1stH: 15-28 53.6%  2ndH: 17-28 60.7%  OT:  0-0 00.0%  Game: 57.1% Deadbl
3pt-FG 1stH:  1-4  25.0%  2ndH:  5-7  71.4%  OT:  0-0 00.0%  Game: 54.5%  Rebs
FThrow 1stH:  6-8  75.0%  2ndH: 10-13 76.9%  OT:  0-0 00.0%  Game: 76.2%   3
-----------------------------------------------------------------------------
HOME TEAM: #2 Tennessee 11-1, 1-0 SEC
                    TOT-FG  3-PT         REBOUNDS
No.    N A M E      FG-FGA FG-FGA FT-FTA OF DE TOT PF  TP  A TO BLK S MIN
13 JACKSON, Gwen   f  3-11  0-2   4-5    2  1   3  3  10  1  1  2  0  27
43 ELY, Shyra      f  4-9   0-0   0-0    2  2   4  3   8  3  3  0  1  24
00 SNOW, Michelle  c  5-15  0-0   4-5    2  5   7  2  14  1  3  1  1  31
10 McDIVITT, April g  2-4   2-4   0-0    0  3   3  1   6  1  1  0  1  23
20 LAWSON, Kara    g  6-14  1-5   4-4    3  4   7  3  17  3  1  0  1  35
03 BUTTS, Tasha       2-3   1-2   0-1    0  0   0  0   5  1  0  0  0   8
04 DAVIS, LaToya      2-4   0-0   0-0    0  0   0  1   4  0  0  0  1  15
21 MOORE, Loree       1-4   1-1   0-0    1  2   3  1   3  4  2  0  3  17
25 JACKSON, Brittany  1-1   1-1   0-0    0  0   0  1   3  0  0  0  0   6
33 ROBINSON, Ashley   0-2   0-0   0-0    1  2   3  1   0  0  1  1  0   8
42 McDANIEL, Courtney 1-5   0-0   0-0    1  0   1  1   2  0  0  0  0   6
TEAM ...................................   2  0   2
TOTALS               27-72  6-15 12-15  14 19  33 17  72 14 12  4  8 200

TOT-FG 1stH: 12-37 32.4%  2ndH: 15-35 42.9%  OT:  0-0 00.0%  Game: 37.5% Deadbl
3pt-FG 1stH:  3-7  42.9%  2ndH:  3-8  37.5%  OT:  0-0 00.0%  Game: 40.0%  Rebs
FThrow 1stH:  4-6  66.7%  2ndH:  8-9  88.9%  OT:  0-0 00.0%  Game: 80.0%   0
-----------------------------------------------------------------------------
OFFICIALS:  June Corteau, Patty Broderick, Bryan Enterline
TECHNICAL FOULS:
#1 Connecticut       -  none
#2 Tennessee         -  none
ATTENDANCE: 24611
SCORE BY PERIODS:          1st   2nd  OT1  OT2  OT3  OT4   TOTAL
#1 Connecticut             37    49                          86
#2 Tennessee               31    41                          72

Largest women's collegiate basketball crowd all-time
Jones (UConn) fouled out at 2:53 in the 2nd half
```

OFFICIAL NCAA BA. .TBALL BOX SCORE   03-29-02   San Antonio, Texas
Licensed To: XstreamSports   FINAL BOX
VISITORS: Tennessee 29-5

NO PLAYER	FG	FGA	3P	3PA	FT	FTA	OR	DR	TOT	PF	PTS	A	TO	BLK	S	MIN
13 Gwen Jackson	2	3	0	0	0	0	0	0	0	3	4	0	1	0	0	12
25 Brittany Jackson	2	11	1	6	3	4	0	6	6	1	8	2	4	1	1	30
00 Michelle Snow	2	7	0	0	2	2	3	5	8	3	6	0	2	1	0	29
20 Kara Lawson	4	13	0	2	1	2	4	1	5	1	9	0	3	0	0	30
10 April McDivitt	0	4	0	1	0	0	0	3	3	2	0	2	1	0	1	17
21 Loree Moore	3	5	1	1	0	0	1	2	3	2	7	2	4	0	2	20
43 Shyra Ely	3	6	0	0	0	1	2	2	4	2	6	1	1	1	0	18
03 Tasha Butts	2	8	1	4	2	2	2	3	5	3	7	0	0	0	0	15
42 Courtney McDaniel	4	8	0	0	1	2	3	1	4	2	9	1	0	2	0	14
14 Michelle Munoz	0	2	0	0	0	2	1	1	2	1	0	0	1	0	1	4
33 Ashley Robinson	0	2	0	0	0	0	0	0	0	1	0	0	1	0	0	5
04 LaToya Davis	0	1	0	0	0	0	0	2	2	0	0	1	0	0	0	3
50 Shalon Pillow	0	0	0	0	0	0	0	0	0	0	0	0	0	0	1	2
11 Amanda Canon	0	0	0	0	0	0	0	0	0	0	0	0	0	0	0	1
TEAM							4	2	6	0		0				
TOTALS	22	70	3	14	9	15	20	28	48	21	56	9	18	5	6	200

FG 1st (11/ 38) 28.9   2nd (11/ 32)   34.4 OT .   Game (22/ 70) 31.4 DEADBALL
3PT 1st (1/ 6) 16.7   2nd (2/ 8)   25.0 OT   Game (3/ 14) 21.4 REBOUNDS 2
FT 1st (2/ 6) 33.3   2nd (7/ 9)   77.8 OT   Game (9/ 15) 60.0

HOME: Connecticut 38-0

NO PLAYER	FG	FGA	3P	3PA	FT	FTA	OR	DR	TOT	PF	PTS	A	TO	BLK	S	MIN
32 Swin Cash	4	10	0	1	5	7	1	3	4	1	13	5	1	4	1	34
34 Tamika Williams	2	4	0	0	4	5	4	5	9	3	8	2	2	2	1	29
15 Asjha Jones	8	17	0	0	2	2	0	10	10	4	18	1	3	2	1	29
03 Diana Taurasi	7	16	3	7	0	1	2	8	10	2	17	5	3	0	2	31
10 Sue Bird	7	15	4	8	0	0	3	1	4	1	18	5	2	0	4	38
31 Jessica Moore	1	1	0	0	1	4	1	2	3	1	3	0	0	2	0	13
05 Maria Conlon	0	1	0	1	0	0	0	0	0	0	0	0	1	0	0	15
22 Ashley Battle	0	1	0	0	2	2	1	0	1	2	2	1	0	0	0	8
02 Ashley Valley	0	0	0	0	0	0	0	2	2	0	0	0	0	0	0	2
12 Stacey Marron	0	0	0	0	0	0	0	0	0	0	0	0	0	0	0	1
20 Morgan Valley	DNP-															
TEAM							0	1	1	0		0				
TOTALS	29	65	7	17	14	21	12	32	44	14	79	19	12	10	9	200

FG 1st (16/ 33) 48.5   2nd (13/ 32)   40.6 OT   Game (29/ 65) 44.6 DEADBALL
3PT 1st (4/ 8) 50.0   2nd (3/ 9)   33.3 OT   Game (7/ 17) 41.2 REBOUNDS 3
FT 1st (2/ 4) 50.0   2nd (12/ 17)   70.6 OT   Game (14/ 21) 66.7

Attendance: 29,619
OFFICIALS   SCORE BY PERIODS   1   2   OT   OT   OT   FINAL
#1- Sally Bell   Tennessee   25   31   56
#2- Lawson Newton   Connecticut   38   41   79
#3- Angie Lewis

TECHNICAL FOULS: NONE

POINTS OFF TURNOVERS: Connecticut 19 Tennessee 14
SECOND CHANCE POINTS: Connecticut 10 Tennessee 18

2002 NCAA Women's National Semifinal

Women's Final Four attendance record.
Largest collegiate women's basketball crowd.

              This report produced by @game(tm) Basketball DOS 6.01.165c.FWNSICHBO
          55 Technology Drive, Lowell, MA 01851 Tel: (978) 275-0200 Fax: (978) 275-0202

```
Official Baske  ll Box Score -- GAME TOTALS -- FINAL STATIS  CS
TENNESSEE vs CONNECTICUT
1/4/03 2:00 p.m. at Hartford Civic Center  Hartford, CT
------------------------------------------------------------------------------
VISITORS: TENNESSEE 9-3
                           TOT-FG   3-PT        REBOUNDS
## Player Name             FG-FGA FG-FGA FT-FTA OF DE TOT PF  TP  A TO BLK S MIN
13 Jackson, Gwen....... f   1-6    0-1    0-0    0  0   0  1   2  0  2   0 1  16
33 Robinson, Ashley.... c   6-13   0-0    3-6    3  1   4  3  15  0  1   1 1  38
03 Butts, Tasha........ g   3-6    0-1    2-3    3  5   8  1   8  1  1   0 0  32
20 Lawson, Kara........ g   5-19   1-7    2-2    4  5   9  0  13  3  0   0 1  41
21 Moore, Loree........ g   3-7    2-4    0-0    1  4   5  3   8  4  4   0 2  33
04 Davis, Latoya.......      0-0    0-0    0-0    0  0   0  0   0  0  0   0 0   1
05 Zolman, Shanna......      3-6    0-0    2-2    2  1   3  2   8  1  2   0 1  19
25 Jackson, Brittany...      0-1    0-0    0-0    0  0   0  1   0  2  0   0 0   9
34 McDaniel, Courtney..      0-0    0-0    0-0    0  0   0  0   0  0  0   1 1   5
43 Ely, Shyra..........      3-10   0-0    2-2    2  4   6  1   8  2  3   1 2  31
   TEAM................                           3  2   5               2
   Totals..............     24-68   3-13  11-15  18 24  42 12  62 13 15   3 8 225

TOTAL FG% 1st Half: 11-28 39.3%   2nd Half: 11-34 32.4%   OT: 2-6  33.3%   Game: 35.3%   DEADB
3-Pt. FG% 1st Half:  1-7  14.3%   2nd Half:  2-4 50.0%    OT: 0-2   0.0%   Game: 23.1%   REBS
F Throw % 1st Half:  3-4  75.0%   2nd Half:  6-9 66.7%    OT: 2-2 100 %    Game: 73.3%    2

------------------------------------------------------------------------------
HOME TEAM: CONNECTICUT 12-0
                           TOT-FG   3-PT        REBOUNDS
## Player Name             FG-FGA FG-FGA FT-FTA OF DE TOT PF  TP  A TO BLK S MIN
22 Battle, Ashley...... f   2-8    0-0    1-3    4  1   5  0   5  3  4   1 0  30
43 Strother, Ann....... f   4-11   0-4    2-2    2  3   5  1  10  2  4   0 0  40
31 Moore, Jessica...... c   2-4    0-0    0-0    1  7   8  3   4  2  1   1 1  33
03 Taurasi, Diana...... g   9-17   4-7    3-4    0  8   8  3  25  3  6   4 0  42
05 Conlon, Maria....... g   3-6    3-5    0-0    0  2   2  2   9  1  5   0 1  41
23 Crockett, Willnett..      1-3    0-0    1-2    1  5   6  2   3  1  0   1 0  23
33 Turner, Barbara.....      2-6    1-3    2-2    1  1   2  1   7  0  0   0 1  16
   TEAM................                           2  1   3
   Totals..............     23-55   8-19   9-13  11 28  39 12  63 12 20   7 3 225

TOTAL FG% 1st Half: 10-24 41.7%   2nd Half: 10-24 41.7%   OT: 3-7  42.9%   Game: 41.8%   DEADB
3-Pt. FG% 1st Half:  4-8  50.0%   2nd Half:  3-10 30.0%   OT: 1-1 100 %    Game: 42.1%   REBS
F Throw % 1st Half:  5-6  83.3%   2nd Half:  4-7 57.1%    OT: 0-0   0.0%   Game: 69.2%    1

------------------------------------------------------------------------------
Officials: Lisa Mattingly, Dennis DeMayo, Bill Titus
Technical fouls: TENNESSEE-None. CONNECTICUT-None.
Attendance: 16294
Score by Periods            1st  2nd   OT    Total
TENNESSEE....................  26   30    6   -   62
CONNECTICUT..................  29   27    7   -   63
Points in the paint-TENN 28,UCONN 24. Points off turnovers-TENN 19,UCONN 9.
2nd chance points-TENN 5,UCONN 11. Fast break points-TENN 9,UCONN 2.
Bench points-TENN 16,UCONN 10. Score tied-13 times. Lead changed-7 times.
Last FG-TENN OT-01:22, UCONN OT-00:51.
```

04/08/2003 8:30pm (EDT)
Final Box Score

Georgia Dome
Atlanta, GA

No.	Tennessee Lady Vols	Total FG		3-point		FT	FTA	Rebounds			F	TP	A	TO	BLK	STL	MIN
		FG	FGA	FG	FGA			Off	Def	Tot							
13	Gwen Jackson (F)	6	14	0	2	3	6	6	3	9	3	15	4	2	1	0	35:45
43	Shyra Ely (F)	3	6	0	0	0	0	0	2	2	1	6	0	2	0	1	24:54
3	Tasha Butts (G)	2	4	0	0	0	0	1	0	1	3	4	2	1	0	1	16:39
20	Kara Lawson (G)	5	13	3	8	5	5	1	4	5	1	18	5	3	0	1	40:00
21	Loree Moore (G)	2	4	1	1	0	0	1	1	2	1	5	1	1	0	3	23:56
4	LaToya Davis	0	0	0	0	0	0	0	0	0	0	0	0	0	0	0	DNP
5	Shanna Zolman	0	0	0	0	0	0	1	1	2	2	0	0	1	0	1	11:18
25	Brittany Jackson	4	10	3	7	2	2	1	4	5	3	13	0	3	0	0	20:45
33	Ashley Robinson	1	2	0	0	1	6	4	4	8	2	3	1	1	0	0	17:03
34	Courtney McDaniel	1	3	0	0	0	0	1	1	2	2	2	0	0	0	0	5:34
50	Tye'sha Fluker	1	1	0	0	0	0	1	0	1	0	2	0	0	0	0	4:06
	Team (Included in Totals)							3	0	3				1			
	Totals	25	57	7	18	11	19	20	20	40	18	68	13	15	1	7	200

Total FG%: 1st half 12 - 29 (41.4%)   2nd half 13 - 28 (46.4%)   Game 25 - 57 (43.9%)   Deadball
3Pt FG%: 1st half 3 - 8 (37.5%)   2nd half 4 - 10 (40.0%)   Game 7 - 18 (38.9%)   rebounds
FT%: 1st half 3 - 4 (75.0%)   2nd half 8 - 15 (53.3%)   Game 11 - 19 (57.9%)   3

No.	Connecticut Huskies	Total FG		3-point		FT	FTA	Rebounds			F	TP	A	TO	BLK	STL	MIN
		FG	FGA	FG	FGA			Off	Def	Tot							
3	Diana Taurasi (G/F)	8	15	4	9	8	8	1	3	4	2	28	1	3	1	0	37:00
33	Barbara Turner (F/G)	5	7	0	0	0	0	1	0	1	3	10	1	2	0	0	20:47
31	Jessica Moore (C)	2	5	0	0	0	0	1	3	4	2	4	3	3	0	0	34:54
5	Maria Conlon (G)	3	7	3	5	2	4	0	4	4	2	11	6	0	0	2	39:15
43	Ann Strother (G)	6	11	3	7	2	2	0	3	3	2	17	3	1	0	0	32:19
2	Ashley Valley	0	0	0	0	0	0	0	0	0	0	0	0	0	0	0	DNP
12	Stacey Marron	0	0	0	0	0	0	0	0	0	0	0	0	0	0	0	DNP
20	Morgan Valley	0	0	0	0	0	0	0	0	0	0	0	0	0	0	0	DNP
21	Nicole Wolff	0	0	0	0	0	0	0	0	0	0	0	0	0	0	0	DNP
22	Ashley Battle	0	3	0	0	0	0	0	0	0	0	0	1	1	0	2	11:46
23	Willnett Crockett	1	1	0	0	1	2	2	4	6	5	3	0	1	0	0	23:59
	Team (Included in Totals)							0	0	0				0			
	Totals	25	49	10	21	13	16	5	17	22	16	73	15	11	1	4	200

Total FG%: 1st half 14 - 26 (53.8%)   2nd half 11 - 23 (47.8%)   Game 25 - 49 (51.0%)   Deadball
3Pt FG%: 1st half 6 - 12 (50.0%)   2nd half 4 - 9 (44.4%)   Game 10 - 21 (47.6%)   rebounds
FT%: 1st half 1 - 2 (50.0%)   2nd half 12 - 14 (85.7%)   Game 13 - 16 (81.3%)   2

Technical Fouls: None
Attendance: 28,210
Officials: Lisa Mattingly, Melissa Barlow, Wesley Dean

Score by Period	1st H	2nd H	Final	Record	Overall	Conf
Connecticut Huskies	35	38	73	Huskies	37-1	
Tennessee Lady Vols	30	38	68	Lady Vols	33-5	

	Huskies	Lady Vols		Huskies	Lady Vols		Huskies	Lady Vols
Points off Turnovers	16	16	Second Effort Points	6	16	Bench Points	3	20
Points in the Paint	20	26	3 Point Points	30	21	Free Throw Points	13	11
Largest Lead	47	34 (13 pts)	Lead Changes	0		Number of Ties	4	

Game comments:

```
OFFICIAL BASKETBALL BOX SCORE -- G A M E   T O T A L S
#4/3 Connecticut vs #1/1 Tennessee
02/05/04 7 p.m. at Thompson-Boling Arena, Knoxville, Tenn.
-------------------------------------------------------------------------
VISITORS: #4/3 Connecticut 17-2
                     TOT-FG  3-PT         REBOUNDS
No.      N A M E     FG-FGA FG-FGA FT-FTA OF DE TOT PF  TP  A TO BLK S MIN
33 TURNER, Barbara  f 6-16   1-2    3-9    3  6   9  4  16  3  1  0  1 32
43 STROTHER, Ann    f 6-14   3-9    2-2    3  4   7  4  17  0  2  1  1 35
31 MOORE, Jessica   c 2-3    0-0    1-3    2  5   7  4   5  1  1  1  0 30
03 TAURASI, Diana   g 4-13   3-7    7-9    2  3   5  5  18  5  3  1  2 30
05 CONLON, Maria    g 3-6    2-4    0-1    1  2   3  1   8  3  0  0  1 32
22 BATTLE, Ashley     5-12   1-1    0-0    3  2   5  1  11  1  1  0  3 22
23 CROCKETT, Willnett 1-2    0-0    4-4    1  1   2  3   6  0  0  0  1 17
34 SHERWOOD, Liz      0-0    0-0    0-0    0  0   0  0   0  0  0  0  0  2
TEAM ........................................  2  2   4
TOTALS              27-66  10-23  17-28   17 25  42 22  81 13  8  3  9 200

TOT-FG 1stH: 16-40 40.0%  2ndH: 11-26 42.3%  OT: 0-0 00.0%  Game: 40.9% Deadbl
3pt-FG 1stH:  6-13 46.2%  2ndH:  4-10 40.0%  OT: 0-0 00.0%  Game: 43.5% Rebs
FThrow 1stH:  3-9  33.3%  2ndH: 14-19 73.7%  OT: 0-0 00.0%  Game: 60.7%   5

-------------------------------------------------------------------------
HOME TEAM: #1/1 Tennessee 18-2
                     TOT-FG  3-PT         REBOUNDS
No.      N A M E     FG-FGA FG-FGA FT-FTA OF DE TOT PF  TP  A TO BLK S MIN
25 JACKSON, Brittany f 3-9    2-5    2-2    0  0   0  1  10  2  5  0  1 27
43 ELY, Shyra       f 4-9    0-0    2-2    5  9  14  4  10  2  1  0  0 36
33 ROBINSON, Ashley c 4-5    0-0    0-0    1  1   2  5   8  1  0  0  2 18
03 BUTTS, Tasha     g 1-8    1-4    3-5    2  5   7  4   6  4  1  0  0 37
05 ZOLMAN, Shanna   g 5-11   2-3    2-2    1  4   5  4  14  3  1  1  0 37
01 SPENCER, Sidney    0-3    0-1    5-6    2  3   5  2   5  4  2  1  0 22
04 DAVIS, LaToya      0-0    0-0    0-0    0  0   0  1   0  0  2  0  0  2
13 REDDING, Dominique 0-1    0-1    0-0    0  0   0  0   0  0  0  0  0  1
50 FLUKER, Tye'sha    5-10   0-0    4-4    0  4   4  2  14  0  3  3  0 20
TEAM ........................................  0  2   2             1
TOTALS              22-56   5-14  18-21   11 28  39 23  67 16 16  5  3 200

TOT-FG 1stH: 10-27 37.0%  2ndH: 12-29 41.4%  OT: 0-0 00.0%  Game: 39.3% Deadbl
3pt-FG 1stH:  3-7  42.9%  2ndH:  2-7  28.6%  OT: 0-0 00.0%  Game: 35.7% Rebs
FThrow 1stH: 10-10 100.%  2ndH:  8-11 72.7%  OT: 0-0 00.0%  Game: 85.7%   1

-------------------------------------------------------------------------
OFFICIALS:  Sally Bell, Wesley Dean, John Morningstar
TECHNICAL FOULS:
#4/3 Connecticut      -  none
#1/1 Tennessee        -  none
ATTENDANCE:  22,515
SCORE BY PERIODS:          1st  2nd  OT1  OT2  OT3  OT4   TOTAL
#4/3 Connecticut           41   40                        81
#1/1 Tennessee             33   34                        67

ID-216031
Turnstile: 20,961 UT's Ashley Robinson fouls out @ 3:23/2nd
UConn's Diana Taurasi fouls out @ :46.0/2nd
```

fícial Basketbaì Box Score -- GAME TOTALS -- FINAL STATIS⸴ ⸴S
⸴nnecticut vs Tennessee
4/6/04 7:39 PM CDT at New Orleans Arena, New Orleans, LA

VISITORS: Connecticut (31-4)

## Player Name		TOT-FG FG-FGA	3-PT FG-FGA	FT-FTA	REBOUNDS OF	DE	TOT	PF	TP	A	TO	BLK	S	MIN
33 TURNER,Barbara......	f	4-12	1-2	3-6	1	8	9	2	12	4	0	2	2	33
31 MOORE,Jessica.......	c	6-9	0-0	2-2	6	3	9	3	14	1	2	0	2	30
03 TAURASI,Diana.......	g	6-11	3-7	2-4	0	3	3	1	17	2	3	0	0	37
05 CONLON,Maria........	g	1-4	1-2	4-4	0	2	2	0	7	5	1	0	2	33
43 STROTHER,Ann........	g	5-8	1-2	3-3	0	2	2	1	14	2	1	0	0	37
22 BATTLE,Ashley.......		1-4	1-1	0-0	0	1	1	1	3	0	1	0	1	15
23 CROCKETT,Willnett...		1-3	0-0	1-1	0	2	2	1	3	1	2	0	0	15
TEAM................						3	3							
Totals.............		24-51	7-14	15-20	7	24	31	10	70	15	10	2	7	200

TOTAL FG% 1st Half: 11-23 47.8%   2nd Half: 13-28 46.4%   Game: 47.1%   DEADB
3-Pt. FG% 1st Half: 5-9 55.6%   2nd Half: 2-5 40.0%   Game: 50.0%   REBS
F Throw % 1st Half: 3-4 75.0%   2nd Half: 12-16 75.0%   Game: 75.0%   3

HOME TEAM: Tennessee (31-4)

## Player Name		TOT-FG FG-FGA	3-PT FG-FGA	FT-FTA	REBOUNDS OF	DE	TOT	PF	TP	A	TO	BLK	S	MIN
04 DAVIS,LaToya........	f	3-8	0-0	0-0	1	0	1	5	6	7	3	0	4	30
43 ELY,Shyra...........	f	4-10	0-0	2-4	2	5	7	2	10	0	3	0	0	26
33 ROBINSON,Ashley.....	c	6-10	0-0	1-4	4	3	7	1	13	1	1	2	0	39
03 BUTTS,Tasha.........	g	1-10	0-6	6-6	3	3	6	2	8	2	1	0	3	32
05 ZOLMAN,Shanna.......	g	6-11	3-6	4-4	2	7	9	2	19	1	1	0	1	37
01 SPENCER,Sidney......		0-1	0-0	0-0	0	1	1	4	0	0	0	0	0	14
13 REDDING,Dominique...		0-1	0-0	0-0	0	0	0	0	0	1	0	0	0	3
25 JACKSON,Brittany....		1-7	1-4	0-0	0	1	1	2	3	1	2	0	0	11
50 FLUKER,Tye'sha......		1-3	0-0	0-0	1	0	1	0	2	0	0	0	0	8
TEAM................					4	2	6							
Totals.............		22-61	4-16	13-18	17	22	39	18	61	13	11	2	8	200

TOTAL FG% 1st Half: 11-33 33.3%   2nd Half: 11-28 39.3%   Game: 36.1%   DEADB
3-Pt. FG% 1st Half: 1-6 16.7%   2nd Half: 3-10 30.0%   Game: 25.0%   REBS
F Throw % 1st Half: 1-4 25.0%   2nd Half: 12-14 85.7%   Game: 72.2%   3

Officials: Lisa Mattingly, Denise Kantner, Bryan Enterline
Technical fouls: Connecticut-None. Tennessee-None.
Attendance: 18211
Score by Periods   1st   2nd   Total
Connecticut................... 30   40 -   70
Tennessee..................... 24   37 -   61
Points in the paint-UCONN 28,UT 28. Points off turnovers-UCONN 14,UT 15.
2nd chance points-UCONN 11,UT 18. Fast break points-UCONN 0,UT 6.
Bench points-UCONN 6,UT 5. Score tied-3 times. Lead changed-2 times.
Last FG-UCONN 2nd-03:01, UT 2nd-01:19.

Official Basketball Box Score -- GAME TOTALS -- FINAL STATISTICS
Tennessee vs Connecticut
1/8/05 2:00 p.m. at Hartford, Conn. (Hartford Civic Center)

VISITORS: Tennessee 10-3

		TOT-FG	3-PT		REBOUNDS									
##	Player Name	FG-FGA	FG-FGA	FT-FTA	OF	DE	TOT	PF	TP	A	TO	BLK	S	MIN
43	ELY, Shyra.......... f	4-9	0-0	3-4	3	6	9	3	11	3	2	0	2	30
55	ANOSIKE, Nicky...... f	2-7	0-0	4-8	3	3	6	2	8	3	2	0	0	26
50	FLUKER, Tye'sha..... c	3-7	0-0	5-8	3	3	6	1	11	0	0	0	1	24
21	MOORE, Loree........ g	5-11	2-5	0-0	2	0	2	4	12	3	2	1	1	36
25	JACKSON, Brittany... g	0-3	0-1	0-0	1	0	1	0	0	0	3	0	0	11
01	SPENCER, Sidney.....	0-1	0-0	0-0	0	1	1	0	0	0	0	2	0	4
05	ZOLMAN, Shanna......	0-4	0-2	0-0	0	0	0	1	0	0	1	0	0	13
13	REDDING, Dominique..	0-0	0-0	0-0	0	0	0	1	0	0	0	0	0	4
14	HORNBUCKLE, Alexis..	5-8	0-0	4-5	2	4	6	3	14	4	3	0	2	27
15	WILEY-GATEWOOD, S...	4-8	3-6	1-1	1	0	1	1	12	1	1	0	1	23
33	DOSTY, Sybil........	0-0	0-0	0-0	1	0	1	0	0	0	0	0	1	2
	TEAM................				3	2	5							
	Totals..............	23-58	5-14	17-26	19	19	38	16	68	14	14	3	8	200

TOTAL FG% 1st Half: 11-33 33.3%   2nd Half: 12-25 48.0%   Game: 39.7%   DEADB
3-Pt. FG% 1st Half: 1-7 14.3%   2nd Half: 4-7 57.1%   Game: 35.7%   REBS
F Throw % 1st Half: 4-9 44.4%   2nd Half: 13-17 76.5%   Game: 65.4%   2

HOME TEAM: Connecticut 8-4

		TOT-FG	3-PT		REBOUNDS									
##	Player Name	FG-FGA	FG-FGA	FT-FTA	OF	DE	TOT	PF	TP	A	TO	BLK	S	MIN
24	HOUSTON, Charde..... f	8-14	0-0	3-5	2	4	6	4	19	1	3	0	2	24
43	STROTHER, Ann....... f	5-11	3-8	3-6	0	2	2	4	16	7	1	0	5	39
23	CROCKETT, Willnett.. c	1-3	0-0	2-2	2	3	5	4	4	2	4	4	0	32
02	VALLEY, Ashley...... g	0-0	0-0	0-0	0	0	0	0	0	0	1	0	0	6
21	WOLFF, Nicole....... g	2-5	0-3	0-0	0	2	2	1	4	0	1	3	1	33
11	SWANIER, Ketia......	0-3	0-0	2-2	0	2	2	2	2	1	2	0	1	16
13	SADIQ, Rashidat.....	0-0	0-0	0-0	0	0	0	1	0	0	0	1	0	2
22	BATTLE, Ashley......	6-10	1-2	2-2	2	4	6	1	15	1	2	0	0	26
31	MOORE, Jessica......	3-5	0-0	1-2	1	4	5	4	7	3	1	1	0	22
	TEAM................				3	2	5				2			
	Totals..............	25-51	4-13	13-19	10	23	33	21	67	15	17	9	9	200

TOTAL FG% 1st Half: 14-28 50.0%   2nd Half: 11-23 47.8%   Game: 49.0%   DEADB
3-Pt. FG% 1st Half: 3-6 50.0%   2nd Half: 1-7 14.3%   Game: 30.8%   REBS
F Throw % 1st Half: 5-6 83.3%   2nd Half: 8-13 61.5%   Game: 68.4%   3

Officials: Lisa Mattingly, Sue Blauch, Mark Zentz
Technical fouls: Tennessee-None. Connecticut-None.
Attendance: 16294

Score by Periods	1st	2nd	Total
Tennessee....................	27	41	- 68
Connecticut..................	36	31	- 67

Points in the paint-TENN 28,UCONN 24. Points off turnovers-TENN 20,UCONN 17.
2nd chance points-TENN 18,UCONN 13. Fast break points-TENN 10,UCONN 4.
Bench points-TENN 26,UCONN 24. Score tied-3 times. Lead changed-3 times.
Last FG-TENN 2nd-00:15, UCONN 2nd-01:50.

Official Basketba `. Box Score -- GAME TOTALS -- FINAL STATIF `CS
#7 Connecticut v. `ENNESSEE
01/07/06 2:05 p.m. at Thompson-Boling Arena, Knoxville, Tenn.

VISITORS: #7 Connecticut 12-2

		TOT-FG	3-PT		REBOUNDS									
## Player Name		FG-FGA	FG-FGA	FT-FTA	OF	DE	TOT	PF	TP	A	TO	BLK	S	MIN
33 TURNER, Barbara..... f		1-8	0-3	4-8	2	5	7	5	6	3	2	0	1	27
43 STROTHER, Ann....... f		9-22	5-15	2-3	1	4	5	5	25	4	3	0	0	40
20 MONTGOMERY, Renee... g		0-0	0-0	0-0	1	0	1	1	0	3	2	0	1	23
21 WOLFF, Nicole....... g		1-1	0-0	2-2	0	1	1	0	4	1	2	0	0	16
25 THOMAS, Mel........ g		1-2	1-1	2-2	1	0	1	3	5	3	1	0	0	27
11 SWANIER, Ketia......		2-5	1-2	0-0	0	1	1	4	5	2	3	0	0	18
23 CROCKETT, Willnett..		1-1	0-0	0-0	0	0	0	3	2	0	0	1	0	5
24 HOUSTON, Charde.....		7-10	0-0	5-8	2	6	8	5	19	1	3	0	1	20
32 GREENE, Kalana......		1-1	0-0	0-0	0	0	0	3	2	0	0	0	0	6
44 HUNTER, Brittany....		5-7	0-0	2-2	0	3	3	1	12	0	1	1	0	18
TEAM................					5	4	9							
Totals.............		28-57	7-21	17-25	12	24	36	30	80	17	17	2	3	200

TOTAL FG% 1st Half: 14-26 53.8%   2nd Half: 14-31 45.2%   Game: 49.1%   DEADB
3-Pt. FG% 1st Half: 4-11 36.4%   2nd Half: 3-10 30.0%   Game: 33.3%   REBS
F Throw % 1st Half: 9-12 75.0%   2nd Half: 8-13 61.5%   Game: 68.0%   4

HOME TEAM: TENNESSEE 15-0

		TOT-FG	3-PT		REBOUNDS									
## Player Name		FG-FGA	FG-FGA	FT-FTA	OF	DE	TOT	PF	TP	A	TO	BLK	S	MIN
01 SPENCER, Sidney..... f		6-9	5-5	4-4	4	2	6	2	21	2	1	1	0	35
03 PARKER, Candace..... f		5-9	0-0	3-4	0	1	1	5	13	3	1	1	1	26
55 ANOSIKE, Nicky...... c		1-6	0-0	4-7	2	2	4	1	6	2	1	1	3	25
05 ZOLMAN, Shanna...... g		1-10	1-7	10-10	0	1	1	2	13	2	2	0	1	39
14 HORNBUCKLE, Alexis.. g		1-6	0-1	6-6	5	9	14	3	10	9	3	0	4	37
13 REDDING, Dominique..		3-3	1-1	0-0	1	1	2	0	7	0	0	0	0	6
21 MOSS, Lindsey.......		0-1	0-1	0-0	0	0	0	0	0	0	0	0	0	1
33 DOSTY, Sybil........		3-4	0-0	0-1	3	1	4	4	6	0	2	1	0	5
44 FULLER, Alex........		0-1	0-0	0-0	0	1	1	0	0	0	0	0	0	5
50 FLUKER, Tye'sha.....		4-10	0-0	5-9	1	2	3	4	13	0	1	0	1	21
TEAM................					2	1	3							
Totals.............		25-63	7-15	32-41	18	21	39	21	89	18	10	5	9	200

TOTAL FG% 1st Half: 15-39 38.5%   2nd Half: 10-24 41.7%   Game: 39.7%   DEADB
3-Pt. FG% 1st Half: 4-9 44.4%   2nd Half: 3-6 50.0%   Game: 46.7%   REBS
F Throw % 1st Half: 5-10 50.0%   2nd Half: 27-31 87.1%   Game: 78.0%   5

Officials: Lisa Mattingly, Dee Kantner, Bryan Enterline
Technical fouls: #7 Connecticut-None. TENNESSEE-None.
Attendance: 24653
Score by Periods   1st   2nd   Total
#7 Connecticut...............   41   39   -   80
TENNESSEE....................   39   50   -   89
ID-367659
Turnstile: 22,415 (2500 tickets were held for UT students)
UConn's #33 fouls out @ 1:38/2 and #43 fouls out @ 16.1/2, 24 @ 5.9/2
UT's #03 fouls out @8.7/2
Points in the paint-UCONN 32,UT 34. Points off turnovers-UCONN 9,UT 19.
2nd chance points-UCONN 8,UT 14. Fast break points-UCONN 2,UT 8.
Bench points-UCONN 40,UT 26. Score tied-3 times. Lead changed-6 times.
Last FG-UCONN 2nd-01:34, UT 2nd-00:59.
Largest lead-UCONN by 5 1st-12:09, UT by 9 2nd-00:06.

Official Basketball Box Score -- GAME TOTALS -- FINAL STATISTICS
Tennessee vs UConn Huskies
1/6/07 4:00 pm at Hartford Civic Center

VISITORS: Tennessee 14-1

## Player Name		TOT-FG FG-FGA	3-PT FG-FGA	FT-FTA	OF	DE	TOT	PF	TP	A	TO	BLK	S	MIN
01 SPENCER, Sidney.....	f	4-13	3-7	3-4	4	5	9	3	14	3	1	0	3	37
03 PARKER, Candace.....	f	12-22	0-0	6-9	7	5	12	3	30	4	2	6	1	40
55 ANOSIKE, Nicky......	c	3-9	0-0	0-0	3	0	3	2	6	0	2	3	1	24
00 BOBBITT, Shannon....	g	3-7	3-6	0-0	0	1	1	1	9	2	1	0	1	34
14 HORNBUCKLE, Alexis..	g	2-10	0-2	2-2	3	3	6	4	6	3	2	1	1	33
02 MCMAHAN, Cait.......		0-0	0-0	0-0	0	0	0	0	0	0	1	0	1	5
13 REDDING, Dominique..		0-0	0-0	0-0	0	1	1	1	0	0	0	0	0	4
33 AUGUSTE, Alberta....		1-6	0-0	0-0	2	0	2	1	2	1	1	0	0	9
44 FULLER, Alex........		1-3	1-2	0-0	0	2	2	1	3	1	0	0	0	14
TEAM..............					4	4								
Totals.............		26-70	7-17	11-15	19	21	40	16	70	14	10	10	8	200

TOTAL FG% 1st Half: 16-41 39.0%   2nd Half: 10-29 34.5%   Game: 37.1%   DEADB
3-Pt. FG% 1st Half: 6-12 50.0%   2nd Half: 1-5 20.0%   Game: 41.2%   REBS
F Throw % 1st Half: 3-3 100 %   2nd Half: 8-12 66.7%   Game: 73.3%   0

HOME TEAM: UConn Huskies 12-1

## Player Name		TOT-FG FG-FGA	3-PT FG-FGA	FT-FTA	OF	DE	TOT	PF	TP	A	TO	BLK	S	MIN
24 HOUSTON, Charde.....	f	10-18	0-0	3-6	0	8	8	2	23	2	4	2	1	37
41 MCLAREN, Kaili......	f	3-7	0-0	0-0	3	2	5	2	6	1	1	0	0	16
20 MONTGOMERY, Renee...	g	2-11	0-5	0-0	2	3	5	1	4	6	1	0	3	39
25 THOMAS, Mel........	g	2-5	2-4	2-2	0	0	0	0	8	1	2	0	1	28
32 GREENE, Kalana......	g	3-9	0-2	0-0	0	2	2	1	6	3	3	0	0	31
11 SWANIER, Ketia......		1-1	0-0	2-2	0	4	4	2	4	2	2	0	2	19
31 CHARLES, Tina.......		3-4	0-0	1-4	3	1	4	0	7	0	0	0	0	11
44 HUNTER, Brittany....		2-5	0-0	2-3	4	2	6	4	6	2	1	3	0	19
TEAM..............					3	7	10	1						
Totals.............		26-60	2-11	10-17	15	29	44	13	64	17	14	5	7	200

TOTAL FG% 1st Half: 11-29 37.9%   2nd Half: 15-31 48.4%   Game: 43.3%   DEADB
3-Pt. FG% 1st Half: 1-6 16.7%   2nd Half: 1-5 20.0%   Game: 18.2%   REBS
F Throw % 1st Half: 6-10 60.0%   2nd Half: 4-7 57.1%   Game: 58.8%   5

Officials: Dee Kantner, Lisa Mattingly, Denise Brooks-Clauser
Technical fouls: Tennessee-None. UConn Huskies-TEAM.
Attendance: 16294
Score by Periods   1st 2nd   Total
Tennessee...................   41   29 - 70
UConn Huskies...............   29   35 - 64
ID-473851
Points in the paint-TENN 30,UCONN 40. Points off turnovers-TENN 22,UCONN 12.
2nd chance points-TENN 9,UCONN 14. Fast break points-TENN 15,UCONN 20.
Bench points-TENN 5,UCONN 17. Score tied-4 times. Lead changed-1 time.
Last FG-TENN 2nd-01:59, UCONN 2nd-00:23.
Largest lead-TENN by 18 2nd-17:55, UCONN by 5 1st-15:09.